THE O'LEARY SERIES

Microsoft® Access 2000

Brief Version

Timothy J. O'Leary
Arizona State University

Linda I. O'Leary

Boston   Burr Ridge, IL   Dubuque, IA   Madison, WI   New York
San Francisco   St. Louis   Bangkok   Bogotá   Caracas   Lisbon
London   Madrid   Mexico City   Milan   New Delhi   Seoul
Singapore   Sydney   Taipei   Toronto

McGraw-Hill Higher Education

A Division of The **McGraw-Hill** *Companies*

MICROSOFT® ACCESS 2000, BRIEF EDITION

Disclaimer: This book is designed to help you improve your computer use. However, the author and publisher assume no responsibility whatsoever for the uses made of this material or for decisions based on their use, and make no warranties, either expressed or implied, regarding the contents of this book, its merchantability, or its fitness for any particular purpose.

Neither the publisher nor anyone else who has been involved in the creation, production, or delivery of this product shall be liable for any direct, incidental, or consequential damages, such as, but not limited to, loss of anticipated profits or benefits or benefits resulting from its use or from any breach of any warranty. Some states do not allow the exclusion or limitation of direct, incidental, or consequential damages, so the above disclaimer may not apply to you. No dealer, company, or person is authorized to alter this disclaimer. Any representation to the contrary will not bind the publisher or author.

This book is printed on acid-free paper.

2 3 4 5 6 7 8 9 0 BAN/BAN 9 0 9 8 7 6 5 4 3 2 1 0 9

ISBN 0-07-233751-6

Vice president/Editor-in-chief: *Michael W. Junior*
Publisher: *David Brake*
Sponsoring editor: *Trisha O'Shea*
Developmental editor: *Stephen Fahringer*
Senior marketing manager: *Jodi McPherson*
Senior project manager: *Beth Cigler*
Manager, new book production: *Melonie Salvati*
Freelance design coordinator: *Gino Cieslik*
Cover design: *Francis Owens*
Cover Illustration: *Paul Wiley*
Supplement coordinator: *Marc Mattson*
Compositor: *Rogondino & Associates*
Typeface: *11/13 Century Book*
Printer: *The Banta Book Group*

Library of Congress Catalog Card Number 99-62021

http://www.mhhe.com

THE O'LEARY SERIES

Microsoft® Access 2000

Brief Version

Timothy J. O'Leary
Arizona State University

Linda I. O'Leary

Irwin McGraw-Hill

Boston   Burr Ridge, IL   Dubuque, IA   Madison, WI   New York
San Francisco   St. Louis   Bangkok   Bogotá   Caracas   Lisbon
London   Madrid   Mexico City   Milan   New Delhi   Seoul
Singapore   Sydney   Taipei   Toronto

At McGraw-Hill Higher Education, we publish instructional materials targeted at the higher education market. In an effort to expand the tools of higher learning, we publish texts, lab manuals, study guides, testing materials, software, and multimedia products.

At **Irwin/McGraw-Hill** (a division of McGraw-Hill Higher Education), we realize that technology has created and will continue to create new mediums for professors and students to use in managing resources and communicating information with one another. We strive to provide the most flexible and complete teaching and learning tools available as well as offer solutions to the changing world of teaching and learning.

Irwin/McGraw-Hill is dedicated to providing the tools for today's instructors and students to successfully navigate the world of Information Technology.

- **Seminar series**—Irwin/McGraw-Hill's Technology Connection seminar series offered across the country every year demonstrates the latest technology products and encourages collaboration among teaching professionals.

- **Osborne/McGraw-Hill**—This division of The McGraw-Hill Companies is known for its best-selling Internet titles *Harley Hahn's Internet & Web Yellow Pages* and the *Internet Complete Reference*. Osborne offers an additional resource for certification and has strategic publishing relationships with corporations such as Corel Corporation and America Online. For more information visit Osborne at **www.osborne.com**.

- **Digital solutions**—Irwin/McGraw-Hill is committed to publishing digital solutions. Taking your course online doesn't have to be a solitary venture, nor does it have to be a difficult one. We offer several solutions that will allow you to enjoy all the benefits of having course material online. For more information visit **www.mhhe.com/solutions/index.mhtml**.

- **Packaging options**—For more about our discount options, contact your local Irwin/McGraw-Hill Sales representative at 1-800-338-3987 or visit our Web site at **www.mhhe.com/it**.

Preface

Goals/Philosophy

The goal of **The O'Leary Series** is to give students a basic understanding of computing concepts and to build the skills necessary to ensure that information technology is an advantage in whatever path they choose in life. Because we believe that students learn better and retain more information when concepts are reinforced visually, we feature a unique visual orientation coupled with our trademark "learn by doing" approach.

Approach

The O'Leary Series is the true *step-by-step way to develop computer application skills*. The new Microsoft Office 2000 design emphasizes the step-by-step instructions with full screen captures that illustrate the results of each step performed. Each Tutorial (chapter) follows the "learn by doing" approach in combining conceptual coverage with detailed, software-specific instructions. A running case study that is featured in each tutorial highlights the real-world capabilities of each of the software applications and leads students step by step from problem to solution.

About the Book

The O'Leary Series offers 2 *levels* of instruction: Brief and Introductory. Each level builds upon the previous level.

- **Brief**—This level covers the basics of an application and contains two to three chapters.

- **Introductory**—This level includes the material in the Brief textbook plus two to three additional chapters. The Introductory text prepares students for the *Microsoft Office User Specialist Exam (MOUS Certification)*.

Each tutorial features:

- **Common Office 2000 Features**—This section provides a review of several basic procedures and Windows features. Students will also learn about many of the features that are common to all Microsoft Office 2000 applications.

- **Overview**—The Overview contains a "Before You Begin" section which presents both students and professors with all the information they need to know before starting the tutorials, including hardware and software settings. The Overview appears at the beginning of each lab manual and describes (1) what the program is,

(2) what the program can do, (3) generic terms the program uses, and (4) the Case Study to be presented.

- **Working Together sections**—These sections provide the same hands-on visual approach found in the tutorials to the integration and new collaboration features of Office 2000.

- **Glossary**—The Glossary appears at the end of each text and defines all key terms that appear in boldface type throughout the tutorials and in the end-of-tutorial Key Terms lists.

- **Index**—The Index appears at the end of each text and provides a quick reference to find specific concepts or terms in the text.

Brief Version

The Brief Version is divided into three tutorials, followed by Working Together, which shows the integration of Access 2000 with Word 2000.

Tutorial 1: You will learn how to design and create the structure for a computerized database and you will enter and edit records in the database. You will also print a table of the records you enter in the database file.

Tutorial 2: You will continue to build, modify, and use the employee database of records. You will learn how to sort the records in a database file to make it easier to locate records. Additionally, you will create a form to make it easier to enter and edit data in the database file.

Tutorial 3: You will learn how to query the database to locate specific information. You will also learn how to create a report and link multiple tables.

Working Together: After querying the database to create a list of all employees who have 5 years service with the club, you will need to send the query results to Brian, the Club owner, along with a brief memo. You will learn how to share information between applications while you create the memo.

Each tutorial features:

- **Step-by-step instructions**—Each tutorial consists of step-by-step instructions along with accompanying screen captures. The screen captures represent how the student's screen should appear after completing a specific step.

- **Competencies**—Listed at the beginning of each tutorial, the Competencies describe what skills will be mastered upon completion of the tutorial.

- **Concept Overview**—Located at the start of each tutorial, the Concept Overviews provide a brief introduction to the concepts to be presented.

■ **Concept boxes**—Tied into the Concept Overviews, the Concept boxes appear throughout the tutorial and provide clear, concise explanations of the concepts under discussion, which makes them a valuable study aid.

■ **Marginal notes**—Appearing throughout the tutorial, marginal notes provide helpful hints, suggestions, troubleshooting advice, and alternative methods of completing tasks.

■ **Case study**—The running case study carried throughout each tutorial and is based on real use of software in a business setting.

■ **End-of-tutorial material**—At the end of each tutorial the following are provided:

> **Concept Summary**—This two-page spread presents a visual summary of the concepts presented in the tutorial and can be used as a study aid for students.

> **Key Terms**—This page-referenced list is a useful study aid for students.

> **Matching/Multiple Choice/True False Questions**

> **Command Summary**—The Command Summary includes keyboard and toolbar shortcuts.

> **Screen Identifications**—These exercises ask students to demonstrate their understanding of the applications by identifying screen features.

> **Discussion Questions**—These questions are designed to stimulate in-class discussion.

> **Hands-On Practice Exercises**—These detailed exercises of increasing difficulty ask students to create Office documents based on the skills learned in the tutorial.

> **On Your Own**—These problems of increasing difficulty ask students to employ more creativity and independence in creating Office documents based on new case scenarios.

Acknowledgments

The new edition of the Microsoft Office 2000 has been made possible only through the enthusiasm and dedication of a great team of people. Because the team spans the country, literally from coast to coast, we have utilized every means of working together including conference calls, FAX, e-mail, and document collaboration . . . we have truly tested the team approach and it works!

Leading the team from Irwin/McGraw-Hill are Kyle Lewis, Senior Sponsoring Editor, Trisha O'Shea, Sponsoring Editor, and Steve Fahringer, Developmental Editor. Their renewed commitment, direction, and support have infused the team with the excitement of a new project.

The production staff is headed by Beth Cigler, Senior Project Manager whose planning and attention to detail has made it possible for us to successfully meet a very challenging schedule. Members of the production team include: Gino Cieslik and Francis Owens, art and design, Pat Rogondino, layout, Susan Defosset and Joan Paterson, copy editing. While all have contributed immensely, I would particularly like to thank Pat and Susan . . . team members for many past editions whom I can always depend on to do a great job. My thanks also go to the project Marketing Manager, Jodi McPherson, for her enthusiastic promotion of this edition.

Finally, I am particularly grateful to a small but very dedicated group of people who helped me develop the manuscript. My deepest appreciation is to my co-author, consultant, and lifelong partner, Tim, for his help and support while I have been working on this edition. Colleen Hayes, who has been assisting me from the beginning, continues to be my right arm, taking on more responsibility with each edition. Susan Demar and Carol Dean have also helped on the last several editions and continue to provide excellent developmental and technical support. New to the project this year are Bill Barth, Kathi Duggan, and Steve Willis, who have provided technical expertise and youthful perspective.

Reviewers

We would also like to thank the reviewers for their insightful input and criticism. Their feedback has helped to make this edition even stronger.

Josephine A. Braneky, *New York City Technical College*
Robert Breshears, *Maryville University*

Gary Buterbaugh, *Indiana University of Pennsylvania*
Mitchell M. Charkiewicz, *Bay Path College*
Seth Hock, *Columbus State Community College*
Katherine S. Hoppe, *Wake Forest University*
Lisa Miller, *University of Central Oklahoma*
Anne Nelson, *High Point University*
Judy Tate, *Tarrant County Junior College*
Dottie Sunio, *Leeward Community College*
Charles Walker, *Harding University*
Mark E. Workman, *Blinn College*

Additionally, each semester I hear from students at Arizona State University who are enrolled in the Introduction to Computers course. They constantly provide great feedback from a student's perspective . . . I thank you all.

Finally, I would like to thank Keri Howard, Manager for the Coffee Plantation, for her evaluation and input into the Downtown Internet Café case study.

Features of This Text

Concept Boxes identify the most important concepts in each Tutorial.

Concept ⑤ Automatic Grammar Check

The automatic grammar-checking feature advises you of incorrect grammar as you create and edit a document, and proposes possible corrections. If Word detects grammatical errors in subject-verb agreements, verb forms, capitalization, or commonly confused words, to name a few, they are identified with a wavy green line. You can correct the grammatical error by editing it or you can display a suggested correction. Not all grammatical errors identified by Word are actual errors. Use discretion when correcting the errors. Grammar checking does not occur until after you enter punctuation or end a line.

suggested correction

2 ■ Right-click on Announcing four to display the Grammar shortcut menu.

Your screen should be similar to Figure 1–10.

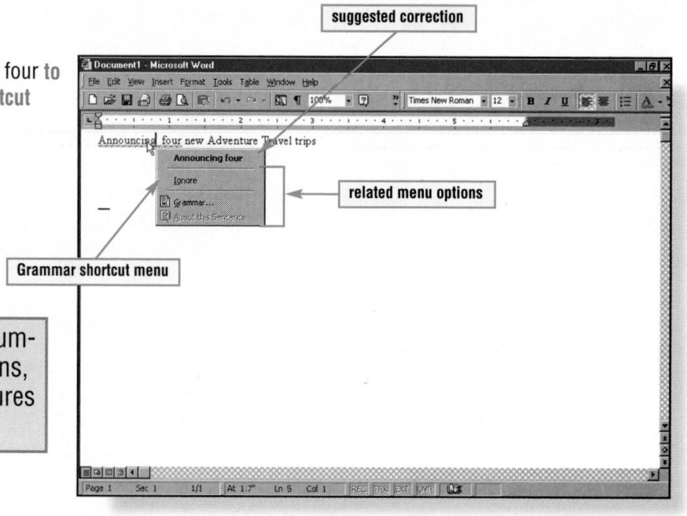

related menu options

Grammar shortcut menu

Tables provide quick summaries of toolbar buttons, key terms, and procedures for specific tasks.

Figure 1–10

Yellow **Additional Information** boxes appear throughout each tutorial and explain additional uses of the application or of a specific topic.

A shortcut menu showing a suggested correction is displayed. The Grammar shortcut menu also includes several related menu options described below.

Additional Information

A dimmed option means it is currently unavailable.

Option	Effect
Ignore	Instructs Word to ignore the grammatical error in this sentence.
Grammar	Opens the Grammar Checker and displays an explanation of the error.
About this Sentence	If the Office Assistant feature is on, this option is available. It also provides a detailed explanation of the error.

Because you cannot readily identify the reason for the error, you will open the Grammar Checker.

Other Features

Real World Case—Each O'Leary Lab Manual provides students with a fictitious running case study. This case study provides students with the real-world capabilities for each software application. Each tutorial builds upon the gained knowledge of the previous tutorial with a single case study running throughout each Lab Manual.

End-of-Chapter Material—Each tutorial ends with a visual **Concept Summary**. This two-page spread presents a concept summary of the concepts presented in the tutorial and can be used as a study aid for

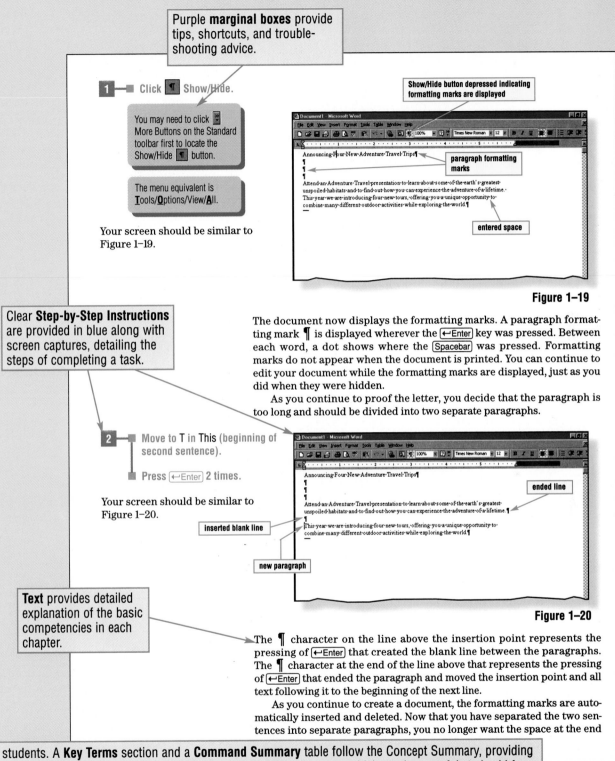

Purple **marginal boxes** provide tips, shortcuts, and troubleshooting advice.

Clear **Step-by-Step Instructions** are provided in blue along with screen captures, detailing the steps of completing a task.

Text provides detailed explanation of the basic competencies in each chapter.

1 ▪ Click ¶ Show/Hide.

You may need to click » More Buttons on the Standard toolbar first to locate the Show/Hide ¶ button.

The menu equivalent is Tools/Options/View/All.

Your screen should be similar to Figure 1–19.

Show/Hide button depressed indicating formatting marks are displayed

paragraph formatting marks

entered space

Figure 1–19

The document now displays the formatting marks. A paragraph formatting mark ¶ is displayed wherever the ⟨←Enter⟩ key was pressed. Between each word, a dot shows where the ⟨Spacebar⟩ was pressed. Formatting marks do not appear when the document is printed. You can continue to edit your document while the formatting marks are displayed, just as you did when they were hidden.

As you continue to proof the letter, you decide that the paragraph is too long and should be divided into two separate paragraphs.

2 ▪ Move to T in This (beginning of second sentence).

▪ Press ⟨←Enter⟩ 2 times.

Your screen should be similar to Figure 1–20.

inserted blank line

ended line

new paragraph

Figure 1–20

The ¶ character on the line above the insertion point represents the pressing of ⟨←Enter⟩ that created the blank line between the paragraphs. The ¶ character at the end of the line above that represents the pressing of ⟨←Enter⟩ that ended the paragraph and moved the insertion point and all text following it to the beginning of the next line.

As you continue to create a document, the formatting marks are automatically inserted and deleted. Now that you have separated the two sentences into separate paragraphs, you no longer want the space at the end

students. A **Key Terms** section and a **Command Summary** table follow the Concept Summary, providing a list of page-referenced terms and keyboard and toolbar shortcuts which can be a useful study aid for students. **Screen Identification**, **Matching**, **Multiple Choice**, and **True False Questions** provide additional reinforcement to the tutorial material. **Discussion Questions**, **Hands-on Practice Exercises**, and **On Your Own Exercises** develop critical thinking skills and offer step-by-step practice. These exercises have a rating system from Easy to Difficult and test the student's ability to apply the knowledge they have gained in each tutorial. Each O'Leary Lab Manual provides at least two **On the Web** exercises where students are asked to use the Web to solve a particular problem.

Teaching Resources

The following is a list of supplemental material that can be used to help teach this course.

Active Testing and Learning Assessment Software (ATLAS)

Available for The O'Leary Series is our cutting edge "Real Time Assessment" ATLAS software. ATLAS is web enabled and allows students to perform timed tasks while working live in an application. ATLAS will track how a specific task is completed and the time it takes to complete that task and so measures both proficiency and efficiency. ATLAS will provide full customization and authoring capabilities for professors and can include content from any of our application series.

Instructor's Resource Kits

Instructor's Resource Kits provide professors with all of the ancillary material needed to teach a course. Irwin/McGraw-Hill is committed to providing instructors with the most effective instructional resources available. Many of these resources are available at our Information Technology Supersite, found at **www.mhhe.com/it**. Our Instructor's Resource Kits are available on CD-ROM and contain the following:

- **Diploma by Brownstone**—Diploma is the most flexible, powerful, and easy to use computerized testing system available in higher education. The Diploma system allows professors to create an exam as a printed version, as a LAN-based Online version, or as an Internet version. Diploma also includes grade book features, which automate the entire testing process.

- **Instructor's Manual**—The Instructor's Manual includes solutions to all lessons and end of the unit material, teaching tips and strategies, and additional exercises.

- **Student Data Files**—Students must have student data files in order to complete practice and test sessions. The instructor and students using this text in classes are granted the right to post student data files on any network or stand-alone computer, or to distribute the files on individual diskettes. The student data files may be downloaded from our IT Supersite at **www.mhhe.com/it**.

- **Series Web site**—Available at **www.mhhe.com/cit/oleary**.

Digital Solutions

- **Pageout Lite**—This software is designed for you if you're just beginning to explore Web site options. Pageout Lite will help you to easily post your own material online. You may choose one of three templates, type in your material, and Pageout Lite will instantly convert it to HTML.

- **Pageout**—Pageout is our Course Web Site Development Center. Pageout offers a syllabus page, Web site address, Online Learning Center content, online exercises and quizzes, gradebook, discussion board, an area for students to build their own Web pages, plus all features of Pageout Lite. For more information please visit the Pageout Web site at **www.mhla.net/pageout**.

- **OLC/Series Web Sites**—Online Learning Centers (OLCs)/series sites are accessible through our Supersite at **www.mhhe.com/it**. Our Online Learning Centers/series sites provide pedagogical features and supplements for our titles online. Students can point and click their way to key terms, learning objectives, chapter overviews, PowerPoint slides, exercises, and Web links.

- **The McGraw-Hill Learning Architecture (MHLA)**—MHLA is a complete course delivery system. MHLA gives professors ownership in the way digital content is presented to the class through on-line quizzing, student collaboration, course administration, and content management. For a walk-through of MHLA, visit the MHLA Web site at **www.mhla.net**.

Packaging Options

For more about our discount options, contact your local Irwin/McGraw-Hill sales representative at 1-800-338-3987 or visit our Web site at **www.mhhe.com/it**.

Contents

Introducing Common Office 2000 Features

This section will review several basic procedures and windows features. In addition you will learn about many of the features that are common to all Microsoft Office 2000 applications. Although Access 2000 will be used to demonstrate how the features work, only common features will be addressed. The features that are specific to the application itself will be introduced individually in each tutorial.

Turning on the Computer

If necessary, follow the procedure below to turn on your computer.

Do not have any disks in the drives when you start the computer.

1 ■ **Turn on the power switch.** The power switch is commonly located on the back or right side of your computer. It may also be a button that you push on the front of your computer.

■ **If necessary, turn your monitor on and adjust the contrast and brightness.** Generally, the button to turn on the monitor is located on the front of the monitor. Use the dials (generally located in the panel on the front of the monitor) to adjust the monitor.

Press [Tab ⇄] to move to the next box.

■ **If you are on a network, you may be asked to enter your User Name and Password.** Type the required information in the boxes. When you are done, press [← Enter].

The Windows program is loaded into the main memory of your computer and the Windows desktop is displayed.

Your screen should be similar to Figure 1.

Figure 1

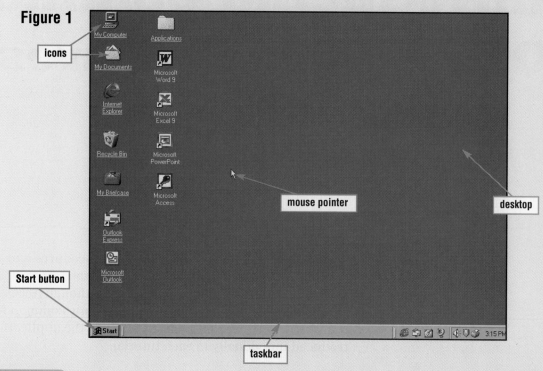

The **desktop** is the opening screen for Windows and is the place where you begin your work using the computer. Figure 1 shows the Windows 98 desktop. If you are using Windows 95 your screen will look slightly different. Small pictures, called **icons**, represent the objects on the desktop. Your desktop will probably display many different icons than shown here. At the bottom of the desktop screen is the taskbar. It contains buttons that are used to access programs and features. The **Start button** on the left end of the bar is used to start a program, open a document, get help, find information, and change system settings.

> If a Welcome box is displayed, click ☒ (in the upper right corner of the box) to close it.

> If you are already familiar with using a mouse, skip to the section Loading an Office Application.

Using a Mouse

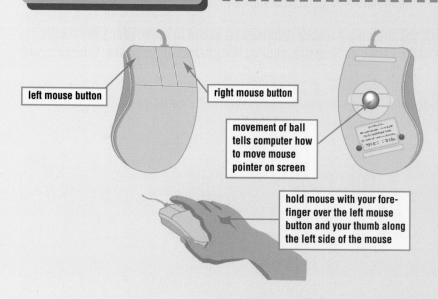

The arrow-shaped symbol on your screen is the **mouse pointer**. It is used to interact with objects on the screen and is controlled by the hardware device called a **mouse** that is attached to your computer.

The mouse pointer changes shape on the screen depending on what it is pointing to. Some of the most common shapes are shown in the table below.

Pointer Shape	Meaning
↖	Normal select
🖑	Link select
⧗	Busy
⃠	Area is not available

On top of the mouse are two or three buttons that are used to choose items on the screen. The mouse actions and descriptions are shown in the table below.

If your system has a stick, ball or touch pad, the buttons are located adjacent to the device.

Action	Description
Point	Move the mouse so the mouse pointer is positioned on the item you want to use.
Click	Press and release a mouse button. The left mouse button is the primary button that is used for most tasks.
Double-click	Quickly press and release the left mouse button twice.
Drag	Move the mouse while holding down the mouse button.

Throughout the labs, click means to use the left mouse button. If the right mouse button is to be used, the directions will tell you to right-click on the item.

1 Move the mouse in all directions (up, down, left, and right) and note the movement of the mouse pointer.

Point to the My Computer My Computer icon.

Your screen should be similar to Figure 2.

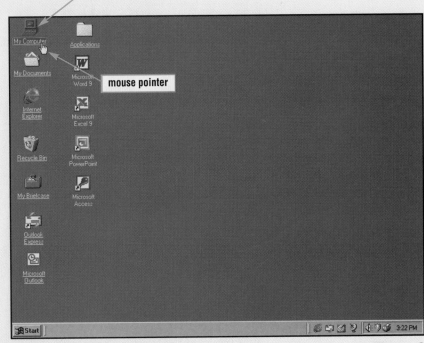

Figure 2

Depending on the version of Windows you are using and the setup, the mouse pointer may be ⬚ and you will need to click on the icon to select it.

The pointer on the screen moved in the direction you moved the mouse and currently appears as a ⬚. The icon appears highlighted, indicating it is the selected item and ready to be used. A **ScreenTip** box containing a brief description of the item you are pointing to may be displayed.

Loading an Office Application

There are several ways to start an Office application. One is to use the Start/New Office Document command and select the type of document you want to create. Another is to use Start/Documents and select the document name from the list of recently used documents. This starts the associated application and opens the selected document at the same time. The two most common ways to start an Office 2000 application are by choosing the application name from the Start menu or by clicking a desktop shortcut for the program if it is available.

Point to a Start menu option to select it; click it to choose it.

If you are using Windows 98, depending on your setup, you may only need to single-click the shortcut.

1 ■ Click **Start** to display the Start menu.

■ Select **Programs**

■ Choose **Microsoft Access**.

or

■ Double-click the **Microsoft Access** shortcut.

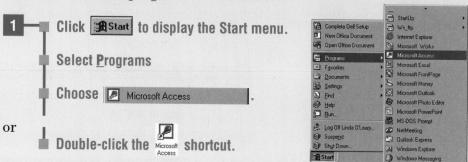

After a few moments, the Access 2000 application window is displayed.

2 ■ Click **Cancel** to close the dialog box.

Your screen should be similar to Figure 3.

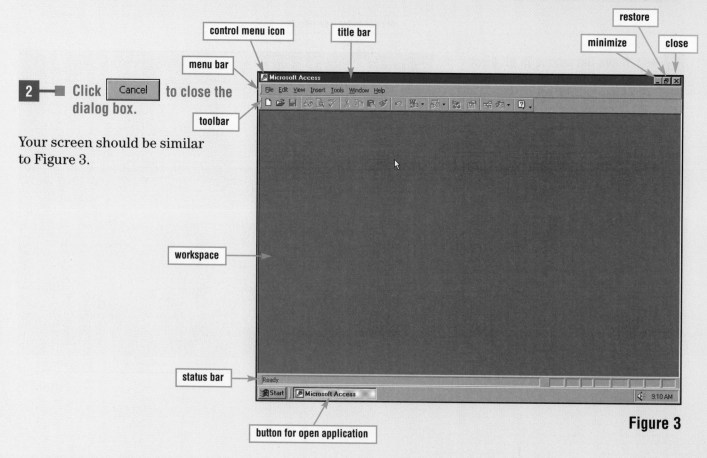

Figure 3

The Access 2000 application is loaded and displayed in a window on the desktop. The taskbar displays a button for the open window.

Basic Windows Features

As you can see, many of the features in the Access window are the same as in other Windows applications. Among those features is a title bar, a menu bar, toolbars, a document window, scroll bars, and mouse compatibility. You can move and size Office application windows, select commands, use Help, and switch between files and programs, just as you can in Windows. The common user interface makes learning and using new applications much easier.

TITLE BAR

The Access window **title bar** displays the program name, Microsoft Access. The left end of the title bar contains the Access application window ▨ Control-menu icon, and the right end displays the ▣ Minimize, ▣ Restore, and ☒ Close buttons. They perform the same functions and operate in the same way as in Windows 95 and Windows 98.

> **1** ━■ If necessary, click ▣ in the title bar to maximize the application window.

MENU BAR

The **menu bar** below the title bar displays the Access program menu, which consists of seven menus. The right end will display the document window ☒ Close button when a document is open. As you use the Office applications you will see that the menu bar contains many of the same menus, such as File, Edit and Help. You will also see several menus that are specific to each application. You will learn about using the menus in the next section.

TOOLBARS

The **toolbar** located below the menu bar contain buttons that are mouse shortcuts for many of the menu items. Commonly, the Office applications will display two toolbars when the application is first opened; Standard and Formatting. They may appear together on one row or on separate rows. Access 2000 initially displays a single toolbar named Database. You will learn about using the toolbars shortly.

WORKSPACE

The **workspace** is the large center area of the Access application window is where documents are displayed in open windows. Currently there is no document open. Multiple documents can be open and displayed in the work area at the same time.

STATUS BAR

The **status bar** at the bottom of the window displays location information and the status of different settings as they are used. Different information is displayed in the status bar for different applications.

Using Office 2000 Features

MENUS

A **menu** is one of many methods you can use to tell a program what you want it to do. When opened, a menu displays a list of commands. Most menus appear in a menu bar. Other menus pop up when you right-click (click the right mouse button) on an item. This type of menu is called a **shortcut menu**.

1 ■ Click Tools to open the Tools menu.

Your screen should be similar to Figure 4.

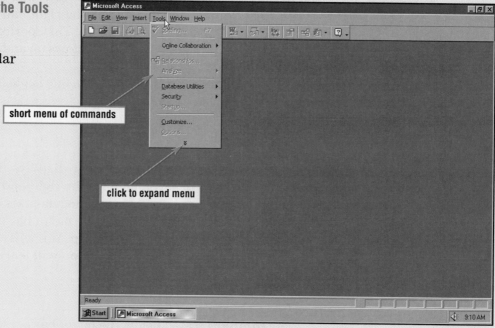

Figure 4

When some menus first open, a short list of commands is displayed. The short menu displays basic commands when the application is first used. As you use the application, those commands you use frequently are listed on the short menu and others are hidden. Because the short menu is personalized automatically to the user's needs different commands may be listed on your Tools menu than appear in Figure 4 above.

An expanded version will display automatically after the menu is opened for a few seconds (see Figure 5). If you do not want to wait for the expanded version to appear, you can click ≈ at the bottom of the menu and the menu list expands to display all commands.

Additional Information

You can also double-click the menu name to show the expanded menu immediately.

Your screen should be similar to Figure 5.

Figure 5

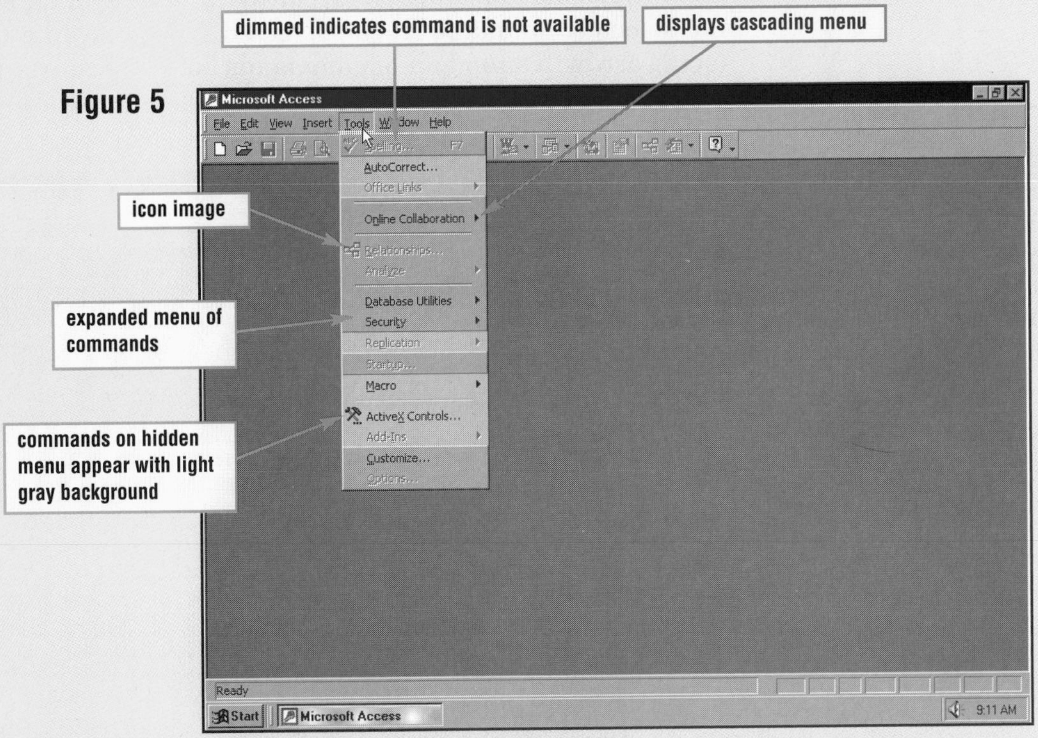

dimmed indicates command is not available

displays cascading menu

icon image

expanded menu of commands

commands on hidden menu appear with light gray background

The commands that are in the hidden menu appear on a light gray background. Additionally, because you do not have a document open, many of the commands are not available and appear dimmed. Once one menu is expanded, others are expanded automatically until you choose a command or perform another action.

2 ■ Point to each menu in the menu bar to see the expanded menu for each.

■ Point to the Tools menu again.

Many commands have images next to them so you can quickly associate the command with the image. The same image appears on the toolbar button for that feature.

Menus may include the following features (not all menus include all features):

Feature	Meaning
Ellipses (...)	Indicates a dialog box will be displayed
▶	Indicates a cascading menu will be displayed
Dimmed	Indicates the command is not available for selection until certain other conditions are met
Shortcut key	A key or key combination that can be used to execute a command without using the menu
Checkmark (✔)	Indicates a toggle type of command. Selecting it turns the feature on or off. A checkmark indicates the feature is on.

Once a menu is open, you can *select* a command from the menu by pointing to it. A colored highlight bar, called the **selection cursor**, appears over the selected command. If the selected command line displays a right-facing arrow, a submenu of commands automatically appears when the command is selected. This is commonly called a **cascading menu**.

3 ■ Point to the Online Collaboration command to display the cascading menu.

Your screen should be similar to Figure 6.

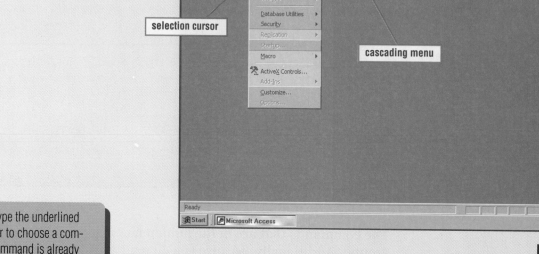

selection cursor

cascading menu

Figure 6

You can also type the underlined command letter to choose a command. If the command is already selected, you can press [←Enter] to choose it.

Then to choose a command you click on it. When the command is chosen, the associated action is performed. You will use a command in the Help menu to access the Microsoft Office Assistant and Help feature.

4 ■ Point to Help.

■ Choose Show the <u>O</u>ffice Assistant.

If the Assistant does not appear, your school has disabled this feature. If this is the case, Choose **H**elp/Microsoft Access **H**elp and skip to the section Using Help.

If the Office Assistant feature is on this command does not appear on the Help menu and the Office Assistant should already be displayed on your screen.

Your screen should be similar to Figure 7.

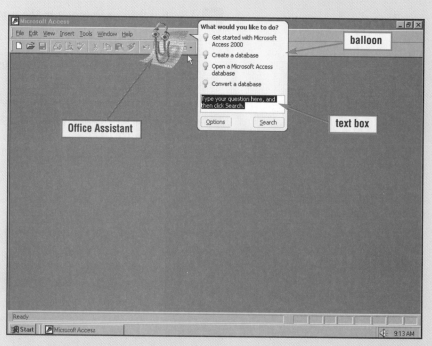

balloon

Office Assistant

text box

Figure 7

The command to display the assistant has been executed and the Office Assistant character is displayed. Because there are a variety of Assistant characters, your screen may display a different character than shown here.

Using the Office Assistant

When the Office Assistant is on, it automatically suggests help topics as you work. It anticipates what you are going to do and then makes suggestions on how to perform a task. In addition, you can activate the Assistant at any time to get help on features in the Office application you are using. When active, the Office Assistant balloon appears and displays a prompt and a text box in which you can type the topic you want help on.

1 ■■ **If the balloon is not displayed as in Figure 7, click the Office Assistant character to activate it.**

You will ask the Office Assistant to provide information on the different ways you can get help while using the program.

2 ■ **Click in the text box and type How do I get help?**

■ Click [Search].

Your screen should be similar to Figure 8.

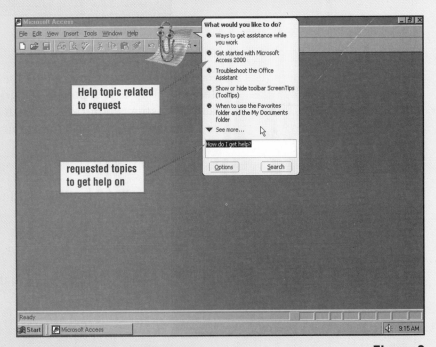

Figure 8

The balloon displays a list of related topics from which you can select.

3 ■ Click "Ways to get assistance while you work."

Your screen should be similar to Figure 9.

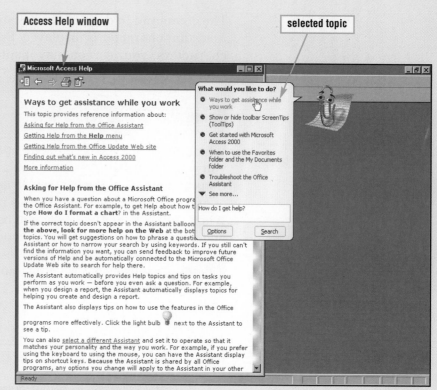

Figure 9

Additional Information

You can also press F1 to open Help if the Office Assistant is not on.

Additional Information

The Options button is used to change the Office Assistant settings so it provides different levels of help, or to select a different Assistant character.

The Help program has been opened and displays the selected topic. Because Help is a separate program it appears in its own window. The taskbar displays a button for both open windows. Now that Help is open, you no longer need to see the Assistant.

4 ■ Click Search .

■ Select **U**se the Office Assistant to clear the checkmark and turn off this feature.

■ Click OK .

■ Click 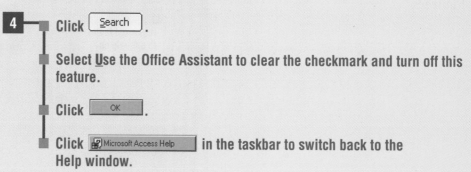 in the taskbar to switch back to the Help window.

Using Help

In the Help window, the toolbar buttons help you use different Help features and navigate within Help. The ⬅▤ Show button displays the Help tabs frame.

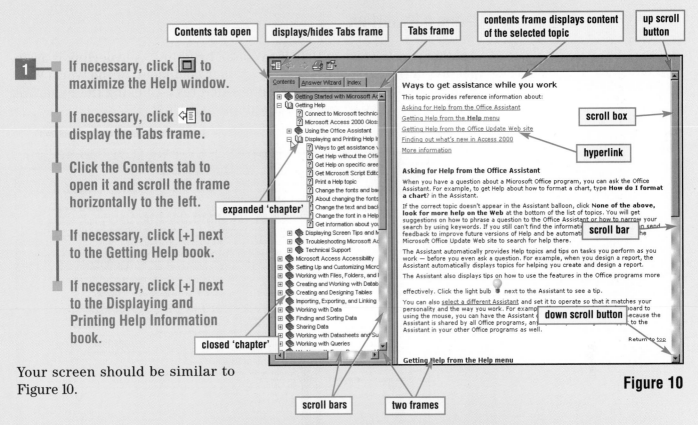

1 If necessary, click ▢ to maximize the Help window.

If necessary, click ◁▤ to display the Tabs frame.

Click the Contents tab to open it and scroll the frame horizontally to the left.

If necessary, click [+] next to the Getting Help book.

If necessary, click [+] next to the Displaying and Printing Help Information book.

Your screen should be similar to Figure 10.

Figure 10

The Help window is divided into two vertical frames. **Frames** divide a window into separate, scrollable areas that can display different information. The left frame in the Help window is the Tabs frame. The three folder-like tabs, Contents, Index and Search, in the left frame are used to access the three different means of getting Help information. The open tab appears in front of the other tabs and displays the available options for the feature.

The Contents tab displays a table of contents listing of topics in Help. Clicking on an item preceded with a 📖 opens a "chapter" which expands to display additional "chapters" or specific Help topics. Chapters are preceded with a 📖 icon and topics with a ? icon.

The right frame, commonly called the content frame, displays the located information. It contains more information than can be displayed at one time. A **scroll bar** is used with a mouse to bring additional lines of information into view in a window. It consists of **scroll arrows** and a **scroll box**. Clicking the arrows moves the information in the direction of the arrows, allowing new information to be displayed in the space. You can also move to a general location within the area by dragging the scroll box up or down the scroll bar. The location of the scroll box on the scroll bar indicates your relative position within the area of available information. Scroll bars can run vertically along the right side or horizontally along the bottom of a window. The vertical scroll bar is used to move vertically and the horizontal scroll bar moves horizontally in the space.

2 Use the scroll bar in the content frame to scroll to the bottom of the Help topic.

Scroll back to the top of the Help topic.

Using a Hyperlink

Another way to move in Help is to click a hyperlink. A **hyperlink** is a connection in the current document, another document, or the World Wide Web. It appears as colored or underlined text. Clicking the hyperlink moves to the location associated with the hyperlink.

1 **Click the** Asking for Help from the Office Assistant **hyperlink.**

The mouse pointer appears as 🖑 when pointing to a hyperlink.

Your screen should be similar to Figure 11.

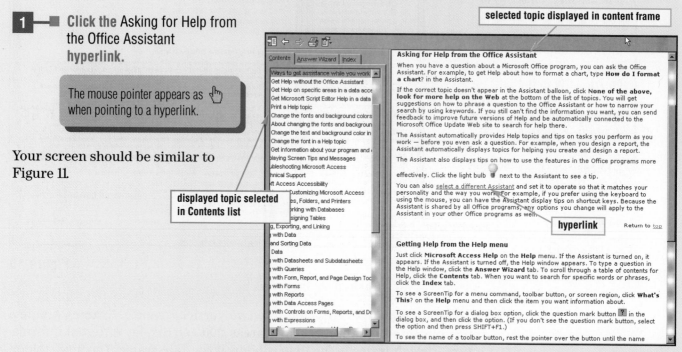

selected topic displayed in content frame

displayed topic selected in Contents list

hyperlink

Figure 11

Help quickly jumps to the selected topic and displays the topic heading at the top of the frame. Notice the Contents list now highlights this topic indicating it is the currently selected topic.

2 **Read the information displayed on this topic.**

Click the select a different Assistant **hyperlink.**

Your screen should be similar to Figure 12.

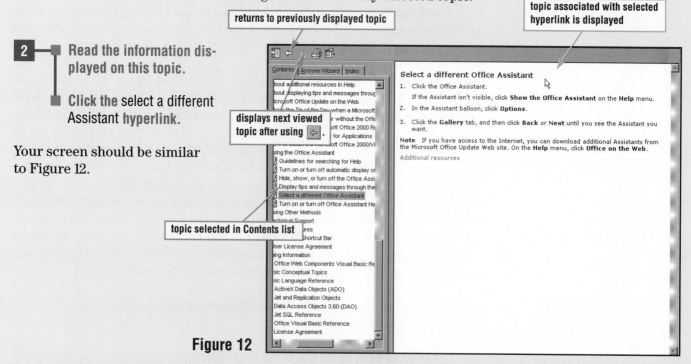

returns to previously displayed topic

topic associated with selected hyperlink is displayed

displays next viewed topic after using ⬅.

topic selected in Contents list

Figure 12

The help topic about selecting a different Assistant is displayed. Other hyperlinks will display a definition of a term in a pop-up box.

To quickly return to the previous topic,

The ⇨ Forward button is available after using ⇦ Back and can be used to move to the next viewed topic.

3 ─■ Click ⇦ Back.

The previous topic is displayed again.

Using the Index Tab

To search for Help information by entering a word or phrase for a topic, you can use the Index tab.

1 ─■ Open the Index tab.

Your screen should be similar to Figure 13.

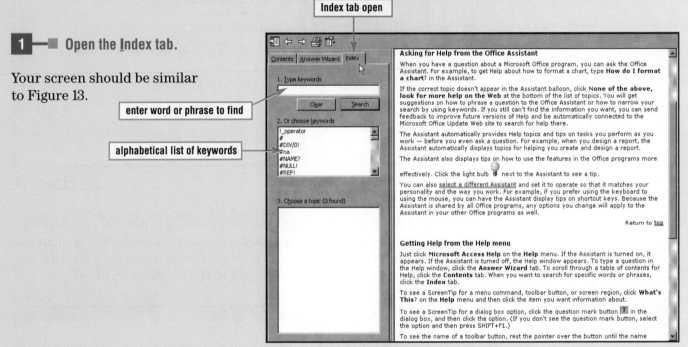

Figure 13

The Index tab consists of a text box where you can type a word or phrase that best describes the topic you want to locate and a list box displaying a complete list of Help keywords in alphabetical order. You want to find information about using the Index tab.

2 ─■ Type **index** in the text box.

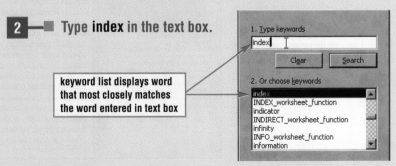

The keyword list jumps to the word index. To locate all Help topics containing this word,

3 ■ **Click** Search .

Your screen should be similar to Figure 14.

63 topics found

selected topic displayed

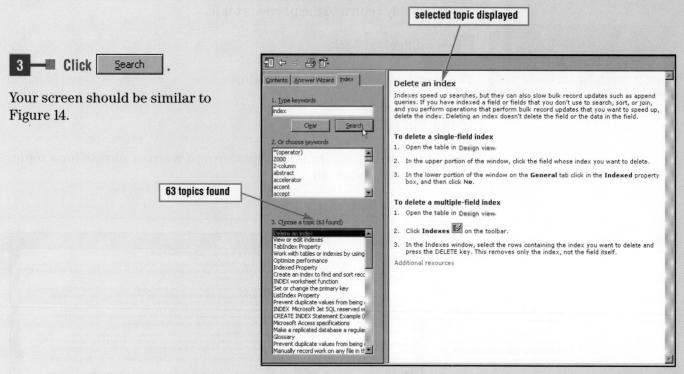

Figure 14

The topic list displays 63 Help topics containing this word and displays the information on the first topic in the content frame. However, many of the located topics are not about the Help Index feature. To narrow the search more, you can add another word to the keyword text box.

4 ■ **Type help in the keyword text box following the word index.**

■ **Click** Search .

Your screen should be similar to Figure 15.

more words define search better

search narrrowed and locates 12 topics

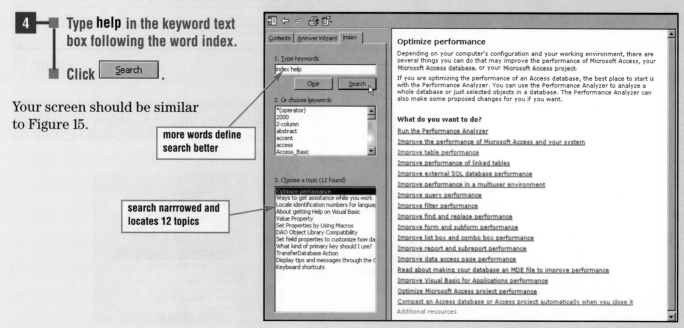

Figure 15

Now only 12 topics were located that contain both keywords. You can then click on a topic to display the information in the contents frame.

Using the Answer Wizard

Another way to locate Help topics is to use the Answer Wizard tab. This feature works just like the Office Assistant to locate topics. You will use this method to locate Help information on toolbars.

1 ■ Open the <u>A</u>nswer Wizard tab.

■ Type **How do toolbars work?** in the text box.

■ Click Search .

> The search term does not need to be worded as a question. It can also be a word or phrase.

Your screen should be similar to Figure 16.

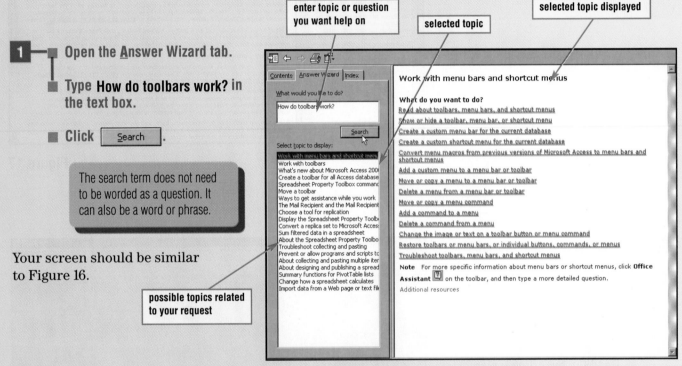

Figure 16

The topic list box displays all topics that the Answer Wizard considers may be related to the question you entered. The first topic is selected and displayed in the content frame.

2 ■ **Click** Read about toolbars, menus, and shortcut menus from the list of topics in the content frame.

Your screen should be similar to Figure 17.

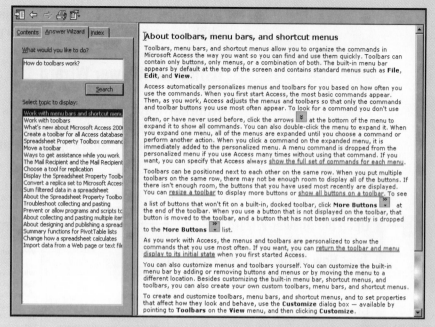

Figure 17

Database toolbar

3 ■ **Click** 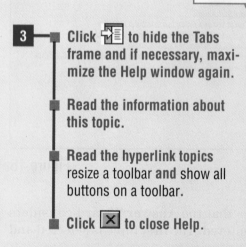 to hide the Tabs frame and if necessary, maximize the Help window again.

■ **Read the information about this topic.**

■ **Read the hyperlink topics** resize a toolbar **and** show all buttons on a toolbar.

■ **Click** ⊠ **to close Help.**

Your screen should be similar to Figure 18.

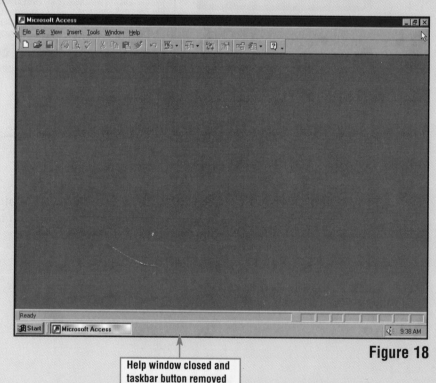

Figure 18

Help window closed and taskbar button removed

The Help window is closed and the Access window is displayed again.

Using Toolbars

While using Office 2000, you will see that many toolbars open automatically as different tasks are performed. Toolbars initially display the basic buttons. Like menus they are personalized automatically ... displaying those buttons you use frequently and hiding others. If there is not enough space to fully display all its buttons, a More Buttons ⨠ button appears at the end of the toolbar. Clicking it displays a drop-down button list of those buttons that are not displayed. When you use a button from this list, it then is moved to the toolbar and a button that has not been used recently is moved to the More Buttons list.

Initially, Access displays the Database toolbar on one row below the menu bar (see Figure 18). This toolbar contains buttons that are used to complete the most frequently used menu commands. If you right-click on a toolbar, the toolbar shortcut menu is displayed. Using this menu you can see which toolbars are available and select those you want displayed.

1 ── Right-click on the toolbar.

> The menu equivalent is **V**iew/**T**oolbars.

Your screen should be similar to Figure 19.

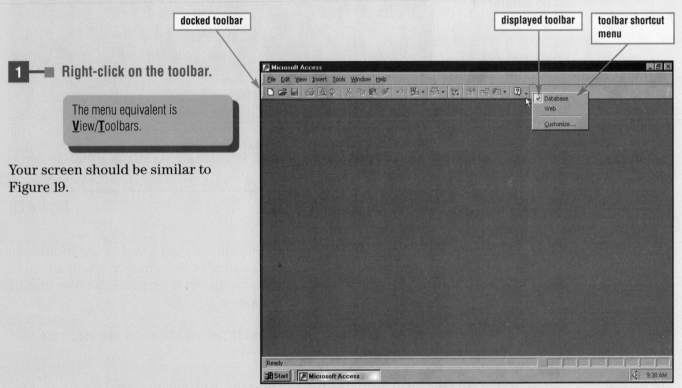

Figure 19

The toolbar shortcut menu lists only two available toolbars. The currently displayed toolbar is checked. Clicking on a toolbar name from the list will display it onscreen. Likewise, clicking on a checked toolbar will hide the toolbar.

2 ── Press Esc to clear the shortcut menu.

When a toolbar is opened, it may appear docked or floating. When **docked** they are fixed to an edge of the window and display the move handle ▯. Dragging this bar up or down allows you to move the toolbar. When docked, multiple toolbars share the same row and dragging the bar left or right adjusts the size of the toolbar. When **floating** they appear in a separate window that can be moved by dragging the title bar.

3 ── ■ Drag the move handle of the Database toolbar into the workspace.

> The mouse pointer appears as ✛ when you can move the toolbar.

Your screen should be similar to Figure 20.

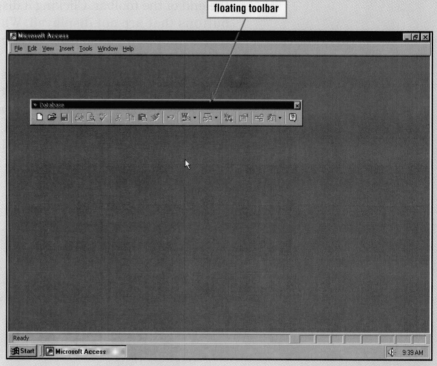

floating toolbar

Figure 20

The Database toolbar is now floating and can be moved to any location in the workspace. If you move it to the edge of the window, it will attach to that location and become a docked toolbar. A floating toolbar can also be sized by dragging the edge of the toolbar.

4 ── ■ Move the floating toolbar back to the left end of the row below the menu bar.

To quickly identify the toolbar buttons, you can display the button name by pointing to the button.

5 ── ■ Point to any button on the Database toolbar to see the ScreenTip displaying the button name.

Exiting an Office Application

The Exit command on the File menu can be used to quit most windows programs. In addition, you can click the ☒ Close button in the application window title bar.

1 ─ ■ Click ☒ Close.

The application window is closed and the desktop is visible again.

Key Terms

cascading menu xxviii	mouse xxii	status bar xxvi
desktop xxii	mouse pointer xxii	taskbar xxii
docked xxxviii	ScreenTip xxiv	title bar xxv
floating xxxviii	scroll arrows xxxi	toolbar xxv
frame xxxi	scroll bar xxxi	workspace xxv
hyperlink xxxii	scroll box xxxi	
icon xxii	selection cursor xxviii	
menu xxvi	shortcut menu xxvi	
menu bar xxv	Start button xxii	

Command Summary

Command	Shortcut Keys	Button	Action
[Start]/Programs			Opens program menu
File/E**x**it	Alt + F4	☒	Exits Access program
View/**T**oolbars			Hides or displays toolbars
Help/Microsoft Access **H**elp	F1		Opens Help window
Help/Show the **O**ffice Assistant.			Displays Help's office assistant

Overview

What Is a Database?

Somewhere at home, or maybe in your office, you probably have a file cabinet or desk drawer filled with information. Perhaps you have organized the information into drawers of related information, and further categorized that information into file folders. This is a database.

As organized as you might be, it takes time to locate a specific piece of information by manually opening drawers and searching through the folders. You can just imagine how much time would be required for a large company to manually search through its massive amounts of data. These companies use electronic database management systems. Now you, too, can use electronic database management systems to store, organize, access, manipulate, and present information in a variety of ways.

In this series of tutorials you will learn how to design and create a computerized database using Access 2000, and you will quickly appreciate the many advantages of a computerized database.

Database table

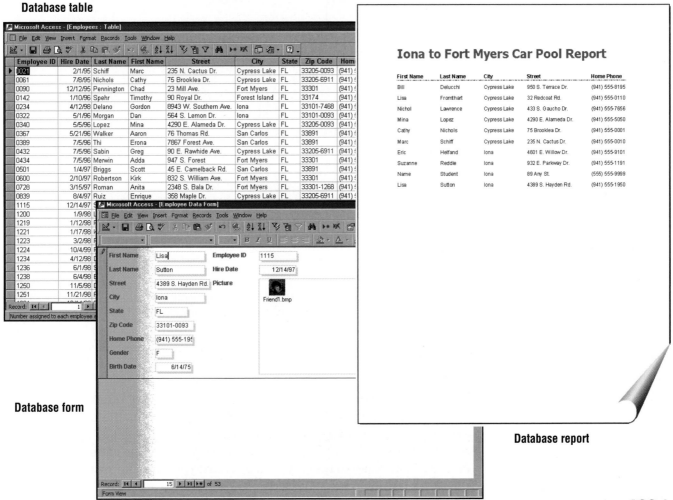

Database form

Database report

Access 2000 Features

Access 2000 is a relational database management system. In relational database systems, data is organized in tables that are related or linked to one another. Each table consists of rows, called records, and columns, called fields.

For example, a state's motor vehicle department database might have an address table. Each row (record) in the table would contain complete address information about one individual. Each column (field) would contain one piece of address information, such as a name. The address table would be linked to other tables in the database by common fields. For example, the address table might be linked to a vehicle owner's table by name and linked to an outstanding citation table by license number (see example below).

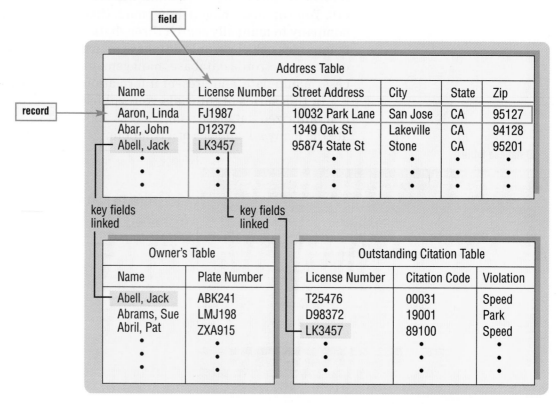

Access 2000 is a powerful program with numerous easy-to-use features, including the ability to quickly locate information, add, delete, and modify records, sort records, analyze data, and produce professional-looking reports. Some of the basic Access 2000 features are described next.

FIND INFORMATION

Once you enter data into the database table, you can quickly search the table to locate a specific record based on the data in a field. In a manual system, you can usually locate a record by knowing one key piece of information. For example, if the records are stored in a file cabinet alphabetically by last name, to quickly find a record you must know the last name.

In a computerized database, even if the records are sorted or organized by last name, you can still quickly locate a record using information in another field.

ADD, DELETE, AND MODIFY RECORDS

Using Access, it is also easy to add and delete records from the table. Once you locate a record, you can edit the contents of the fields to update the record or delete the record entirely from the table. You can also add new records to a table. When you enter a new record, it is automatically placed in the correct organizational location within the table.

SORT RECORDS

The capability to arrange or sort records in the table according to different fields of data helps provide more meaningful information. You can organize records by name, department, pay, class, or any other category you need at a particular time. Sorting the records in different ways can provide information to different departments for different purposes.

ANALYZE DATA

Using Access, you can analyze the data in a table and perform calculations on different fields of data. Instead of pulling each record from a filing cabinet, recording the piece of data you want to use, and then performing the calculation on the recorded data, you can simply have the database program perform the calculation on all the values in the specified field. Additionally, you can ask questions or query the table to find only certain records that meet specific conditions to be used in the analysis. Information that was once costly and time-consuming to get is now quickly and readily available.

GENERATE REPORTS

Access includes many features that help you quickly produce reports ranging from simple listings to complex, professional-looking reports. You can create a simple report by asking for a listing of specified fields of data and restricting the listing to records meeting designated conditions. You can create a more complex, professional report using the same restrictions or conditions as the simple report, but you can display the data in different layout styles, or with titles, headings, subtotals, or totals.

Case Study for Access 2000 Tutorials

You have recently accepted a job as employment administrator for Lifestyle Fitness Club. The Club has recently purchased Microsoft Access 2000, and you are using it to update their manual system for recording employee information.

Before You Begin

- -

To the Student

The following assumptions have been made:

■ Microsoft Access 2000 has been properly installed on the hard disk of your computer system.

■ The data disk contains the data files needed to complete the series of tutorials and practice exercises. These files are supplied by your instructor.

■ You are already familiar with how to use Windows and a mouse.

To the Instructor

By default, Office 2000 installs the most commonly used components and leaves others to be installed when first accessed. It is assumed that these additional features have been installed prior to students using the tutorials.

Please be aware that the following settings are assumed to be in effect for the Access 2000 program. These assumptions are necessary so that the screens and directions in the manual are accurate.

■ The Startup dialog box appears when Access first loads.

■ The ScreenTips feature is active. (Use Tools/Customize/Options.)

■ The Office Assistant feature is not on. (Click on the Assistant, click [Options], and clear the Use the Office Assistant option.)

■ The status bar is displayed.

■ All default datasheet settings are in effect, including font settings of Arial 10 pt.

■ In addition, all figures in the manual reflect the use of a standard VGA display monitor set at 800×600. If another monitor setting is used, there may be more or fewer lines displayed in the windows than in the figures. This setting can be changed using Windows setup.

Microsoft Office Shortcut Bar

- -

The Microsoft Office Shortcut Bar (shown on the next page) may be displayed automatically on the Windows desktop. Commonly, it appears on the right side of the desktop, but it may appear in other locations, depending upon your setup. The Shortcut Bar on your screen may display different buttons. This is because the Shortcut Bar can be customized to display other toolbar buttons.

The Office Shortcut Bar makes it easy to open existing documents or to create new documents using one of the Microsoft Office applications. It can also be used to send e-mail, add a task to a to-do list, schedule appointments using Schedule+, or access Office Help.

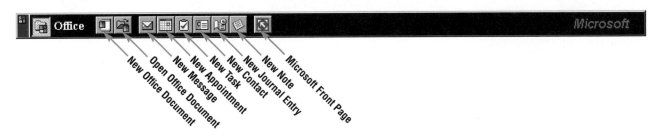

Instructional Conventions

Hands-on instructions you are to perform appear as a sequence of numbered blue steps. Within each step, a series of pink bullets identifies the specific actions that must be performed. Step numbering starts over within each main topic heading throughout the tutorial.

Command sequences you are to issue appear following the word "Choose." Each menu command selection is separated by a /. If the menu command can be selected by typing a letter of the command, the letter will appear underlined and bold. Items that need to be highlighted will follow the word "Select." You can select items with the mouse or directional keys.

EXAMPLE

1 — ■ Choose **F**ile/**O**pen.

   ■ Select Trip Flyer

Commands that can be initiated using a button and the mouse appear following the word "Click. " The icon (and the icon name if the icon does not include text) is displayed following Click. The menu equivalent and keyboard shortcut appear in a margin note when the action is first introduced.

> The menu equivalent is **F**ile/**O**pen and the keyboard shortcut is (Ctrl) + O.

EXAMPLE

1 — ■ Click 📂 Open

Black text identifies items you need to select or move to. Information you are asked to type appears in black and bold.

EXAMPLE

1 — ■ Move to the A in Announcing.

   ■ Type **Adventure Travel presents four new trips**.

Creating a Database

Competencies

After completing this tutorial, you will know how to:

1. Plan and create a database.
2. Create a table.
3. Save the table structure.
4. Change views.
5. Enter and edit data.
6. Insert a picture.
7. Adjust column widths.
8. Add records in Data Entry.
9. Preview and print a table.
10. Close and open a database.

Case Study

You have recently accepted a new job as employment administrator with Lifestyle Fitness Club. Like many fitness centers, Lifestyle Fitness Club includes exercise equipment, free weights, aerobic classes, tanning and message facilities, swimming pool, steam room and sauna, and child care facilities. In addition, they promote a healthy lifestyle by including educational seminars on good nutrition and proper exercise. They also have a small snack bar that serves healthy drinks, sandwiches, and snacks.

The Lifestyle Fitness Clubs is a franchised chain of clubs that are individually owned. The club you work at is owned by Brian and Cindy

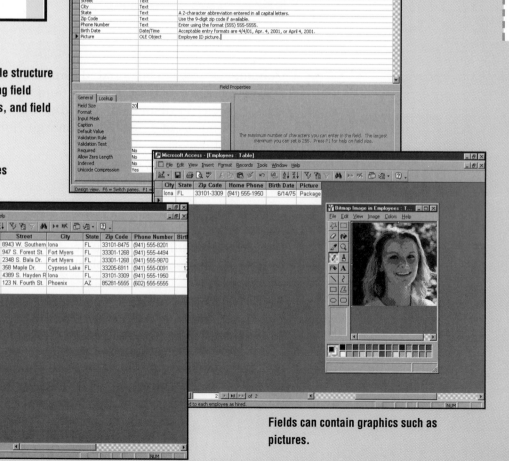

Designing the table structure consists of defining field names, data types, and field properties.

Entering data in a table creates records of information.

Fields can contain graphics such as pictures.

Birch, who also own two others in Florida. Accounting and employment functions for all three clubs are handled centrally at the Fort Myers location.

You are responsible for maintaining the employment records for all employees, as well as traditional employment activities such as hiring and benefits. Currently the Club employment records are maintained on paper forms and stored in file cabinets organized alphabetically by last name. Although the information is well organized, it still takes time to manually leaf through the folders to locate the information you need and to compile reports from this data.

The Club has recently purchased new computers, and the owners want to update the employee record-keeping system to an electronic database management system. The software tool you will use to create the database is the database application Access 2000. In this tutorial, you will learn about entering, editing, previewing, and printing a document while you create the employee database and a table (shown below) of basic employee information.

Employees   1/21/01

Employee ID	Hire Date	Last Name	First Name	Street	City	State
0434	7/5/96	Merwin	Adda	947 S. Forest St.	Fort Myers	FL
0728	3/15/97	Roman	Anita	2348 S. Bala Dr.	Fort Myers	FL
0839	8/4/97	Ruiz	Enrique	358 Maple Dr.	Cypress Lake	FL
1115	10/14/97	Sutton	Lisa	4389 Hayden Rd.	Iona	FL
1228	4/12/98	Delano	Gordon	8943 W. Southern Ave.	Iona	FL
9999	2/12/01	Name	Student	55 Any St.	Any Town	FL

Employees   1/21/01

Zip Code	Home Phone	Birth Date	Picture
33301-1268	(941) 555-4494	4/20/70	
33301-7985	(941) 555-9870	3/15/61	
33205-6911	(941) 555-0091	12/10/63	
33101-3309	(941) 555-1950	6/14/65	Package
33101-8475	(941) 555-8201	8/7/61	
33333-3333	(555) 555-1222	8/7/75	

Concept Overview

The following concepts will be introduced in this lab:

(1) Database   A database is an organized collection of related information.

(2) Database Development   The development of a database follows several steps: plan, create, enter and edit data, and preview and print.

(3) Object   An item, such as a table, or reports, that can be created, selected, and manipulated as a unit.

(4) Field Name   A field name is used to identify the data stored in the field.

(5) Data Type   The data type defines the type of data the field will contain.

(6) Field Property   Field properties are a set of characteristics that are associated with each field.

(7) Primary Key   A primary key is a field that uniquely identifies each record.

(8) Edit and Navigation Modes   The Edit and Navigation modes control how you can move through and make changes to data in a table.

(9) Graphics   A graphic is a non-text element or object, such as a drawing or picture, that can be added to a table.

(10) Column Width   Column width refers to the size of each field column in Datasheet view. It controls the amount of data you can see on the screen.

Exploring the Access 2000 Window

The Fitness Club recently purchased the Office 2000 application software suite and will use the Access 2000 database management program to create several different databases of information.

Concept ① Database

A **database** is an organized collection of related information. Typically, the information in a database is stored in a **table** consisting of vertical columns and horizontal rows. Each row contains a **record**, which is all the information about one person, thing, or place. Each column is a **field**, which is the smallest unit of information about a record. Access databases can contain multiple tables that can be linked to produce combined output from all tables. This type of database is called a **relational database**. See the Overview to Access 2000 for more information about relational databases.

You will begin by creating a database table using Access 2000 to hold the employee data.

1 Start Access 2000.

If necessary, maximize the Access application window.

See Introducing Common Office 2000 Features for information on how to start the application and for a discussion of features that are common to all Office 2000 applications.

Your screen should be similar to Figure 1–1

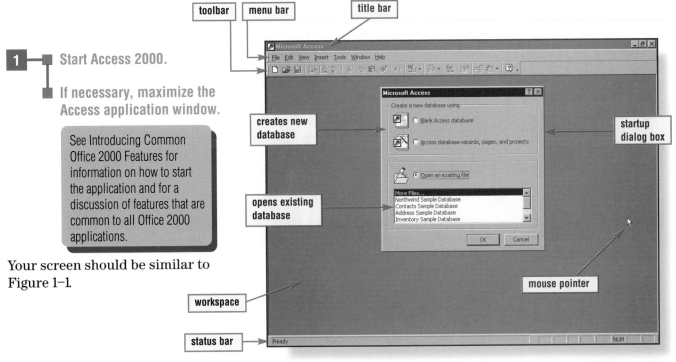

Figure 1–1

Because the Office 2000 applications remember settings that were on when the program was last exited, your screen may look slightly different.

The Microsoft Access 2000 application window with the startup dialog box open in it is displayed. The startup dialog box allows you to create a new database or open an existing database. The menu bar below the title bar displays the Access program menu. It consists of seven menus that provide access to the commands and features you will use to create and modify a database. The menus and commands that are available at any time vary with the task you are performing.

The toolbar, normally located below the menu bar, contains buttons that are mouse shortcuts for many of the menu commands. There are many different toolbars in Access. Most toolbars appear automatically as you perform different tasks and open different windows.

The center area of the window is the workspace where different Access windows are displayed as you are using the program. Just below the workspace, the status bar provides information about the task you are working on and the current Access operation. In addition, the status bar displays messages such as button and command descriptions to help you use the program more efficiently.

The mouse pointer appears as a ☐ on your screen. The mouse pointer changes shape depending upon the task you are performing or where the pointer is located on the window.

Finally, your screen may display the Office Assistant. This feature provides quick access to online Help.

Planning a Database

The Lifestyle Fitness Club plans to use Access 2000 to maintain several different types of databases. The database you will create will contain information about each Club employee. Other plans for using Access include keeping track of members and inventory. To keep the different types of information separate, the club plans to create a database for each group. Creating a new database follows several basic steps.

Concept ② Database Development

The development of a database follows several steps: plan, create, enter, and edit data, and preview and print.

Plan The first step in the development of a database is to understand the purpose of the database and to plan what information it should hold and the output you need from it.

Create After planning the database, you create tables to hold data by defining the table structure.

Enter and Edit Once a table has been set up, you enter the data to complete each record. While entering data, you may make typing and entry errors that need to be corrected. This is one type of editing. Another is to revise the structure of the tables by adding, deleting, or redefining information in the table.

Preview and Print The last step is to print a hard copy of the database or report. This step includes previewing the document onscreen as it will appear when printed. Previewing allows you to check the document's overall appearance and to make any final changes needed before printing.

You will find that you will generally follow these steps in order as you create your database. However, you will probably retrace steps as the final database is developed.

Your first step is to plan the design of your database tables: how many tables, what data they will contain, and how they will be related. You need to decide what information each table in the employee database should contain and how it should be structured or laid out.

You can obtain this information by analyzing the current record-keeping procedures used throughout the company. You need to understand the existing procedures so your database tables will reflect the information that is maintained by different departments. You should be aware of the forms that are the basis for the data entered into the department records, and of the information that is taken from the records to produce periodic reports. You also need to find out what information the department heads would like to be able to obtain from the database that may be too difficult to generate using their current procedures.

After looking over the existing record-keeping procedures and the reports that are created from the information, you decide to create several separate tables of data in the database file. Creating several smaller tables of related data rather than one large table makes it easier to use the tables and faster to process data. This is because you can join several tables together as needed. The main table will include the employee's basic information, such as employee number, name, and address. Another table will contain job-related information, such as department and job title. A third will contain data on pay rate, and another will hold data about the hours worked each week. To clarify the organization of the database, you sketched out the structure for the employee database as shown below.

Employee Database

Employee Table

Emp #	Last Name	First Name	Street	City	State	Zipcode	Phone	Birth Date
7721	Brown	Linda	——	——	——	——	——	——
7823	Duggan	Michael	——	——	——	——	——	——
⋮	⋮	⋮	⋮	⋮	⋮	⋮	⋮	⋮

link on common field

link on common field

Location

Emp #	Location
7721	Iona
7823	Fort Myers
⋮	⋮

Pay Rate

Emp #	Pay	Hours
7721	8.25	30
7823	7.50	20
⋮	⋮	⋮

Creating a Database

Now that you have decided on the information you want to include in the tables, you are ready to create a new database to hold the table information. From the startup dialog box,

1 ■ Select **B**lank Access Database.

   ■ Click   OK   .

Your screen should be similar to Figure 1–2.

> The default location and the folders and files displayed may be different than shown here.

> You can also start a new database using **F**ile/**N**ew/General/**D**atabase.

Additional Information

Windows documents can have up to 256 characters in the file name. Names can contain letters or numbers. Special symbols cannot be used with the exception of the underscore.

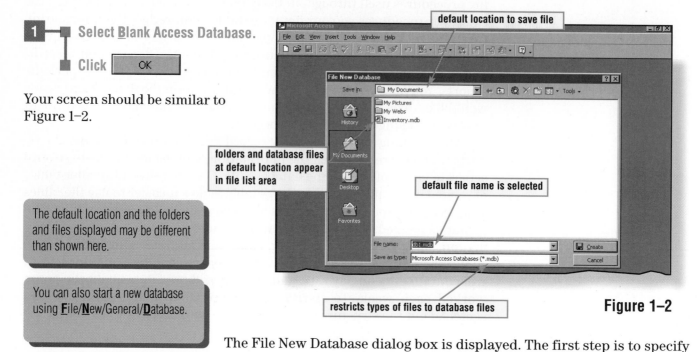

Figure 1–2

The File New Database dialog box is displayed. The first step is to specify a name for the database file and the location where you want the file saved. By default, Access opens the My Documents folder as the location to save the file. The file list section of the dialog box displays the names of folders and database files in the default location. Only database file names are displayed because the file type is restricted to Access Databases in the Save As Type text box. The default file name db1 appears in the File Name text box. You want the program to store the database on your data disk using the name Lifestyle Fitness Employees. Notice the default name is highlighted, indicating it is selected and will be replaced as you type the new name. First you will change the file name.

2 ■ Type **Lifestyle Fitness Employees**.

Your screen should be similar to Figure 1–3.

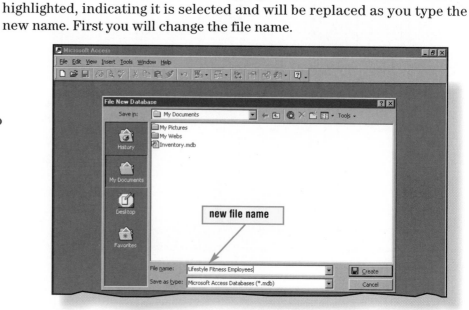

Figure 1–3

The default file name is replaced with the new file name. Next you need to change the location to the drive containing your data disk (A:).

3 ■ Place your data disk in drive A (or the appropriate drive for your system).

■ Open the Save In list box.

■ Select 3 1/2 Floppy (A:) from the Save In drop-down list.

Your screen should be similar to Figure 1–4.

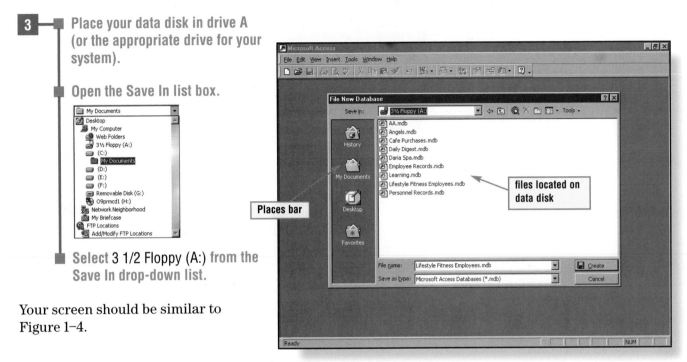

Places bar

files located on data disk

Figure 1–4

Now the file list section displays the names of all Access files on your data disk. You can also select the location to save from the Places bar along the left side of the dialog box. The icons bring up a list of recently accessed files and folders (History), the contents of the My Documents and Favorites folder, and the Windows desktop. Selecting a folder from one of these lists changes to that location. You can also click the ⇐ button in the toolbar to return to folders that were previously opened during the current session.

Notice that the program added the .mdb file extension to the file name. This is the default extension for Access documents.

If your screen does not display file extensions, your Windows program has this option deactivated.

4 ━ ■ Click 💾 Create .

Your screen should be similar to
Figure 1–5.

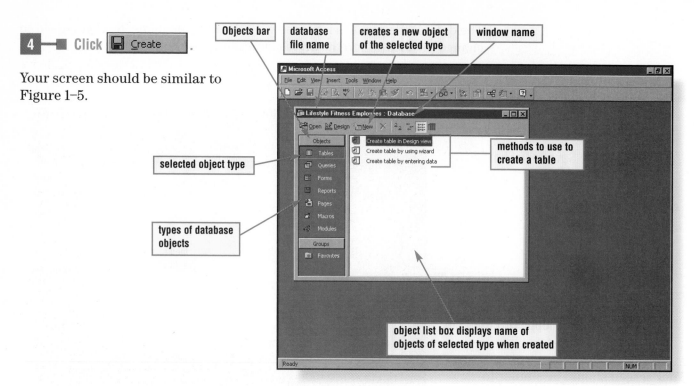

Figure 1–5

Using the Database Window

The Database window displays the name of the database, LifeStyle Fitness
Employees, followed by the name of the window in the window title bar. It
also includes its own toolbar that contains buttons to help you quickly create, open, or manage database objects.

Concept ③ Object

An **object** is an item, such as a table or report, that is made up of many elements and that can be created,
selected, and manipulated as a unit. The **Objects bar** along the left edge of the Database window organizes
the database objects into object types and groups, and is used to quickly access the different database objects. The currently selected object is Tables. The table object is the basic unit of a database and must be
created first, before any other types of objects are created. The **object list box** to the right of the object bar
normally displays a list of objects associated with the selected object type. The Tables object list box displays
three ways you can create a table. It will also display the names of objects of the selected object type once
they are created.

Access displays each different type of object in its own window. You can display multiple object windows
in the workspace; however, you cannot open more than one database file at a time.

Creating a Table

- -

After naming the database, your next step is to create the new table to hold the employee information by defining the structure of the table.

1 ── ■ Click  .

Your screen should be similar to Figure 1–6.

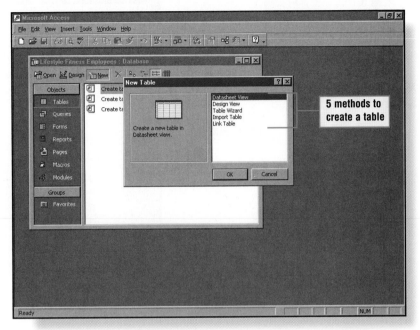

Figure 1–6

Additional Information
- - - - - - - - - - - - - - - - -

Access includes many different Wizards that can be used to create different Access objects.

You will learn more about views later in the lab.

The New Table dialog box provides five different ways to create a table. The first three, Datasheet View, Design View, and Table Wizard, are the most commonly used. They are the same three methods that are listed in the object list box. The Table Wizard option starts the Table Wizard feature, which lets you select from 45 predesigned database tables. The Wizard then guides you through the steps to create a table for you based upon your selections. The Datasheet and Design View options open different windows in which you can create a new custom table from scratch.

You will use the Design View option to create the table.

2 ■ Select Design View.

■ Click ▭OK▭ .

■ If necessary, maximize the Table window.

Your screen should be similar to Figure 1–7.

Table Design toolbar

design grid used to define fields

Help box describes current task of defining a field name

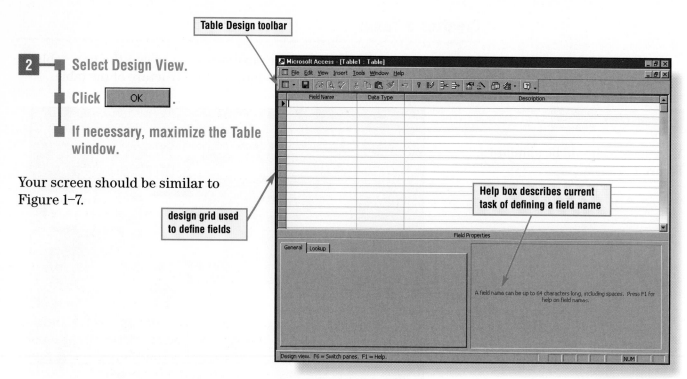

Figure 1–7

The Table Design window is opened and displayed over the Database window in the workspace. This window also has its own toolbar, the Table Design toolbar, which contains the standard buttons as well as buttons (identified below) that are specific to this window.

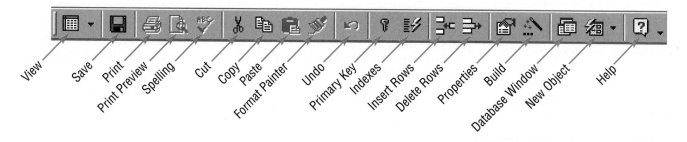

The upper section of the Table Design window consists of a **design grid** where you define each field to include in the table. Each row in the grid is where a field is defined by entering the required information in each of the columns. You decide to include the data currently maintained in the personnel folder on each employee in one table using the following 11 fields: Employee Number, Date Hired, Last Name, First Name, Street, City, State, Zip Code, Phone Number, Birth Date, and Picture.

Defining Field Name

The first step is to give each field a field name.

Concept ④ Field Name

A **field name** is used to identify the data stored in the field. A field name should be descriptive of the contents of the data to be entered in the field. It can be up to 64 characters long and can consist of letters, numbers, spaces, and special characters, except a period, an exclamation point, an accent grave ('), and brackets ([]). You also cannot start a field name with a space. Examples of field names are: Last Name, First Name, Address, Phone Number, Department, Hire Date, or other words that describe the data. It is best to use short field names to make the tables easier to manage.

In the lower right section of the dialog box, a Help box provides information on the task you are performing in the window. Since the insertion point is positioned in the Field Name text box, the Help box displays a brief description of the rules for entering a valid field name.

The first field of data you will enter in the table is the employee number, which is assigned to each employee when hired. Each new employee is given the next consecutive number, so no two employees can have the same number. It is a maximum of four digits. The ▶ to the left of the first row indicates the current field.

> The field name can be typed in uppercase or lowercase letters, and will be displayed exactly as entered.

1 ▬ Type **Employee Number**.

Your screen should be similar to Figure 1–8.

indicates current field

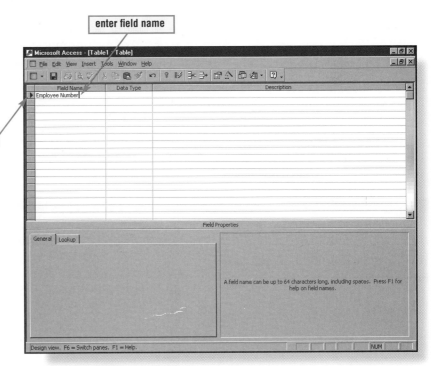

enter field name

Figure 1–8

Since the data you will enter in this field is a maximum of four characters, you decide to change the field name to Employee ID, so the field name is closer in size to the data that will be entered in the field.

To edit the entry,

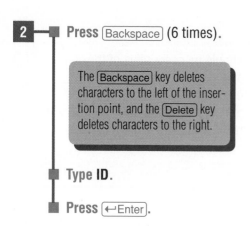

2 ■ Press Backspace (6 times).

> The Backspace key deletes characters to the left of the insertion point, and the Delete key deletes characters to the right.

■ Type **ID**.

■ Press ←Enter.

Your screen should be similar to Figure 1–9.

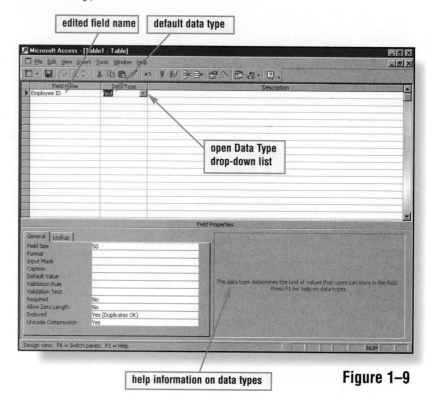

Figure 1–9

The insertion point has moved to the Data Type column, where the default data type of "Text" is automatically entered. The Help box provides a definition of what defining a data type does.

Defining Data Type and Field Properties

To specify the data type for the Employee ID field,

1 ■ Open the Data Type drop-down list.

Your screen should be similar to Figure 1–10.

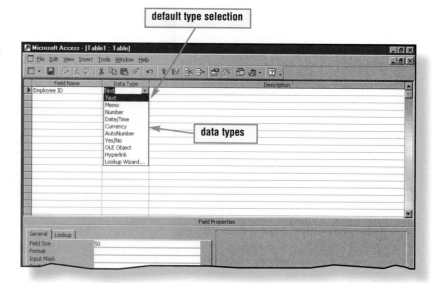

Figure 1–10

Concept ⑤ Data Type

The **data type** defines the type of data the field will contain. Access uses the data type to ensure that the right kind of data is entered in a field. It is important to choose the right data type for a field before you start entering data in the table. You can change a data type after the field contains data, but if the data types are not compatible, such as a text entry in a field whose data type accepts numbers only, you may lose data. The data types are described below.

Data Type	Description
Text	Text entries (words, combinations of words and numbers, numbers that are not used in calculations) up to 255 characters in length (this is the default). Names and phone numbers are examples of Text field entries. Text is the default data type.
Memo	Text that is variable in length and usually too long to be stored in a Text field. A maximum of 65,535 characters can be entered in a Memo field.
Number	Digits only. Number fields are used when you want to perform calculations on the values in the field. Number of Units Ordered is an example of a Number field entry.
Date/Time	Any valid date. Access allows dates from January 1, 100 to December 31, 9999. Access correctly handles leap years and checks all dates for validity.
Currency	Exactly like the Number field, but formatted to display decimal places and a currency symbol.
AutoNumber	A unique, sequential number that is automatically incremented by one whenever a new record is added to a table.
Yes/No	Accepts only Yes/No, True/False, or On/Off entries.
OLE Object	An object, such as a graphic (picture), sound, document, or spreadsheet, that is linked to or embedded in a table.
Hyperlink	Accepts hyperlink entries that are paths to an object, document, Web page, or other destinations.
Lookup Wizard	Displays a list of options you choose from another table in the database. Choosing this data type starts the Lookup Wizard.

Even though a field such as the Employee ID field may contain numeric entries, unless the numbers are used in calculations, the field should be assigned the Text data type. This allows other characters, such as the parentheses or hyphens in a telephone number, to be included in the entry. Also, by specifying the type as Text, any leading zeros (for example, in the zip code 07739) will be preserved, whereas leading zeros in a Number type field are dropped (which would make this zip code incorrectly 7739).

To close the Data Type drop-down menu without changing the selection,

2 ─■ Press Esc.

Your screen should be similar to
Figure 1–11.

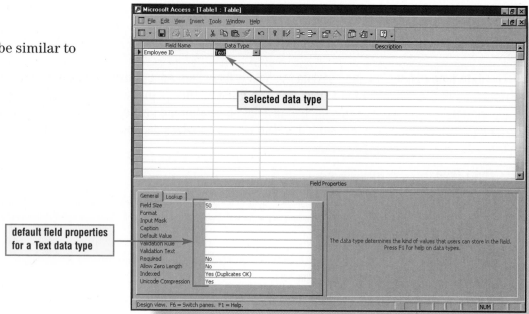

Figure 1–11

Notice in the Field Properties area of the dialog box that the General tab displays the default field property settings associated with a Text data type.

Concept ⑥ Field Property

Field properties are a set of characteristics that are associated with each field. Each data type has a different set of field properties. Setting field properties enhances the way your table works. Some of the more commonly used properties and their functions are described below.

Field Property	Description
Field Size	Sets the maximum number of characters that can be entered in the field.
Format	Specifies how data displays in a table and prints.
Input Mask	Simplifies data entry by controlling what data is required in a field and how the data is to be displayed.
Caption	Specifies a field label other than the field name.
Default Value	Automatically fills in a certain value for this field in new records as you add to the table. You can override a default value by typing a new value into the field.
Validation Rule	Limits data entered in a field to values that meet certain requirements.
Validation Text	Specifies the message to be displayed when the associated Validation Rule is not satisfied.
Required	Specifies whether or not a value must be entered in a field.
Allow Zero Length	Specifies whether or not an entry containing no characters is valid.
Indexed	Sets a field as an index field (a field that controls the order of records). Speeds up searches on fields that are searched frequently.

You need to set the **field size** for the Employee ID field. By default, Access sets a Text field size to 50. Although Access uses only the amount of storage space necessary for the text you actually store in a Text field, setting the field size to the smallest possible size can decrease the processing time required by the program. Additionally, if the field data to be entered is a specific size, setting the field size to that number restricts the entry to the maximum number. Since the Employee ID field will contain a maximum of four characters, you want to change the field size from the default of 50 to 4.

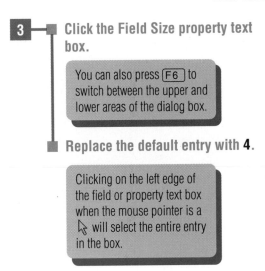

3 ■ **Click the Field Size property text box.**

You can also press F6 to switch between the upper and lower areas of the dialog box.

■ **Replace the default entry with 4.**

Clicking on the left edge of the field or property text box when the mouse pointer is a ⇲ will select the entire entry in the box.

Your screen should be similar to Figure 1–12.

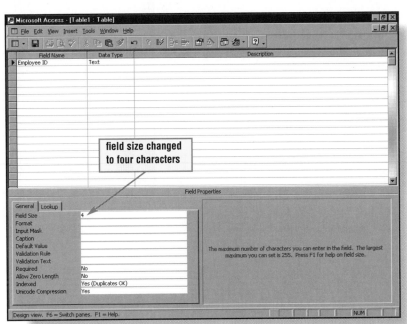

field size changed to four characters

Figure 1–12

Entering a Field Description

To continue defining the Employee ID field, you will enter a description of the field in the Description text box. Although it is optional, a field description makes the table easier to understand and update because the description is displayed in the status bar when you enter data into the table.

1 ■ Click the Description text box for the Employee ID field.

■ Type **A unique 4 digit number assigned to each employee when hired**.

> Text in the Description box scrolls horizontally as needed.

Your screen should be similar to Figure 1–13.

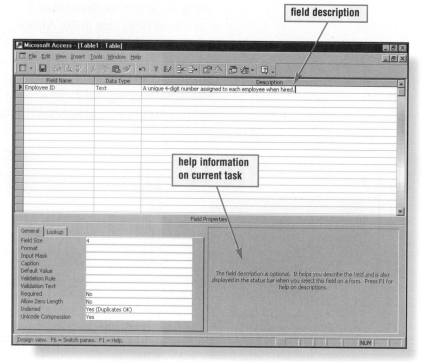

Figure 1–13

Defining a Primary Key Field

Next you want to make the Employee ID field a primary key field.

Concept ⑦ Primary Key

A **primary key** is a field that uniquely identifies each record. Most tables have at least one field that is selected as the primary key. The data in the primary key field must be unique for each record. For example, a Social Security number field could be selected as the primary key because the data in that field is unique for each employee. Other examples of a primary key field are parts numbers or catalog numbers.

A primary key prevents duplicate records from being entered in the table and is used to control the order in which records display in the table. This makes it faster for databases to locate records in the table and to process other operations. The primary key is also used to create a link between tables in a database.

Although any field can be the primary key, traditionally the first field or group of fields in the table is the primary key field.

To define the field as a primary key,

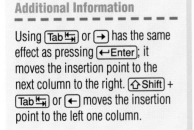

1 Click 🗝️ Primary Key.

The menu equivalent is **E**dit/Primary **K**ey.

Your screen should be similar to Figure 1–14.

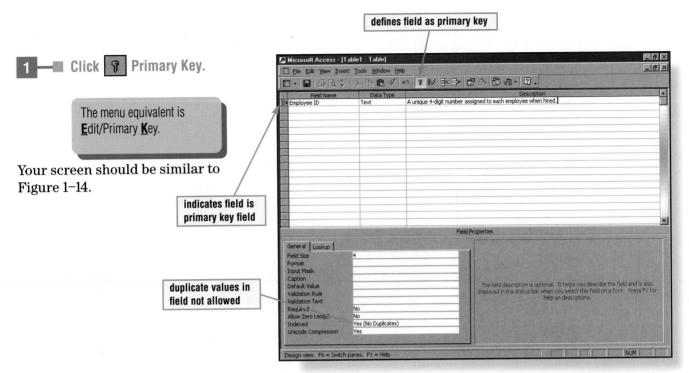

Figure 1–14

The 🗝️ icon appears in the column to the left of the field name, showing that this field is a primary key field. Now that this is the primary key field, the Indexed property setting has changed to Yes (No Duplicates). This setting prohibits duplicate values in a field.

Defining Additional Fields

The second field will display the date the employee started working at Lifestyle Fitness Club in the form of month/day/year. To enter the second field name,

Additional Information

Using `Tab ⇆` or `→` has the same effect as pressing `←Enter`; it moves the insertion point to the next column to the right. `⇧ Shift` + `Tab ⇆` or `←` moves the insertion point to the left one column.

1 Press `←Enter`.

Type Date Hired.

Press `Tab ⇆` or [`→`].

2 ■ Select the Date/Time data type.

Additional Information

You can also enter the data type by typing the first character of the data type option. For example, you can enter "d" for Date/Time.

Your screen should be similar to Figure 1–15.

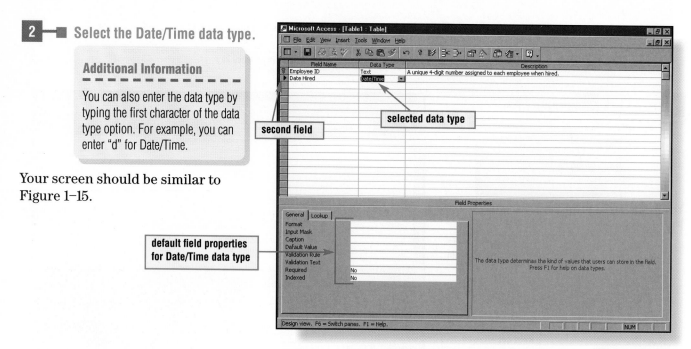

Figure 1–15

You cannot set the field size in Date/Time fields.

The default field properties for the selected data type are displayed. This time you want to change the format of the field so that the date will display as mm/dd/yy, regardless of how it is entered.

3 ■ Select the Format property box.

■ Open the drop-down list of Format options.

Your screen should be similar to Figure 1–16.

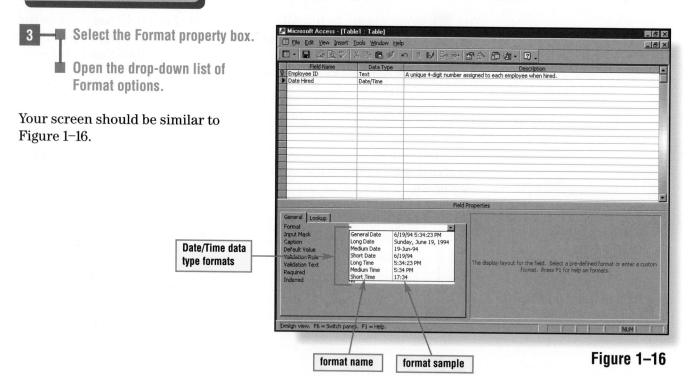

Figure 1–16

The names of the seven predefined layouts for the Date/Time field type are displayed in the list. An example of each layout appears to the right of the name.

4 Choose Short Date.

In the Description text box of the Date Hired field, enter the description: **Acceptable entry formats are 4/4/01, Apr. 4, 2001, or April 4, 2001.**

Your screen should be similar to Figure 1–17.

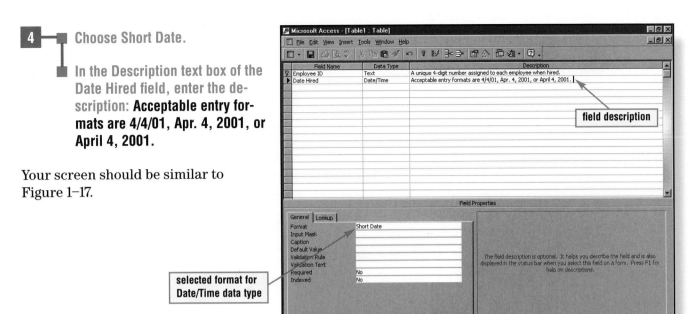

Figure 1–17

The third field is a Text field type that will contain the employee's last name. Because the field name is descriptive of the field contents, a description is not needed.

5 Press ⏎Enter.

Type **Last Name**.

Press ⏎Enter (3 times).

Your screen should be similar to Figure 1–18.

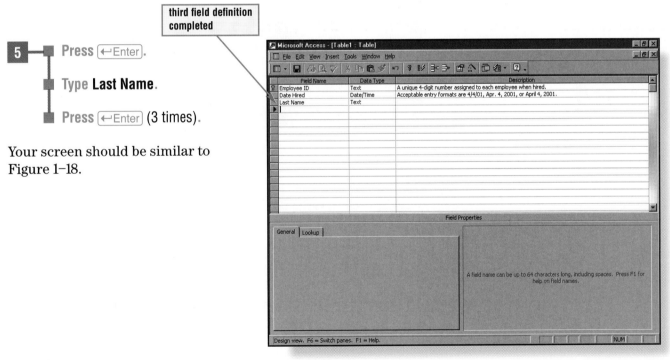

Figure 1–18

6 In the same manner, enter the information shown below for the next seven fields. If you make a typing mistake, use Backspace and Delete to correct errors.

Field Name	Data Type	Description	Field Size/Format
First Name	Text		50
Street	Text		50
City	Text		50
State	Text	A 2-character abbreviation entered in all capital letters.	2
Zip Code	Text	Use the 9-digit zip code if available.	10
Phone Number	Text	Enter using the format (555) 555-5555.	15
Birth Date	Date/Time	Acceptable entry formats are 4/4/01, Apr. 4, 2001, or April 4, 2001.	Short Date
Picture	OLE object	Employee ID picture.	

You can copy the description from the Date Hired field to the Birth Date field.

When you have completed the seven additional fields, your field definition grid should be similar to Figure 1–19.

11 fields defined in table

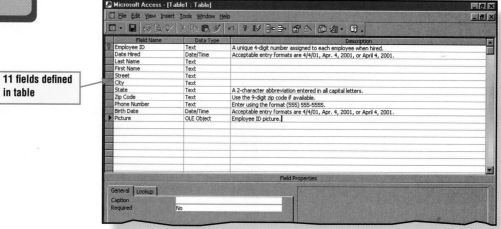

Figure 1–19

Editing Field Definitions

After looking over the fields, you decide to change the field sizes of the Last Name, First Name, and City fields to 20 character entries. Positioning the insertion point in any column of a field will display the properties for that field.

1 ■ Move to any column in the Last Name field.

■ Change the field size to 20.

■ In a similar manner, change the field size for the First Name and City fields to 20.

■ Carefully check your screen to ensure that each field name and field type was entered accurately and make any necessary corrections.

> To delete an entire field, move to the field and choose **E**dit/Delete **R**ows or click ⊟⊁ .

Your screen should be similar to Figure 1–20.

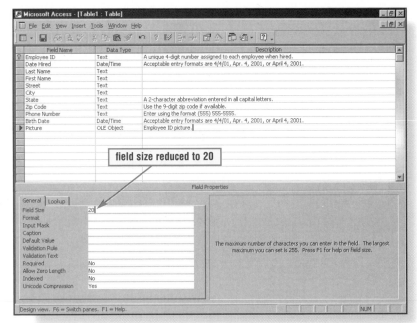

Figure 1–20

Saving the Table Structure

Once you are satisfied that your field definitions are correct, you can save the table design by naming it.

1 ■ Click 🖫 Save.

> The menu equivalent is **F**ile/**S**ave, and the keyboard shortcut is Ctrl + S.

Your screen should be similar to Figure 1–21.

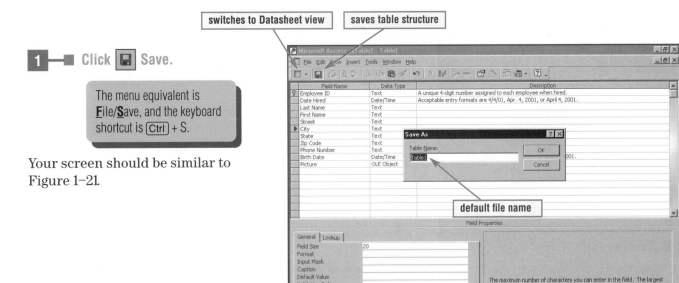

Figure 1–21

In the Save As dialog box, you want to replace the default name, Table 1, with a more descriptive name. A table name follows the same set of standard naming conventions or rules that you use when naming fields. It is acceptable to use the same name for both a table and the database, although each table in a database must have a unique name. You will save the table using the table name Employees.

2 — ■ Type **Employees**.

■ Click [OK].

The table structure is saved with the database file. You have created a table named Employees in the Lifestyle Fitness Employees database file.

Switching Views

Now that the table structure is defined and saved, you can enter the employee data into the new table. You enter and display data in the table in Datasheet view. Access allows you to view the objects in your database in several different window formats, called **views**. Each view includes its own menu and toolbar designed to work with the object in the window. The views that are available change depending on the type of object you are working with. The basic views are described in the table below.

View	Use
Design view	Used to create a table, form, query, or report.
Datasheet view	Provides a row-and-column view of the data in tables, forms, and queries.
Form view	Displays the records in a form.
Preview	Displays a form, report, or datasheet as it will appear when printed.

Opening the 🔲 ▾ View button displays a drop-down list of available views.

The 🔲 ▾ View button is a toggle button that switches between the different available views. The graphic in the button changes to indicate the view that will be displayed when selected. The View button appears as 📐 ▾ for Design view and 🔲 ▾ for Datasheet view.

1 ■ Click [image] ▾ Datasheet View.

■ If necessary, maximize the window.

> The menu equivalent is View/Datasheet View.

Your screen should be similar to Figure 1–22.

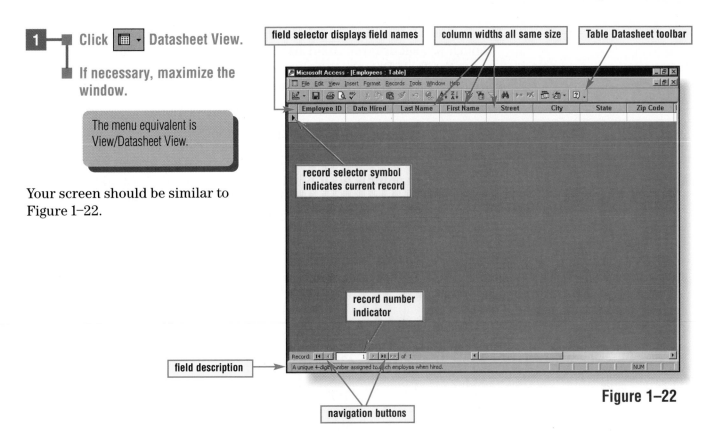

field selector displays field names

column widths all same size

Table Datasheet toolbar

record selector symbol indicates current record

record number indicator

field description

navigation buttons

Figure 1–22

In Table Datasheet view, you can enter and delete records and edit field data in existing records. This view displays the table data in a row-and-column format. Each field is a column of the table, and the field names you entered in Design view are displayed as column headings. The column heading area is called the **field selector** for each column. Below the field selector is a blank row where you will enter the data for a record. To the left of the row is the **record selector** symbol ▶, which indicates which record is the **current record**.

The bottom of the window displays a horizontal scroll bar, navigation buttons, and a record number indicator. The **record number indicator** shows the number of the current record as well as the total number of records in the table. Because the table does not yet contain records, the indicator displays "Record: 1 of 1" in anticipation of your first entry. On both sides of the record number are the **navigation buttons**, which are used to move through records with a mouse.

In addition, this view displays a Table Datasheet toolbar containing the standard buttons as well as buttons (identified below) that are specific to the Table Datasheet view window.

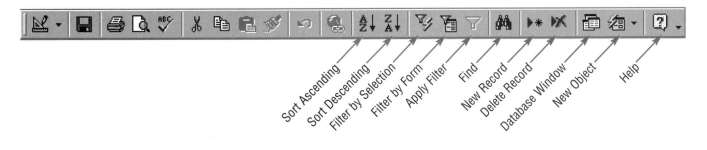

Sort Ascending
Sort Descending
Filter by Selection
Filter by Form
Apply Filter
Find
New Record
Delete Record
Database Window
New Object
Help

Notice also in this view that the column widths are all the same, even though you set different field sizes in the Table Design window. This is because the Table Datasheet view window has its own default column width setting. You will learn how to change the column width later in this tutorial.

Entering and Editing Data

The insertion point is positioned in the Employee ID field, indicating the program is ready to accept data in this field. The status bar displays the description you entered for the field. The data you will enter for the first record is as follows:

Field Name	Data
Employee ID	1151
Date Hired	October 14, 1997
Last Name	Sutton
First Name	Lisa
Street	4389 S. Hayden Rd.
City	Iona
State	FL
Zip Code	33101-3309
Phone Number	(941) 555-1950
Birth Date	June 14, 1975
Picture	friend1.bmp

When you enter data in a record, it should be entered accurately and consistently. The data you enter in a field should be typed exactly as you want it to appear. This is important because any printouts of the data will display the information exactly as entered. It is also important to enter data in a consistent form. For example, if you decide to abbreviate the word "Street" as "St." in the Street field, then it should be abbreviated the same way in every record where it appears. Also be careful not to enter a blank space before or after a field entry. This can cause problems when using the table to locate information.

You will try to enter an Employee ID number that is larger than the field size of 4 that you defined in Table Design view.

1 — Type **11510**.

Press (←Enter).

Your screen should be similar to Figure 1–23.

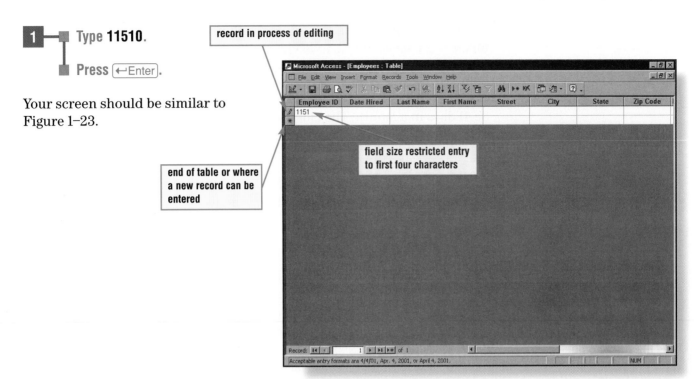

Figure 1–23

The program accepted only the first four digits you typed. The field size restriction helps control the accuracy of data by not allowing an entry larger than specified. Also notice that a second row has appeared in the table. The * symbol in the record selector column indicates the end of the table or where a new record can be entered. In addition, the current record symbol has changed to a ✎. This symbol means the record is in the process of being entered or edited and has not yet been saved.

To enter the date hired (it is intentionally incorrect) for this record,

2 — Type **10/41/97**.

Press (←Enter).

Your screen should be similar to Figure 1–24.

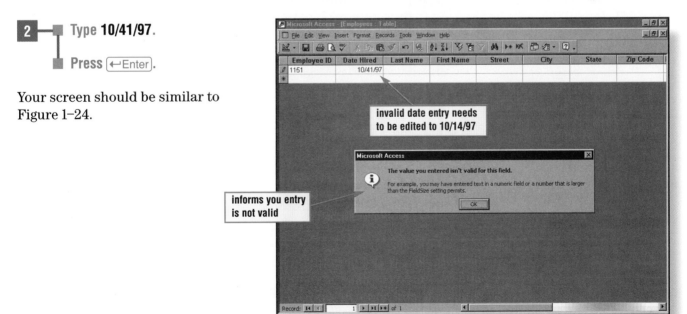

Figure 1–24

An informational message box is displayed. Access automatically performs some basic validity checks on the data as it is entered based upon the field type specified in the table design. This is another way Access helps you control data entry to ensure the accuracy of the data. In this case the date entered (10/41/97) could not be correct because there cannot be 41 days in a month. The close the message box,

3 ━■ **Click**  .

Next you need to edit the entry to correct it. How you edit data in Access depends on which mode of operation is active.

Concept (8) Edit and Navigation Modes

The Edit and Navigation modes control how you can move through and make changes to data in a table. **Edit mode** is used to enter or edit data in a field. In Edit mode the insertion point is displayed in the field so you can edit existing data or enter new data. To position the insertion point in the field entry, click at the location where you want it to appear. The keyboard keys shown in the table below can also be used to move the insertion point in Edit mode and to make changes to individual characters in the entry.

Navigation mode is used to move from field to field and to delete an entire field entry. In Navigation mode the entire field entry is selected (highlighted), and the insertion point is not displayed. You move from field to field using the keyboard keys shown in the table below.

Key	Edit Mode
← or →	Moves insertion point left or right one character.
Ctrl + ← or →	Moves insertion point left or right one word.
↓	Moves insertion point to current field in next record.
Home or End	Moves insertion point to beginning or end of field in single-line field.
Ctrl + Home or End	Moves insertion point to beginning or end of field in multiple-line field.
Delete	Deletes character to right of insertion point.
Backspace	Deletes character to left of insertion point.
Tab ⇄ or ⇧ Shift + Tab ⇄	Ends Edit mode and highlights next or previous field.

Key	Navigation Mode
→ or Tab ⇄	Moves highlight to next field.
← or ⇧ Shift + Tab ⇄	Moves highlight to previous field.
↓	Moves highlight to current field in next record.
Home or End	Moves highlight to first or last field in current record.
Delete or Backspace	Deletes highlighted field contents.

To activate Navigation mode, point to the left edge of a field and click when the pointer is a ✛. To activate Edit mode, click on the field when the mouse pointer is an I-beam. To switch between modes using the keyboard, press F2.

Because you are entering data in a new record, Edit mode is automatically active.

4 ■ Edit the entry to be 10/14/97.

■ Press ⏎Enter.

> You can also press Tab⇥ to move to the next field. → will move to the next field if the insertion point is at the end of the entry or you are in Navigation mode.

Your screen should be similar to Figure 1–25.

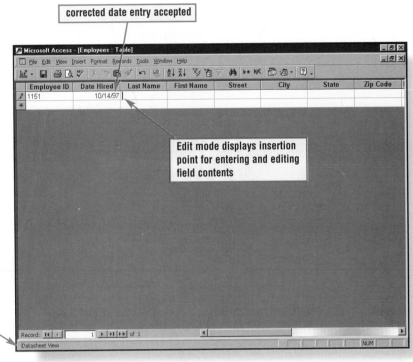

> **corrected date entry accepted**

> **Edit mode displays insertion point for entering and editing field contents**

> **status bar displays name of view when field does not include a description**

Figure 1–25

Additional Information

You can cancel changes you are making in the current field at any time by pressing Esc, and the original entry is restored.

The corrected date is accepted, and the insertion point moves to the Last Name field. Because no description was entered for this field, the status bar displays "Datasheet View," the name of the current view, instead of a field description.

5 ■ Enter the data shown below for the remaining fields, typing the information exactly as it appears.

> The fields will scroll on the screen as you move to the right in the record.

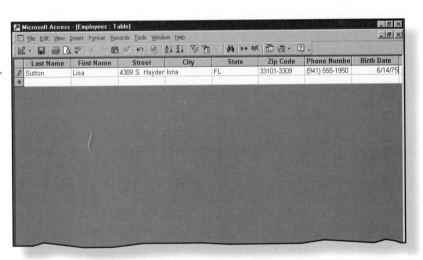

Figure 1–26

Field Name	Data
Last Name	**Sutton**
First Name	**Lisa**
Street	**4389 S. Hayden Rd.**
City	**Iona**
State	**FL**
Zip Code	**33101-3309**
Phone Number	**(941) 555-1950**
Birth Date	**6/14/75**

Your screen should be similar to Figure 1–26.

Inserting a Picture

To complete the information for this record, you need to insert a picture of Lisa in the picture field. A picture is one of several different types of graphic objects that can be added to a database table.

Concept ⑨ Graphics

A **graphic** is a non-text element or object, such as a drawing or picture, that can be added to a table. A graphic can be a simple **drawing object** consisting of shapes such as lines and boxes that can be created using a drawing program such as Paint. A **picture** is an illustration such as a scanned photograph. Most images that are scanned and inserted into documents are stored as Windows bitmap files (.bmp). Other types of objects that can be added are a worksheet created in Excel or a Word document.

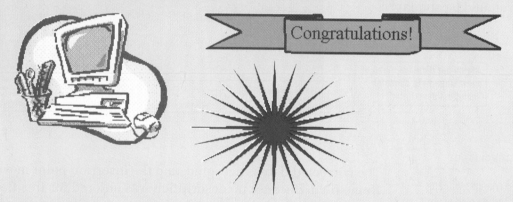

Picture files can be obtained from a variety of sources. Many simple drawings, called **clip art**, are available in the Clip Gallery that comes with Office 2000. You can also create graphic files using a scanner to convert any printed document, including photographs, to an electronic format. All types of graphics, including clip art, photographs, and other types of images can be found on the Internet. These files are commonly stored as .jpg or .pcx files. Keep in mind that any images you locate on the Internet may be protected by copyright and should be used only with permission. You can also purchase CDs containing graphics for your use.

Since you do not have employee pictures yet, you will insert a picture of a friend to demonstrate to the owners how this feature works. Then after the database design is completed, you will arrange to have all employee pictures taken and inserted into the appropriate field. You have a recent photograph of your friend that you scanned and saved as Friend1.jpg. You will insert the picture in the Picture field for Lisa.

1 Move to the Picture field.

Choose Insert/Object.

Your screen should be similar to
Figure 1–27.

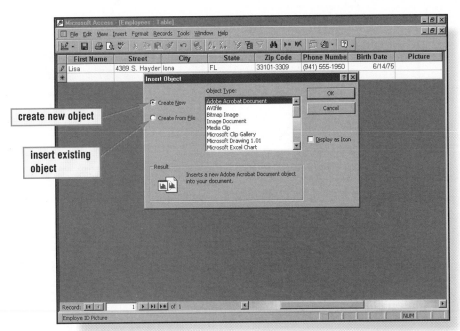

create new object

insert existing
object

Figure 1–27

From the Insert Object dialog box you specify whether you want to create
a new object or insert an existing object. Since the picture is already created and stored on your data disk, you will use the Create from File option
and specify the location of the file.

2 Select Create from File.

Click  .

Your screen should be similar to
Figure 1–28.

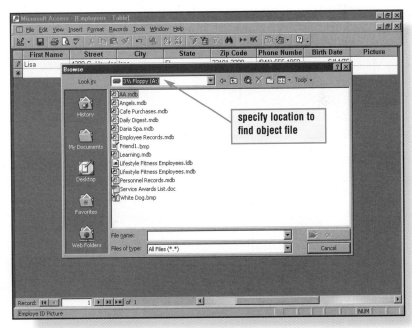

specify location to
find object file

Figure 1–28

This Browse dialog box is used to locate and select the name of the file you
want to insert. The Look In drop-down list box displays the default folder
as the location where the program will look for files, and the file list box
displays the names of all files at that location. First you need to change
the location to the drive containing your data disk.

3 ■ Open the Look In drop-down list box.

■ Choose 3 1/2 Floppy (A:) or the drive containing your data disk.

> If a system error message appears, check that your disk is properly inserted in the drive.

Your screen should be similar to Figure 1–29.

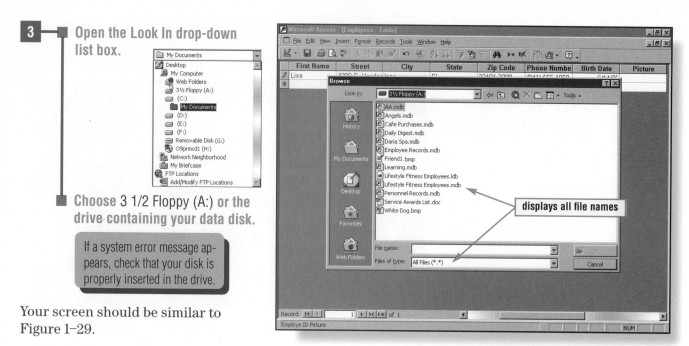

Figure 1–29

Now the file list box displays the names of all files on your data disk. When selecting a file to insert, it may be helpful to see a preview of the file first. To do this you can change the dialog box view.

4 ■ Select Friend1.

> If necessary, scroll the list box until the file name Friend1 is visible. If the file name is not displayed, ask your instructor for help.

■ Open the [⊞] Views drop-down list.

■ Choose Preview.

Your screen should be similar to Figure 1–30.

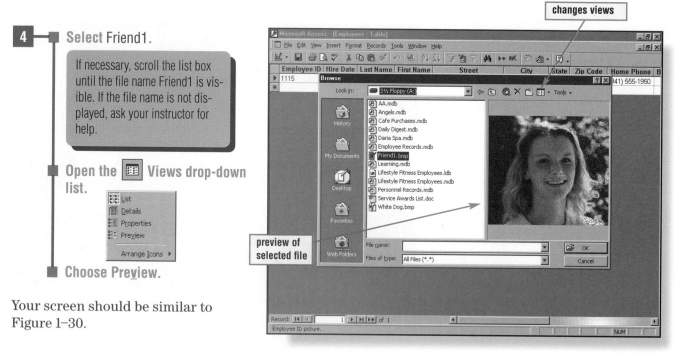

Figure 1–30

A preview of the selected file is displayed in the right side of the dialog box. To return the view to the list of file names and open this file,

5 ■ Click  Views.

■ Choose List.

■ Click ☞ OK .

> You could also double-click the file name to both select it and choose ☞ OK .

Your screen should be similar to Figure 1–31.

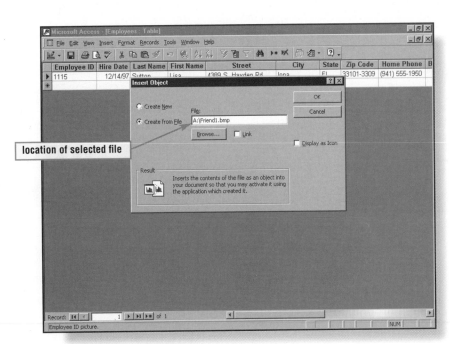

Figure 1–31

> You could also type the path and file name directly in the File text box.

The Insert Object dialog box is displayed again with the path to the selected object displayed in the File text box. When inserting an object, you can specify if you want to display the object as an icon instead of the picture. Using this setting saves a lot of disk space because only an icon appears for the object rather than the complete object. Although the future plan is to include a picture for each employee and display it as an icon, for the test picture you will display the picture.

6 ■ Click OK .

Your screen should be similar to Figure 1–32.

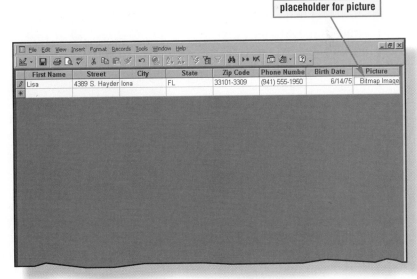

Figure 1–32

In Table Datasheet view, the field displays a text placeholder such as "Package" or "Bitmap Image" instead of the picture. The actual placeholder you will see will depend upon the software your computer used to import the image into Access. Then, to see the picture,

7 ▪ Double-click on the Picture field entry.

Your screen should be similar to Figure 1–33.

Figure 1–33

The picture object is opened and displayed in the associated graphics program, in this case, Paint. Yours may have opened and be displayed in a different graphics program. It can be further manipulated using the program features.

8 ▪ Click ☒ in the Paint window title bar to close the Paint application.

▪ Press ⏎Enter.

Your screen should be similar to Figure 1–34.

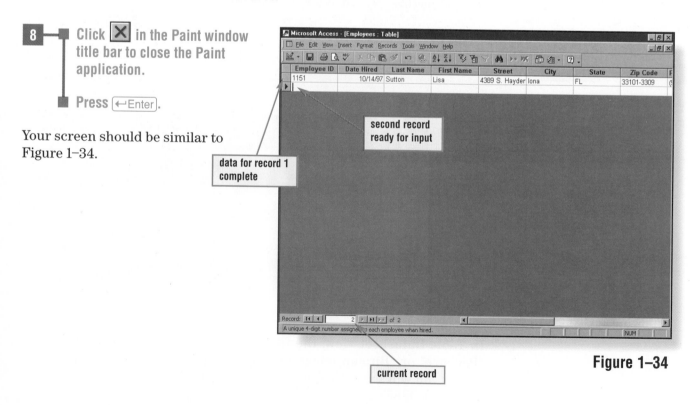

Figure 1–34

Using Navigation Mode

The data for the first record is now complete. The insertion point moves to the first field on the next row and waits for input of the employee number for the next record. As soon as the insertion point moves to another record, the data is saved on the disk and the number of the new record appears in the status bar. The second record was automatically assigned the record number 2.

Next you will check the first record for accuracy.

1 ▪ Point to the left end of the Employee ID field for the first record. When the mouse pointer appears as ⬧, click the mouse button.

Your screen should be similar to Figure 1–35.

entire field is highlighted in Navigation mode

Figure 1–35

The entire field is selected (highlighted), and you have activated Navigation mode. If you type, the entire selection will be replaced with the new text. To select the Street field to check the field contents,

2 ▪ Press → (4 times).

▪ Click the Street field with the mouse pointer shape as an I-beam.

The insertion point is positioned in the field, and you have activated the Edit mode. Now you can edit the field contents if necessary. To move the insertion point to the end of the address so that you can check the rest of the entry,

3 ▪ Press End.

The text scrolled in the field, and the insertion point is positioned at the end of the entry. However, now you cannot see the beginning of the entry. To expand the field box to view the entire entry in the field,

4 ■ Press ⇧Shift + F2.

Your screen should be similar to Figure 1–36.

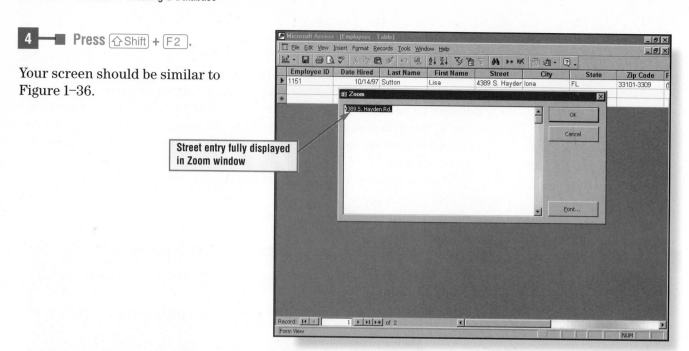

Street entry fully displayed in Zoom window

Figure 1–36

The entry is fully displayed in a separate Zoom window. You can edit in the window just as you would in the field box.

> You can also expand a text box in the same way to make it easier to edit.

5 ■ If the entry contains an error, correct it.

■ Click ⎡ OK ⎤.

■ Press Tab.

■ Continue to check the first record for accuracy and edit as needed.

> You can also use the horizontal scroll bar to scroll the window to check fields that are not visible.

■ Enter the following data for the second record.

> Notice that the date format changed automatically to the format set in the date property field.

Field Name	Data
Employee ID	0434
Date Hired	July 5, 1996
Last Name	Merwin
First Name	Adda
Street	947 S. Forest St.
City	Fort Myers
State	FL
Zip Code	33301-1268
Phone Number	(941) 555-4494
Birth Date	April 20, 1970

6 ■ Press ⌊←Enter⌋ twice.

■ Check the second record for accuracy and edit it if necessary.

Your screen should be similar to Figure 1–37.

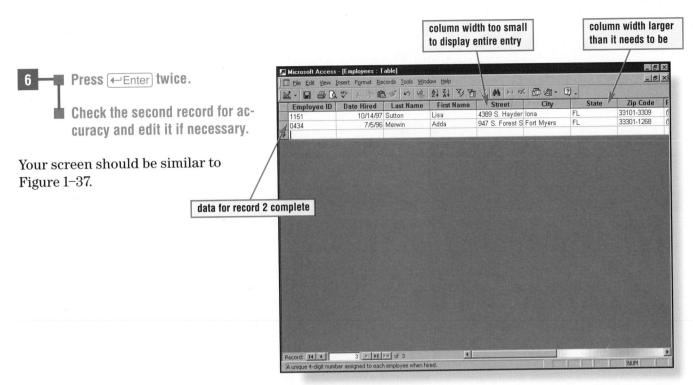

Figure 1–37

Adjusting Column Widths

As you have noticed, some of the fields (such as the Street field) do not display the entire entry, while other fields (such as the State field) are much larger than the field's column heading or contents. This is because the default column width in Datasheet view is not the same size as the field sizes you specified in Design view.

Concept ⑩ Column Width

Column width refers to the size of each field column in Datasheet view. The column width does not affect the amount of data you can enter into a field, but does affect the data that you can see on the screen. The default column width in Datasheet view is set to display 15.6667 characters. You can adjust the column width to change the appearance of the datasheet. It is usually best to adjust the column width so the column is slightly larger than the column heading or longest field contents, whichever is longer. Do not confuse column width with field size. Field size is a property associated with each field; it controls the maximum number of characters that you can enter in the field. If you shorten the field size, you can lose data already entered in the field.

To quickly modify the column width, simply drag the right column border line in the field selector in either direction to increase or decrease the column width. The mouse pointer shape is ✥ when you can drag to size the column. As you drag, a column line appears to show you the new column border. When you release the mouse button, the column width will be set. First you will increase the width of the Street field so the entire address will be visible.

1

■ Point to the right column border line in the field selector for the Street field name.

■ When the mouse pointer is ✥, drag the border to the right until you think the column width will be long enough to display the field contents.

■ Adjust the column width again if it is too wide or not wide enough.

> You can also adjust the column width to a specific number of characters using F**o**rmat/**C**olumn Width.

Your screen should be similar to Figure 1–38.

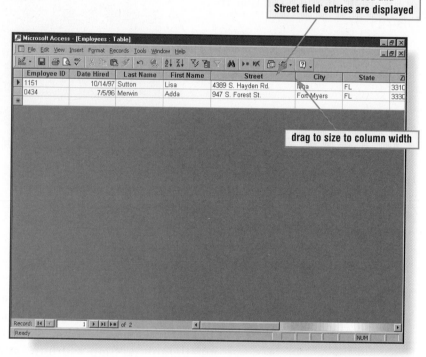

column width increased and Street field entries are displayed

drag to size to column width

Figure 1–38

> The keyboard equivalent for selecting columns is to select a field entry in the first column, press [Ctrl] + [Spacebar], then press [⇧ Shift] + the appropriate arrow key to select multiple columns.

> To clear a selection, click anywhere in the table.

Rather than change the widths of all the other columns individually, you can select all columns and change their widths at the same time. To select multiple columns, point to the column heading in the field selector area of the first or last column you want to select. Then, when the mouse pointer changes to ↓, click, and without releasing the mouse button, drag in either direction across the column headings.

2 ■ Point to the Employee ID field name.

■ When the mouse pointer is ↓, drag to the right across all column headings.

> The fields will scroll horizontally in the window as you drag to select the columns.

■ Use the horizontal scroll bar to bring the first field column back into view in the window.

Your screen should be similar to Figure 1–39.

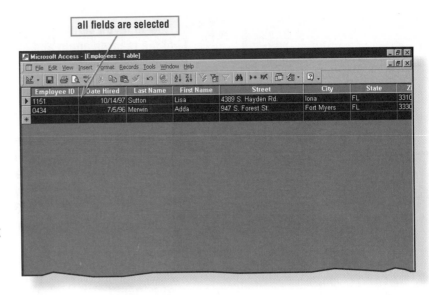

all fields are selected

Figure 1–39

> Clicking the box to the left of the first field name will also select the entire table; however, you cannot use Best Fit when the entire table is selected in this manner.

> The menu equivalent is Format/Column Width. The Column Width command is also on the shortcut menu when an entire column is selected.

Multiple columns are highlighted. Now, if you were to drag the column border of any selected column, all the selected columns would change to the same size. However, you want the column widths to be adjusted appropriately to fit the data in each column. To do this you can double-click the column border to activate the Best Fit feature. The **Best Fit** feature automatically adjusts the column widths of all selected columns to accommodate the longest entry or column heading in each of the selected columns.

3 ■ Double-click any column border line (in the field selector) within the selection when the mouse pointer is ↔.

Your screen should be similar to Figure 1–40.

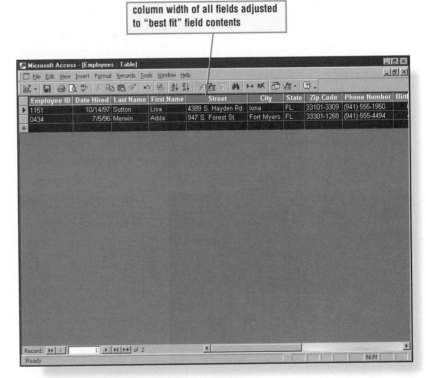

column width of all fields adjusted to "best fit" field contents

Figure 1–40

Clicking anywhere in the table will clear the section.

4 ■ Now that you can see the complete contents of each field, check each of the records again and edit any entries that are incorrect.

■ Add the following record to the table as record 3.

Field Name	Data
Employee ID	0434
Date Hired	April 12, 1998
Last Name	Delano
First Name	Gordon
Street	8943 W. Southern Ave.
City	Iona
State	FL
Zip Code	33101-8475
Phone Number	(941) 555-8201
Birth Date	August 7, 1961

5 ■ Press ⏎Enter twice.

Your screen should be similar to Figure 1–41.

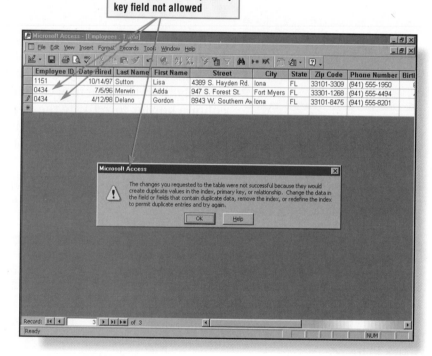

Figure 1–41

As soon as you complete the record, an error message dialog box appears indicating that Access has located a duplicate value in a key field. The key field is Employee ID. You realize you were looking at the employee number from the previous record when you entered the employee number for this record. To clear the message and enter the correct number,

6 ■ Click OK .

■ Change the Employee ID for record 3 to **0234**.

■ Press ↓.

The record is accepted with the new employee number. Notice that the address for this record does not fully display in the Street field. It has a longer address than either of the other two records.

7 ━ **Double-click the right border of the Street field to best fit the field column.**

When you add new records in Datasheet view, the records are displayed in the order you enter them. However, they are stored on disk in order by the primary key field. You can change the display on the screen to reflect the correct order by using the ⇧Shift + F9 key combination.

8 ━ **Press ⇧Shift + F9 .**

Your screen should be similar to Figure 1–42.

records in order by
employee number

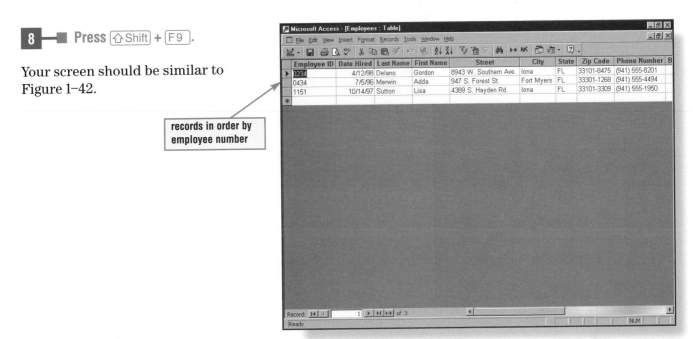

Figure 1–42

The records are now in order by employee number. This is the order determined by the primary key field.

Adding Records in Data Entry

Additional Information

The table order is also updated when you close and then reopen the table.

Next you want to add several more employee records to the table. Another way to add records is to use the Data Entry command on the Records menu. This command does not display existing records, which prevents accidental changes to the table data.

1 ━■ Choose <u>R</u>ecords/<u>D</u>ata Entry.

Your screen should be similar to
Figure 1–43.

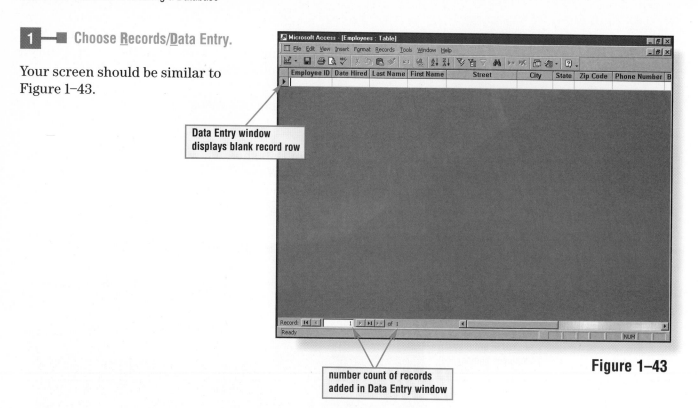

Figure 1–43

The existing records are hidden, and the only row displayed is a blank row
where you can enter a new record. The status bar displays "1 of 1." This
number reflects the number of new records as they are added in Data
Entry rather than all records in the table.

2 — Enter the data for the two records shown below.

Field	Record 1	Record 2
Employee ID	0839	0728
Hire Date	August 14, 1997	March 15, 1997
Last Name	Ruiz	Roman
First Name	Enrique	Anita
Street	358 Maple Dr.	2348 S. Bala Dr.
City	Cypress Lake	Fort Myers
State	FL	FL
Zip Code	33205-6911	33301-1268
Home Phone	(941) 555-0091	(941) 555-9870
Birth Date	December 10, 1963	March 15, 1961

Your screen should be similar to Figure 1–44.

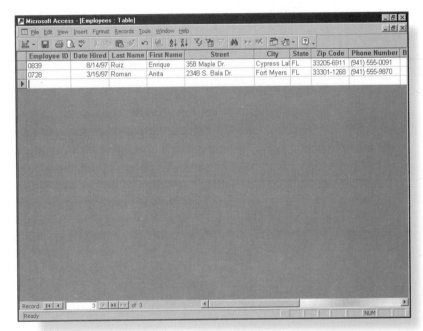

Figure 1–44

3 — Enter a final record using your first and last names. Enter 9999 as your employee number and the current date as your date hired. The information you enter in all other fields can be fictitious.

■ Best fit the City column and any other columns that do not fully display the field contents.

■ Check each of the records and correct any entry errors.

Now that you have entered the new records, you can redisplay all the records in the table. To do this,

4 Choose **Records**/**Remove** Filter/Sort.

Your screen should be similar to Figure 1–45.

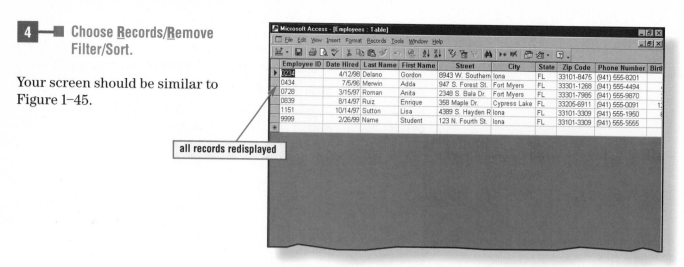

Figure 1–45

The new records are added to the table in order by employee number. If you had added these records in Datasheet view, they would not appear in primary key field order until you updated the table display. This is another advantage of using Data Entry.

Previewing and Printing the Table

If you have printer capability, you can print a copy of the records in this table. Before printing the table, you will preview how it will look when printed using Print Preview view. Previewing the document displays each page of your document in a reduced size so you can see the layout. Then, if necessary, you can make changes to the layout before printing, to both save time and avoid wasting paper.

To preview the Employees table,

1 Click 🔍 Print Preview.

The menu equivalent is **F**ile/Print Pre**v**iew.

Your screen should be similar to Figure 1–46.

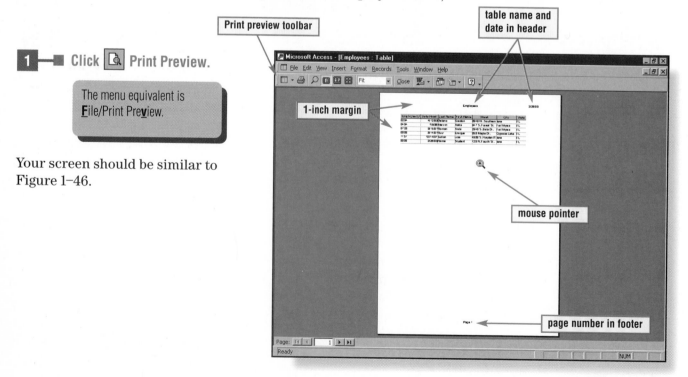

Figure 1–46

The Print Preview window displays a reduced view of how the table will appear when printed. The window also includes its own toolbar. The document will be printed using the default report and page layout settings, which include such items as 1-inch margins, the table name and date displayed in a header, and the page number in a footer.

To better see the information in the table, you can change the magnification level of the Preview window. The current magnification level is Fit as displayed in the Fit button in the toolbar. This setting adjusts the magnification of the page to best fit in the size of the window. Notice that the mouse pointer is a magnifying glass when it is positioned on the page. This indicates that you can click on the page to switch between the Fit magnification level and the last used level.

> Use the Fit Zoom button on the Print Preview toolbar to select a magnification percentage or type.

2 Click on the file name in the header.

> Clicking Zoom will also toggle between the magnification levels.

> The location where you click determines the area that is displayed initially.

Your screen should be similar to Figure 1–47.

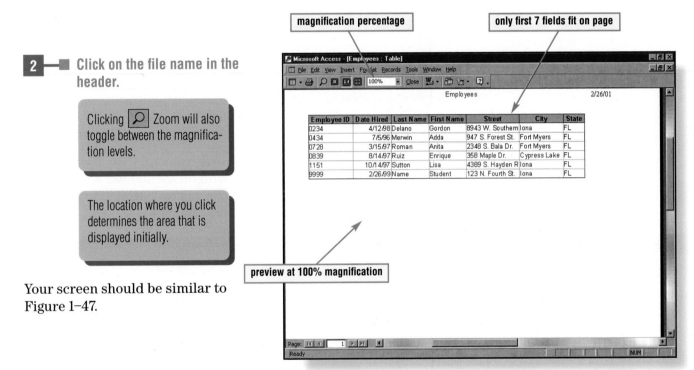

magnification percentage

only first 7 fields fit on page

preview at 100% magnification

Figure 1–47

> Because Access remembers the last zoom percentage, your zoom percentage may be different. Use the Zoom button to change your percentage to 100%.

The table appears in 100% magnification. This is the size it will appear when printed. Notice, however, that because the table is too wide to fit across the width of a page, only the first seven fields are displayed on the page. The rest of the table will be printed on a second page. To see both pages,

 Click 🔲 Two Pages.

Your screen should be similar to Figure 1–48.

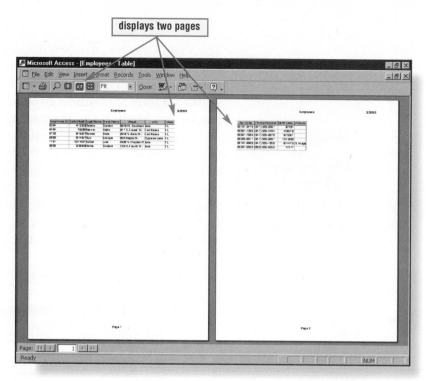

displays two pages

Figure 1–48

The last four field columns are displayed on the second page. Now you are ready to print the table. The 🖨 Print button on the toolbar will immediately start printing the report using the default print settings. To check the print settings first, you need to use the Print command.

4 ─■ Click 🔲 One Page to return the display to a single page.

■ If necessary, make sure your printer is on and ready to print.

■ Choose **File/Print**.

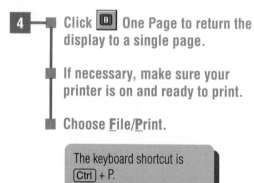

The keyboard shortcut is Ctrl + P.

Your screen should be similar to Figure 1–49.

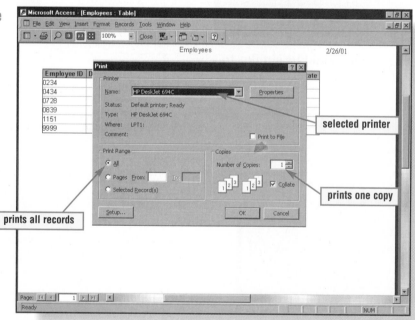

selected printer

prints one copy

prints all records

Figure 1–49

Please consult your instructor for printing procedures that may differ from the directions here.

From the Print dialog box, you need to specify the printer you will be using and the document settings. The printer that is currently selected is displayed in the Name drop-down list box in the Printer section of the dialog box.

5 ━■ If you need to change the selected printer to another printer, open the Name drop-down list box and select the appropriate printer (your instructor will tell you which printer to select).

The Page Range area of the Print dialog box lets you specify how much of the document you want printed. The range options are described in the following table:

Option	Action
All	Prints the entire document.
Pages	Prints pages you specify by typing page numbers in the text box.
Selected Records	Prints selected records only.

The default range setting, All, is the correct setting. In the Copies section, the default setting of one copy of the document is acceptable. To begin printing using the settings in the Print dialog box,

6 ━■ Click  .

Your printer should be printing out the database table report. The printed copy should be similar to the final product shown in the opening case study of this tutorial.

To close the Print Preview window and return to the Datasheet view,

The menu equivalent is **V**iew/Data**s**heet View.

7 ━■ Click Close .

Closing and Opening a Database

- -

To close the table,

The menu equivalent is **F**ile/Close.

1 ━■ Click  (in the Table window).

Because you changed the column widths of the table in Datasheet view, you are prompted to save the layout changes you made before the table is closed. If you do not save the table, your column width settings will be lost.

2 ━■ Click ⬚Yes⬚ .

Your screen should be similar to
Figure 1–50.

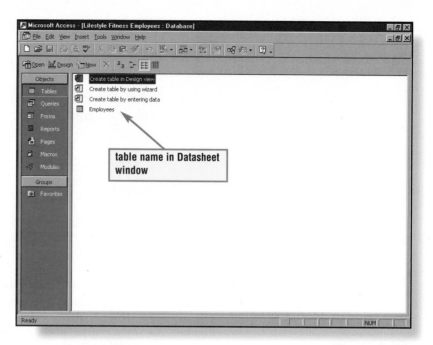

Figure 1–50

The Database window is displayed again. The name of the table you created appears in the Table object list. Now the Open and Design command
buttons can be used to modify the selected table in the list box. To close
the database file,

3 ━■ Click ⊠ (on the menu bar).

Then to open and redisplay the table of employee records,

4 ━■ Click 📂 Open.

━■ If necessary, display the Look In
drop-down list and select the
location of your data disk.

> The menu equivalent is **F**ile/**O**pen
> and the keyboard shortcut is ⌜Ctrl⌝ +
> O. You can also select "Open an ex-
> isting database" from the startup dia-
> log box when Access is first loaded.

Your screen should be similar to
Figure 1–51.

Figure 1–51

Now the name of the database file you just created, as well as others you will use in the labs, is displayed in the list box. To open the database file and the table of employee records,

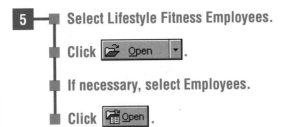

5 ■ Select Lifestyle Fitness Employees.

■ Click [📂 Open ▾].

■ If necessary, select Employees.

■ Click [🗐 Open].

> You can also double-click the table name to open it.

The table of employee records is displayed in Datasheet view again, just as it was before you saved and closed the table.

6 ■ Close the table again.

Notice that this time you were not prompted to save the table because you did not make any changes.

Exiting Access

You will continue to build and use the table of employee records in the next lab. To exit Access and return to the Windows desktop,

> The menu equivalent is File/Exit, and the keyboard shortcut is [Alt] + [F4].

1 ■ Click [X] (in the Access window title bar).

Warning: Do not remove your data disk from the drive until you close the Access application window.

Concept Summary

Tutorial 1: Creating a Database

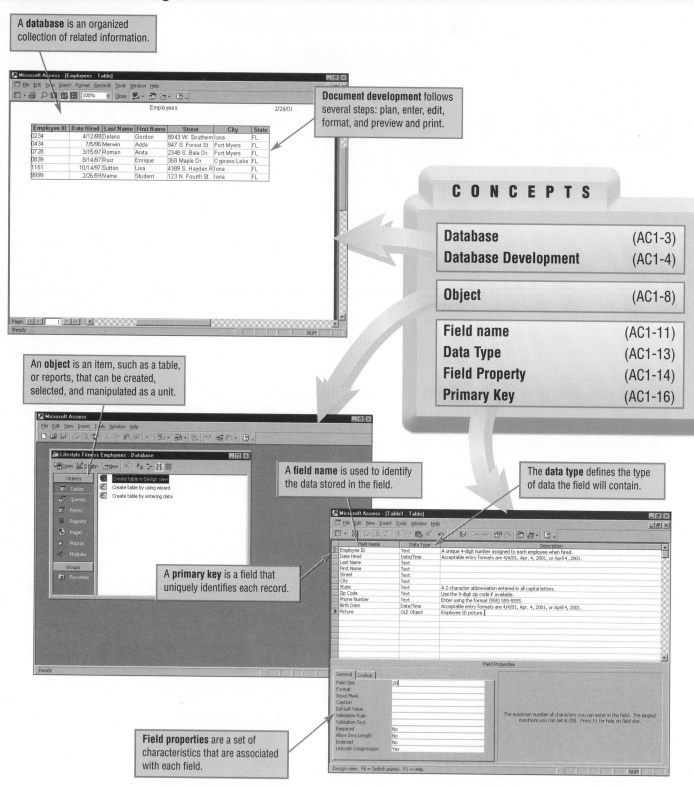

A **database** is an organized collection of related information.

Document development follows several steps: plan, enter, edit, format, and preview and print.

An **object** is an item, such as a table, or reports, that can be created, selected, and manipulated as a unit.

A **field name** is used to identify the data stored in the field.

The **data type** defines the type of data the field will contain.

A **primary key** is a field that uniquely identifies each record.

Field properties are a set of characteristics that are associated with each field.

CONCEPTS

Database	(AC1-3)
Database Development	(AC1-4)
Object	(AC1-8)
Field name	(AC1-11)
Data Type	(AC1-13)
Field Property	(AC1-14)
Primary Key	(AC1-16)

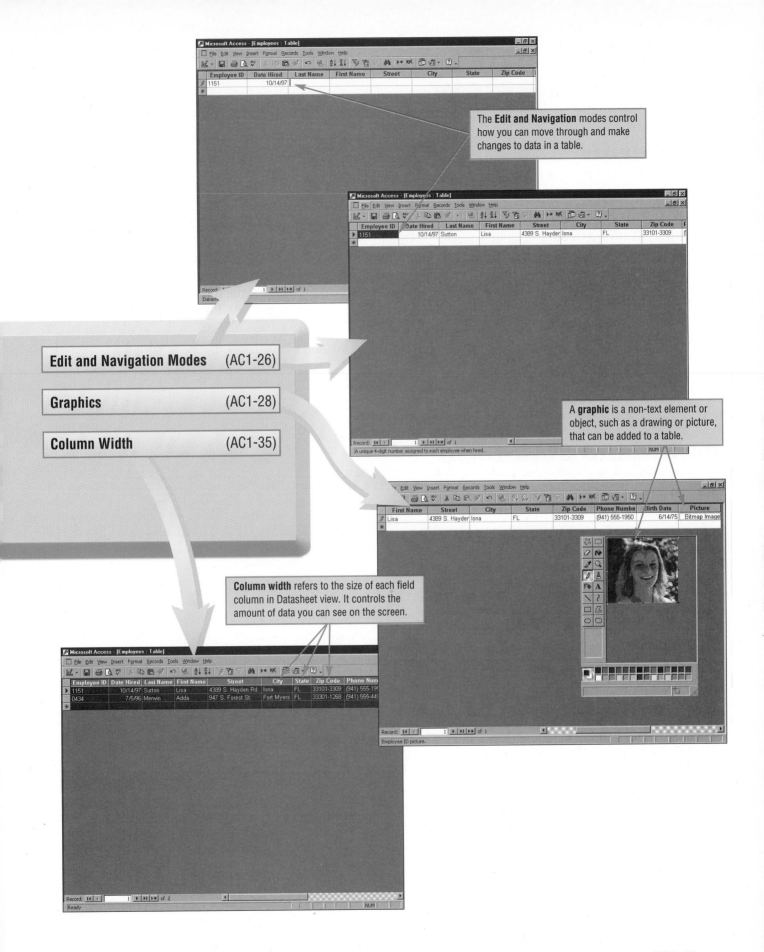

The **Edit and Navigation** modes control how you can move through and make changes to data in a table.

A **graphic** is a non-text element or object, such as a drawing or picture, that can be added to a table.

Column width refers to the size of each field column in Datasheet view. It controls the amount of data you can see on the screen.

Tutorial Review

Key Terms

Best Fit   AC1-37
Clip art   AC1-28
column width   AC1-35
current record   AC1-23
database   AC1-3
data type   AC1-13
design grid   AC1-10
drawing object   AC1-28
Edit mode   AC1-26
field   AC1-3

field name   AC1-11
field property   AC1-14
field selector   AC1-23
field size   AC1-15
graphic   AC1-28
navigation buttons   AC1-23
Navigation mode   AC1-26
object   AC1-8
Object bar   AC1-8
object list box   AC1-8

picture   AC1-28
primary key   AC1-16
record   AC1-3
record number indicator   AC1-23
record selector   AC1-23
relational database   AC1-3
table   AC1-3
view   AC1-22

Command Summary

Command	Shortcut Keys	Button	Action
File/**N**ew	Ctrl + N	🗋	Creates a new database
File/**O**pen	Ctrl + O	📂	Opens an existing database
File/**C**lose			Closes open window
File/**S**ave	Ctrl + S	💾	Saves table
File/Print Pre**v**iew		🔍	Displays file as it will appear when printed
File/**P**rint	Ctrl + P	🖨	Prints contents of file
File/E**x**it		✖	Closes Access and returns to Windows desktop
Edit/Delete **R**ows			Deletes selected field in Design view
Edit/Primary **K**ey		🔑	Defines a field as a primary key field
View/Data**s**heet View		▦ ▾	Displays table in Datasheet view
Insert/**O**bject/Create from **F**ile			Inserts an existing object into current field.
Format/**C**olumn Width			Changes width of table columns in Datasheet view
Format/**C**olumn Width/**B**est Fit			Sizes selected columns to accommodate longest entry or column header
Records/**R**emove Filter/Sort			Displays all records in table
Records/**D**ata Entry			Hides existing records and displays Data Entry window mode

Screen Identification

In the following screen, several items are identified by letters. Enter the correct term for each item in the spaces that follow.

a. _____

b. _____

c. _____

d. _____

e. _____

f. _____

g. _____

h. _____

i. _____

j. _____

k. _____

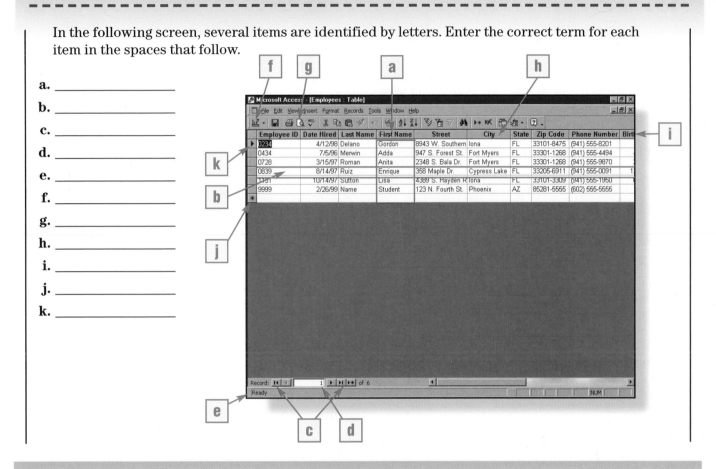

Matching

Match the letter to the correct item in the numbered list.

1. record

2. database

3. field property

4. primary key

5. Best Fit

6. field size

7. data type

8. Design view

9. Datasheet view

10. field

_____ a. specific item of information contained in a record

_____ b. collection of related fields

_____ c. an organized collection of related information

_____ d. used to define the table structure

_____ e. feature used to adjust column width to largest entry

_____ f. controls the type of data a field can contain

_____ g. field used to order records

_____ h. displays table in row and column format

_____ i. characteristics associated with a field

_____ j. controls the maximum number of characters that can be entered in a field

True/False

Circle the correct answer to the following statements.

1. A database is an organized collection of related properties. True False

2. The first step in database development is planning. True False

3. Tables, forms, and reports are objects. True False

4. Field names are used to define properties for a database. True False

5. Text, memo, number, and date/time are data types. True False

6. Data properties are a set of characteristics that are associated with each field. True False

7. A person's first name is often used as the primary key. True False

8. The Edit and Database modes control how you can move through and make changes to data in a table. True False

9. Drawings and pictures can be added to a database. True False

10. While column width does not affect the amount of data that you can see on the screen, it does affect the amount of data that you can enter into a field. True False

Multiple Choice

Circle the letter of the correct answer to the following statements.

1. A(n) _____ is an organized collection of related information.

    a. object
    b. database
    c. property
    d. document

2. The steps of database development include planning, creating, and _____ data.

    a. entering
    b. graphing
    c. developing
    d. organizing

3. Located at the left of the Database window, the Object _____ is used to select the type of object you want to work with.

    a. bar
    b. buttons
    c. properties
    d. tabs

4. A field name is used to identify the _____ stored in a field.

   a. characters
   b. keys
   c. data
   d. graphics

5. The _____ type defines the type of data the field contains.

   a. property
   b. entry
   c. data
   d. specification

6. Field size, format, input mask, caption, and default value are:

   a. key elements
   b. field properties
   c. navigating modes
   d. data types

7. The _____ key uniquely identifies each record.

   a. primary
   b. database
   c. object
   d. premier

8. The _____ mode is used to move from field to field and to delete an entire field entry.

   a. Edit
   b. Browser
   c. Entry
   d. Navigation

9. A(n) _____ is a non-text element or object that can be added to a database.

   a. graphic
   b. data element
   c. property
   d. medium

10. In Datasheet view, _____ refers to the size of each field column.

   a. maximum
   b. content capacity
   c. data range
   d. column width

Fill-In

Complete the following statements by filling in the blanks with the correct terms.

1. A(n)_____ is a collection of organized information. The information is stored in _____.

2. Relational databases define ____ between tables by having common data in the tables.

3. The first step in developing a database is _____.

4. The _____ defines the type of data that can be entered in a field.

5. A(n) _____ is an item made up of different elements.

6. The set of characteristics associated with a field are the _____.

7. A descriptive label called a(n) _____ is used to identify the data stored in a field.

8. The _____ data type is used to format numbers with dollar signs and decimal places.

9. A(n) _____ is a field that uniquely identifies each record in a table.

10. _____ view allows the user to enter, edit, and delete records in a table.

Discussion Questions

1. Discuss several uses you may have for a relational database. Then explain the steps you would follow to create the first table.

2. Discuss why it is important to plan a database before creating it. How can proper planning save you time later?

3. Discuss the difference between Edit mode and Navigation mode.

4. Design view and Datasheet view are two of the Access views. Discuss when it would be appropriate to use each of these views.

5. Discuss why it is important to choose the correct data type for a field. What may happen to the data if you change the data type?

Hands-On Practice Exercises

Step-by-Step

1. After being open for only two months, Daria's Day Spa is quickly becoming recognized for its excellent service to the Madison community. The spa's owner, Daria O'Dell, originally delayed computerizing the spa's operations; however, she now recognizes the numerous benefits she will receive from using a database management system. Ms. O'Dell has asked you to build a database that will enable her to keep information about her clients. When you are finished, your completed database table should look like the table shown here.

Client ID	First Name	Last Name	Home Phone	Work Phone	Street Address	City	State	Zip Code
001	Elaine	Grace	(217) 555-4215	(217) 555-4557	718 North Coltrane	Madison	TX	75380
002	Polly	Trawe	(217) 555-0091	(217) 555-2831	619 Portland Drive	Alison	TX	76890
003	Nadine	Richmond	(217) 555-1748	(217) 555-4279	1248 Trammell Avenue	Alison	TX	76890
004	[Your first name]	[Your last name]	(217) 555-1212	(217) 555-9335	987 Hyde Park	Bakersville	TX	76987

To create the client database, follow these steps:

a. Create a database named Spa. Design a table using the following field information:

Field Data	Type	Description	Field Size
Client ID	Text	A unique 3-digit number	3
First Name	Text		25
Last Name	Text		25
Home Phone			15
Work Phone			15
Street Address	Text		30
City	Text		25
State	Text	2-letter abbreviation	2
Zip Code	Text		10

b. Make the Client ID field the primary key field.

c. Save the table as Clients.

d. Switch to Datasheet view and enter the following records into the table:

Record 1	Record 2	Record 3	Record 4
001	002	003	004
Elaine	Polly	Nadine	[Your first name]
Grace	Trawe	Richmond	[Your last name]
(217) 555-4215	(217) 555-0091	(217) 555-1748	(217) 555-1212
(217) 555-4557	(217) 555-2831	(217) 555-4279	(217) 555-9335
718 North Coltrane	619 Portland Drive	1248 Trammell Avenue	987 Hyde Park
Madison	Alison	Alison	Bakersville
TX	TX	TX	TX
75380	76890	76890	76987

e. Adjust the column widths appropriately.

f. Print, save, and close the table.

2. You work for the Daily Digest, a small, startup publication that is distributed door-to-door in your local town and relies solely on advertising income from local businesses. Your managing editor has asked you to create a database to keep track of advertiser contact information. When you are finished, your completed database table should look like the table shown here.

Advertiser ID	Business Name	Business Type	Contact Name	Phone Number	Billing Street	Billing City	Billing State	Billing Zip
A003	Paper and Pencil	Office Supplies	Sharon Smith	(650) 555-5050	1021 Lakeland Dr.	Middlefield	CA	95054
A340	Fix It Up	Auto Repair	Karen Little	(650) 555-3903	59 Main St.	Temple	CA	95056
B299	Happy Feet	Shoe Repair	[Your name]	(650) 555-3589	344 Park Ave.	Beacon Shores	CA	95055
C101	Discount Drugs	Pharmacy	Dan O'Donald	(650) 555-2233	142 Poppin Ave.	Beacon Shores	CA	95055

To create the advertiser database, follow these steps:

a. Create a database named Digest. Design a table using the following field information:

Field Data	Type	Description	Field Size
Advertiser ID	Text	A unique 4-digit number	4
Business Name	Text		25
Business Type	Text		15
Contact Name	Text		30
Phone Number	Text		15
Billing Street	Text		30
Billing City	Text		25
Billing State	Text		2
Billing Zip	Text		10

b. Make the Advertiser ID field the primary key field.

c. Save the table as Advertisers.

d. Switch to Datasheet view and enter the following records into the table:

Record 1	Record 2	Record 3	Record 4
C101	A340	A003	B299
Discount Drugs	Fix It Up	Paper and Pencil	Happy Feet
Pharmacy	Auto Repair	Office Supplies	Shoe Repair
Dan O'Donald	Karen Little	Sharon Smith	[Your Name]
(650) 555-2233	(650) 555-3903	(650) 555-5050	(650) 555-3589
142 Poppin Ave.	59 Main St.	1021 Lakeland Dr.	344 Park Ave.
Beacon Shores	Temple	Middlefield	Beacon Shores
CA	CA	CA	CA
95055	95056	95054	95055

e. Adjust the column widths appropriately.

f. Display the records in primary key order.

g. Print, save, and close the table.

3. The Downtown Internet Cafe, which you helped the owner, Evan, get off the ground, is an overwhelming success. The clientele is growing every day, as is the demand for the beverages you serve. Up until now, the information about the vendors is kept in an alphabetical card file and a vendor is contacted whenever you need something. This has become quite unwieldy however, and Evan would like a more sophisticated tracking system. For starters, he would like you to create a database containing each purchase item and the contact information for the vendor that sells that item. When you are finished, your completed database table should look like the table shown here.

Vendors : Table

Item #	Description	Vendor Name	Contact	Address	City	State	Zip Code	Phone
1100	Coffee filters	Restaurant Supply	[Your Name]	13990 N. Central Ave.	Phoenix	AZ	84137-7214	(602) 555-0037
1723	Decaf Colombian	Pure Processing	Nancy Young	1124 Mariner Rd.	Half Moon Bay	CA	94019	(640) 555-5689
3527	Kona coffee	Quality Coffee	Fred Wilmington	772 First Street	Seattle	WA	73210-7214	(206) 555-9090
7926	Darjeeling tea	The Beverage Co.	Mae Yung	12 Main Street	Pacifica	CA	94044-3322	(415) 555-1122

To create the database, follow these steps:

a. Create a database named Purchases. Design a table using the following field information:

Field Data	Type	Description	Field Size
Item #	Text	Unique 4-digit product number	4
Description	Text	Name of product	50
Vendor Name	Text	Name of supplier	50
Contact	Text	First & Last Name of contact person	50
Address	Text		50
City	Text		50
State	Text	2-letter abbreviation	2
Zip Code	Text	Include the 4-digit extension number if possible	10
Phone	Text	Include the area code in parentheses: (999) 123-4567	15

b. Make the Item # field the primary key field.

c. Save the table as Vendors.

d. Enter the following records into the table in Datasheet view:

Record 1

3527
Kona coffee
Quality Coffee
Fred Wilmington
772 First Street
Seattle
WA
93210-7214
(206) 555-9090

Record 2

1723
Decaf Colombian
Pure Processing
Nancy Young
1124 Mariner Rd.
Half Moon Bay
CA
94019
(650) 555-5689

e. Add the following records into the table in Data Entry:

Record 1

7926
Darjeeling tea
The Beverage Co.
Mae Yung
12 Main Street
Pacifica
CA
94044-3213
(415) 555-1122

Record 2

1100
Coffee filters
Restaurant Supply
Manny Smith
13990 N. Central Ave.
Phoenix
AZ
84137-7214
(602) 555-0037

f. Return to Datasheet view and display the records in primary key order.

g. Adjust the column widths appropriately.

h. Edit the record for Item # 7926 to change the four-digit zip code extension from 3213 to 3322.

i. Edit the record for Item # 1100 to replace the current Contact name with your name.

j. Preview the table. Print, save, and close the table.

4. You have just been hired by Adventure Travel tours to create and maintain a database containing information about the tours they offer and the clients who have purchased those tours. When you are finished, your completed database table should look like the table shown here.

Clients : Table

Client #	Last Name	First Name	Address	City	State	Zip Code	Phone	Tour Name	Tour Date
009	Crane	Laura	727 N. Hayden Rd.	Mesa	AZ	85205-9999	(602) 555-0932	Dude Ranch	1/23/98
023	[Your name]	[Your name]	12 Central Ave.	Phoenix	AZ	89472-8141	(602) 555-7321	Mountain Magic	7/17/98
090	McMahon	Cynthia	95 Chandler Blvd.	Chandler	AZ	85601-3144	(602) 555-1122	Capital Sites	10/4/98
101	Van Duesen	Mark	2421 Forest St.	Tempe	AZ	85301-7985	(602) 555-3956	Hawaiian Islands	2/25/99

To create the database, follow these steps:

a. Create a database named Adventure. Design a table using the following field information:

Field Data	Data Type	Description	Field Size/Format
Client #	Text	Unique 3-digit number	3
Last Name	Text		50
First Name	Text		50
Address	Text		50
City	Text		50
State	Text	2-letter abbreviation	2
Zip Code	Text	Include the 4-digit extension number if possible	10
Phone	Text	Include the area code in parentheses: (999) 123-4567	15
Tour Name	Text		50
Tour Date	Date/Time		Short Date

b. Make the Client # field the primary key field.

c. Change the Last and First Name fields sizes to 15, the Address field size to 25, and the Tour Name field size to 30.

d. Save the table as Clients.

e. Enter the following records into the table in Table Datasheet view:

Record 1	Record 2
101	009
Van Duesen	Crane
Mark	Lauren
2421 Forest St.	727 N. Hayden Rd.
Tempe	Mesa
AZ	AZ
85301-7985	85205-0346
(602) 555-3956	(602) 555-0932
Hawaiian Islands	Dude Ranch
2/25/99	1/23/98

f. Add the following records into the table in Data Entry:

Record 1	Record 2
023	090
Frazier	McMahon
Barry	Cynthia
12 Central Ave.	95 Chandler Blvd.
Phoenix	Chandler
AZ	AZ
89472-8141	85601-3144
(602) 555-7521	(602) 555-1122
Mountain Magic	Capital Sites
7/17/98	10/4/98

g. Return to Datasheet view and display the records in primary key order.

h. Adjust the column widths appropriately.

i. Edit the record for Client # 023 to replace Barry Frazier's name with your name.

j. Change the four-digit zip code extension in Lauren Crane's record to 9999.

k. Preview and print the table. Save and close the table.

5. As a volunteer at the Animal Angels charity organization, you offer to create an Access database for them, to help them keep track of the animals that are picked up from local shelters. It needs to show when and which animals were boarded at Animal Angels; placed in foster homes; and finally, placed in adoptive homes. When you are finished, your completed database table should look like the table shown here.

Tracking : Table

ID #	Type	Gender	Name	Boarded Date	Foster Date	Adoption Date	Photo
012	Dog	F	Erin	3/2/98	4/1/98		
062	Dog	M	Max	12/9/98			Package
123	Cat	M	Puddy	3/23/98		4/15/98	
199	Cat	F		1/15/99		2/1/99	
345	Rabbit	M	Bunny	5/1/98	12/15/98		
752	Horse	F	[your name's] Pet	2/7/99			

To create the database, follow these steps:

a. Create a database named Animal Angels. Design a table using the following field information:

Field Data	Data Type	Description	Field Size/Format
ID #	Text	Unique 3-digit number given to animal when picked up from shelter	3
Type	Text	Type of animal (cat, dog, horse, etc.)	50
Gender	Text	Enter M (male) or F (female)	1
Name	Text	Name of animal, if any	50
Boarded Date	Date/Time	Date animal was boarded	Short Date
Foster Date	Date/Time	Date animal was placed in foster home	Short Date
Adoption Date	Date/Time	Date animal was adopted	Short Date
Photo	OLE object		

b. Change the field size of Type to 10 and Name to 30.

c. Make the ID # field the primary key field, and save the table as Tracking.

d. Enter six records: two for animals that are still being boarded (make one of these a dog), another two for animals in foster homes, and another two for animals that have been adopted. Enter [your name]'s Pet in the Name field of the last new record you add.

e. In Datasheet View select the Photo field in a record you entered for a dog that is still being boarded. Insert the Whitedog.bmp picture file as an object in the selected field. View the inserted picture.

f. Display the records in primary key order. Adjust the column widths appropriately.

g. Preview and print the table, and then save and close the table.

On Your Own

6. After creating the Adventure Travel database (in Practice Exercise 4), you realize that it does not accommodate clients who have taken more than one tour through your agency. Open the Adventure database and Clients table, change the existing Tour fields to include the number 1, and add four more fields for Tour 2 and Tour 3 names and dates. Adjust the field sizes as appropriate. Edit the existing records to include one or two more tours, and enter two new records. Adjust the column widths as necessary and display the table in primary key order. Preview and print the table. Close the table, saving any changes.

7. When you first started working at Lewis & Lewis, Inc. as an administrative assistant, you knew everyone by name and had no problems taking and transferring calls. However, the company has grown quite a bit and you no longer have everyone's phone extension memorized. Since you are on the computer most of the day, you decide that having this information online would be quite helpful, not only when you receive calls, but also to print out and distribute phone lists within the office. Create a database table that contains employees' last and first names, positions, and extension numbers, with the last name field as the primary key. Enter at least ten records, including one with your name as the employee and a phone extension of 0. Preview and print the table when you are finished.

8. You have been hired to create a patient database by a dentist who just opened his own office. The database table you set up should contain patient identification numbers, last and first names, addresses, phone numbers, "referred by" information, "patient since" dates, and insurance company information. Use appropriate field sizes and make the ID number field the primary key. Enter at least ten records, using both Data Entry and Datasheet view, adjusting the column widths as necessary. Display the table in primary key order. To practice editing data, change two of the records. Add a record that contains your name as the patient. Preview and print the table.

9. National Packing is a nationwide company that sells packing materials to mailing service chains and to businesses that do their own shipping. Based on your excellent reputation as a freelance database developer, the owner of the company has contacted you to create an Access database for tracking sales territories and representatives. First you need to design a table that includes the sales representatives' names, territories, and their customers' company name, contact, and address information. You should enter more than one field for the territory and client information, as the sales representative may cover multiple territories (e.g., Territory 1, Customer 1, Contact 1 . . . and Territory 2, Customer 2, Contact 2 . . .). Assign a primary key and appropriately size the fields. After designing the table, enter at least ten records using both Data Entry and Datasheet view, and adjust the column widths as necessary. Display the table in primary key order, and then edit one of these records so it contains your name as the sales representative or customer contact. Preview and print the table.

10. You work for Oldies But Goodies, a small company that locates and sells vintage record albums. The current method used to keep track of on-hand inventory is a notebook taped to the storeroom wall with a typewritten list where employees check records in and out. The business and inventory has grown large enough now to warrant an online database. Create a database with a table that contains stock identification numbers, record titles, artist, category (such as rock, R&B, and classical) cost, and inventory on hand. Size the fields as appropriate and assign a primary key to one of them. To obtain title, category, and artist information for records you might sell in this type of company, search for "vintage record albums" on the Web and select an appropriate site. Use this information to enter records into your table, adjusting column widths as necessary. Display the table in primary key order, change the artist's name in one of the records to your name, and then preview and print the table.

Modifying a Table and Creating a Form

Competencies

After completing this tutorial, you will know how to:

1. Navigate a large table.
2. Change field properties.
3. Find and replace data.
4. Use Undo.
5. Insert a field.
6. Add validity checks.
7. Hide and redisplay fields.
8. Sort records.
9. Delete records.
10. Create and enter records into a form.
11. Preview, print, close, and save a form.

Case Study

The Lifestyle Fitness Club owners, Brian and Cindy, are very pleased with your plans for the organization of the database and on your progress in creating the first table of basic employee data. As you have seen, creating a database takes planning and a lot of time to set up the structure and enter the

Field properties make a table easier to use and more accurate.

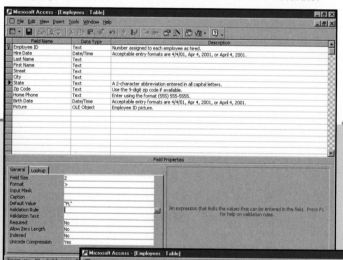

Forms can be used to display information in an easy-to-read manner and make data entry easier.

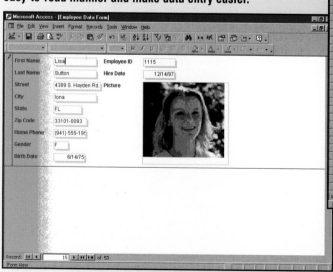

Data can be sorted to make it easier to locate information.

data. As you have continued to add more employee records to the table, you have noticed several errors. You also realize that you forgot to include a field for the employee's sex. Even with the best of planning and care, errors occur and the information may change. You will see how easy it is to modify the database structure and to customize field properties to provide more control over how and what data is entered in a field.

Even more impressive, as you will see in this tutorial, is the program's ability to locate information in the database. This is where all the hard work of entering data pays off. With a click of a button you can find data that might otherwise take hours to locate. The end result both saves time and improves the accuracy of the output.

You will also see how you can make the data you are looking at onscreen more pleasing by creating a form (shown here).

Printed form of employee record.

First Name	Lisa	Employee ID	1115
Last Name	Sutton	Hire Date	12/14/97
Street	4389 S. Hayden Rd.	Picture	
City	Iona		
State	FL		
Zip Code	33101-3309		
Home Phone	(941) 555-19		
Gender			
Birth Date	6/14/75		

Concept Overview

The following concepts will be introduced in this lab:

1 **Format Property**   You can use the Format property to create custom formats that change the way numbers, dates, times, and text display and print.

2 **Default Value Property**   The Default Value property is used to specify a value to be automatically entered in a field when a new record is created.

3 **Find and Replace**   The Find and Replace feature helps you quickly find specific information and automatically replace it with new information.

4 **Validity Check**   Access automatically performs certain checks, called validity checks, on values entered in a field to make sure that the values are valid for the field type.

5 **Sort**   You can quickly reorder records in a table by sorting the table to display in a different record order.

6 **Form**   A form is a database object used primarily to display records onscreen to make it easier to enter new records and to make changes to existing records.

Navigating a Large Table

The database file that contains the additional employee records is on your data disk and is named Employee Records. To open this file,

1 ▪ Load Access 2000. Put your data disk in drive A (or the appropriate drive for your system).

▪ Select Open an Existing Database.

▪ Click   OK .

▪ From the Look In drop-down list box, change the location to the drive containing your data disk.

▪ Select Employee Records.

▪ Click 🗁 Open ▾.

The Database window for the Employee Records file is displayed. To open the table with the additional employee records, Employees,

2 ■ Click 🖻Open .

■ Maximize the Datasheet window.

Your screen should be similar to
Figure 2–1.

records 1–26
displayed

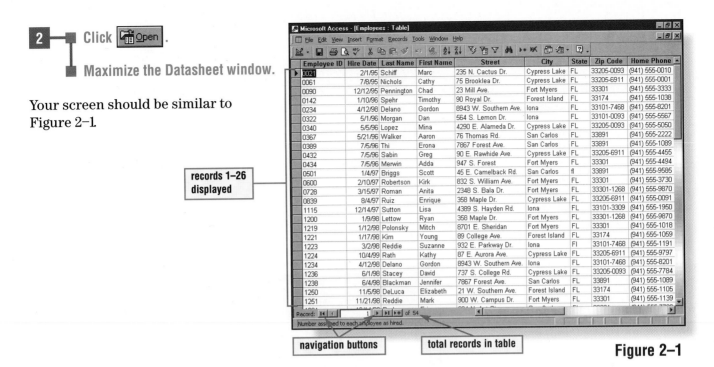

navigation buttons

total records in table

Figure 2–1

By default, the Datasheet view of the Table window is displayed. As you
can see from the record number indicator, there are now 54 records in the
table.

In a large table, there are many methods you can use to quickly navigate, or move, through records in Datasheet view. You can always use the
mouse to move from one field or record to another. However, if the information is not visible in the window, you must scroll the window first. The
table below presents several keyboard methods that make moving around
a table faster in Navigation mode.

Keys	Effect
Page Down	Down one page
Page Up	Up one page
Ctrl + Pg Up	Left one window
Ctrl + Pg Dn	Right one window
End	Last field in record
Home	First field in record
Ctrl + End	Last field of last record
Ctrl + Home	First field of first record
Ctrl + ↑	Current field of first record
Ctrl + ↓	Current field of last record

The Navigation buttons in the status bar also provide navigation shortcuts. These buttons are described on the next page.

Additional Information

You can also type the record number you want to move to in the record indicator box of the status bar.

Throughout this tutorial your screen may display a different number of records, depending upon your system setup.

Button	Effect
◄	First record, same field
◄	Previous record, same field
►	Next record, same field
►►	Last record, same field
►*	New (blank) record

Currently, records 1 through 26 are displayed in the window. To see the next full window of records,

3 ▬ Press [Pg Dn].

Your screen should be similar to Figure 2–2.

records 27–52 displayed

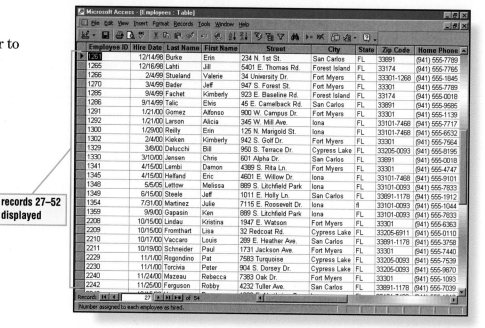

Figure 2–2

Now records 27 through 52 are displayed in the window. The first record in the window is now the current record.

Due to the number and width of the fields, not all fields can be displayed in the window at the same time. Rather than scrolling the window horizontally to see the additional fields, you can quickly move to the right a window at a time.

4 ——■ Press End.

Your screen should be similar to Figure 2–3.

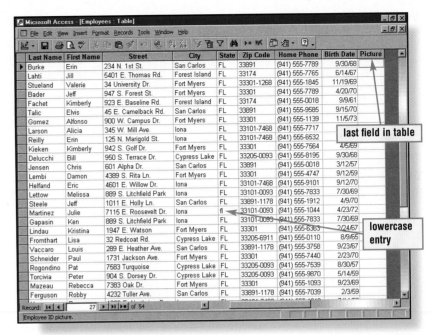

Figure 2–3

The last field in the table is now visible in the window. To quickly move to the same field of the last record and then back to the first field of the first record,

5 ——■ Click ▶|.

——■ Press Ctrl + Home.

Changing Field Properties

As you looked through the records, you noticed that records 12, 22, and 43 have mixed-case entries in the State field. You would like all the State field entries to be in all uppercase letters. Also, rather than having to enter the same state for each record, you want the field to display the state FL automatically. This will make data entry faster because all the stores are located in Florida and it is unlikely that the employees will live in another state.

In Tutorial 1 you set the field properties of several fields. For example, you set the Employee ID field size to 4 so that a larger number could not be entered into the field. In addition, you set the format of the Hire Date field to display a date using the Short Date style. You can also set a field's property to automatically change the entry to uppercase characters. To change the properties of a field, you use Design view.

1 ■ Click 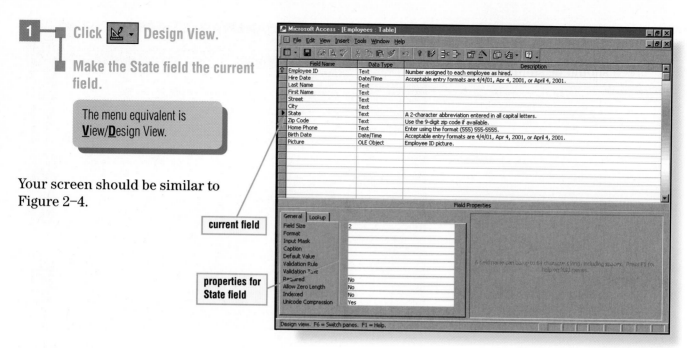 ▾ Design View.

■ Make the State field the current field.

> The menu equivalent is **V**iew/**D**esign View.

Your screen should be similar to Figure 2–4.

Figure 2–4

The properties associated with the State field are displayed in the General tab. The Format property is used to customize the way an entry is displayed.

Concept ① Format Property

You can use the Format property to create custom formats that change the way numbers, dates, times, and text display and print. Format properties do not change the way Access stores data, only how the data is displayed. To change the format of a field, different symbols are entered in the Format text box. Text and Memo Data Types can use any of these four symbols:

Symbol	Meaning	Example
@	A required text character or space	@@@-@@-@@@@ would display 123456789 as 123–45–6789. Nine characters or spaces are required.
>	Forces all characters to uppercase	> would display SMITH whether you entered SMITH, smith, or Smith.
<	Forces all characters to lowercase	< would display smith whether you entered SMITH, smith, or Smith.
&	An optional text character	@@-@@& would display 12345 as 12–345 and 12.34 as 12–34. Four out of five characters are required, and a fifth is optional.

To enter the symbol to change all entries in the field to uppercase,

2 — Move to the Format field property text box.

■ Type **>**

Your screen should be similar to Figure 2–5.

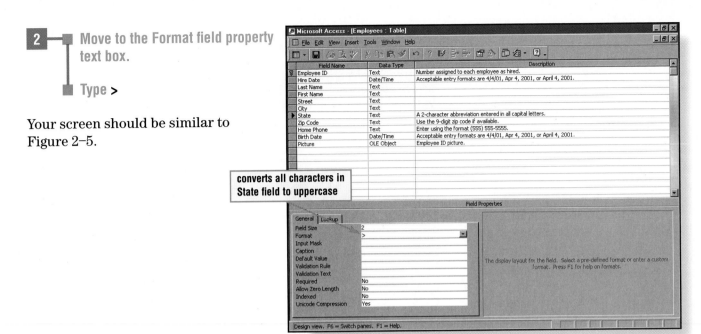

converts all characters in State field to uppercase

Figure 2–5

Next you want to change the State field property to automatically display the default value of FL.

Concept ② Default Value Property

The Default Value property is used to specify a value that is automatically entered in a field when a new record is created. This property is commonly used when most of the entries in a field will be the same for the entire table. That default value is then displayed automatically in the field. When users add a record to the table, they can either accept this value or enter another value. This saves time while entering data.

3 — Move to the Default Value property text box.

■ Type **FL**

■ Press ⏎Enter.

Your screen should be similar to Figure 2–6.

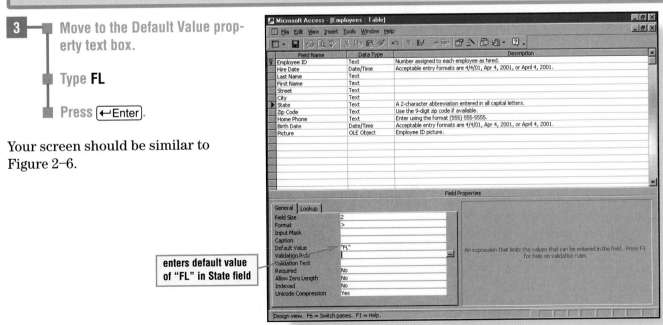

enters default value of "FL" in State field

Figure 2–6

The default value is automatically enclosed in quotes to identify the entry as a group of characters called a **character string**.

4 ■ Click ▦ ▾ Datasheet view.

■ Click ▭Yes▭ to save the table.

Your screen should be similar to Figure 2–7.

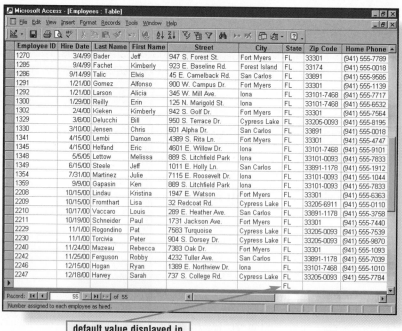

converted to uppercase

Figure 2–7

You can now see that records 12 (Scott Briggs) and 22 (Suzanne Reddie) correctly display the state in capital letters as a result of the format property setting you entered for the State field. To see the default value of FL displayed in a new blank record,

5 ■ Click ▸✱ .

Your screen should be similar to Figure 2–8.

default value displayed in
State field of new record

Figure 2–8

The new blank record at the end of the table displays FL as the default value for the State field.

Finding and Replacing Data

Next you want to update the Zip Code field for the existing records. You have checked with the U.S. Postal Service and found that all zip codes of 33891 have a four-digit extension of 1605. To locate all the records with this zip code, you could look at the Zip Code field for each record to find the match and then edit the field to add the extension. If the table is small, this method would be acceptable. For large tables, however, this method could be quite time consuming and more prone to errors. A more efficient way is to search the table to find specific values in records and then replace the entry with another.

Concept ③ Find and Replace

The Find and Replace feature helps you quickly find specific information and automatically replace it with new information. The Find command will locate all specified values in a field, and the Replace command will both find a value and automatically replace it with another. For example, in a table containing supplier and item prices, you may need to increase the price of all items supplied by one manufacturer. To quickly locate these items, you would use the Find command to locate all records with the name of the manufacturer and then update the price appropriately. Alternatively, you could use the Replace command if you knew that all items priced at $9.95 were increasing to $11.89. This command would locate all values matching the original price and replace them with the new price. Finding and replacing data is fast and accurate, but you need to be careful when replacing not to replace unintended matches.

The Replace command will search the current field to find the specified data and replace it with other data.

1 ■— Move to the Zip Code field of record 1.

■ Choose Edit/Replace.

> The keyboard shortcut is
> Ctrl + H.

Your screen should be similar to Figure 2–9.

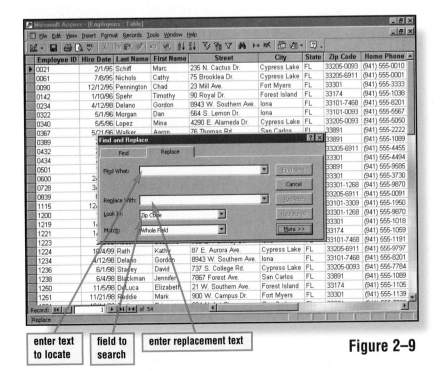

enter text to locate

field to search

enter replacement text

Figure 2–9

The Find and Replace dialog box shows the name of the field it will search in the Look In text box. In the Find What text box, you enter the text you want to locate, and in the Replace With text box, you enter the replacement text exactly as you want it to appear in your document. In addition, you can use the advanced search options to refine the search. To see these options,

2 ── Click [More ⚲] .

Your screen should be similar to Figure 2–10.

additional options to refine search

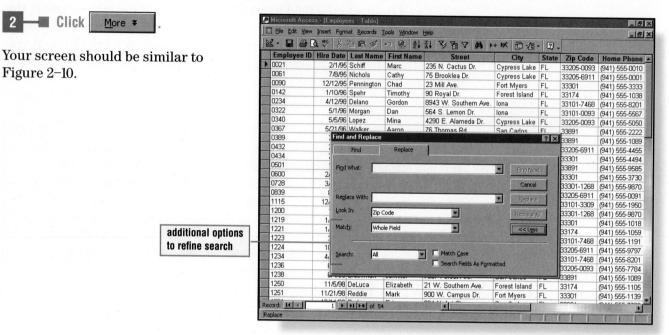

Figure 2–10

The additional options in the Find and Replace dialog box can be combined in many ways to help you find and replace text in documents. They are described in the table below.

Option	Effect on Text
Match	Refines area in field to locate match to the whole field, any part of the field, or the start of the field.
Search	Specifies direction in table to search: All (search all records), Down or Up (search down or up from the current insertion point location in the field).
Match Case	Finds words that have the same pattern of uppercase letters as entered in the Find What text box. Using this option makes the search case sensitive.
Search Fields as Formatted	Finds data based on its display format.

To enter the zip code to find and the replacement zip code, and to search using the default options,

3 Click in the Find What text box.

Type **33891**

Press Tab.

Type **33891-1605**

Click Find Next.

> If necessary, move the dialog box so you can see the located entry.

Your screen should be similar to Figure 2–11.

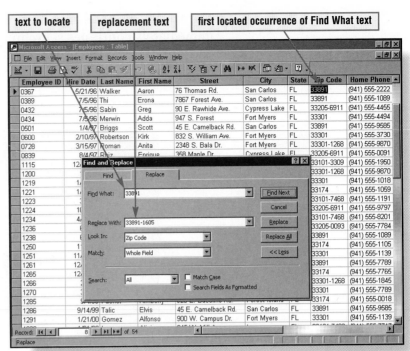

Figure 2–11

Immediately the highlight moves to the first occurrence of text in the document that matches the Find What text and highlights it. To replace the highlighted text,

4 Click Replace.

Your screen should be similar to Figure 2–12.

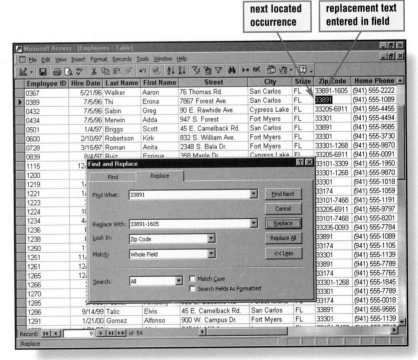

Figure 2–12

The original zip code entry is replaced with the new zip code. The program immediately continues searching and locates a second occurrence of the entry. You decide the program is locating the values accurately, and it will be safe to replace all finds with the replacement value. To do this,

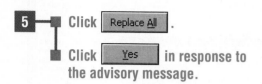

5   Click [Replace All] .

   Click [Yes] **in response to the advisory message.**

Your screen should be similar to Figure 2–13.

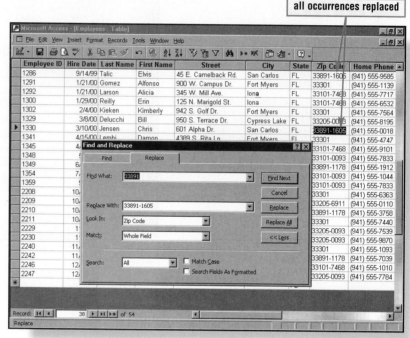

Figure 2–13

All matches are replaced with the replacement text. It is much faster to use Replace All than to confirm each match separately. However, exercise care when using Replace All, because the search text you specify might be part of another field and you may accidentally replace text you want to keep.

6   In the same manner, update the zip code for 33301 to include the extension **1268**.

   Click the [Less ±] button to close the other options portion of the dialog box.

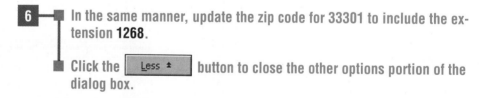

The menu equivalent is Edit/Find, the toolbar button is [🔍], and the keyboard shortcut is [Ctrl] + F.

Over the past few days you have received several change request forms to update the employee records. The first change request is for Melissa Lettow, who recently married and has both a name and address change. To quickly locate this record you will use the Find command. This command works just like the Find and Replace command, except it does not enter a replacement.

7 ▪ Move to the Last Name field of record 1.

▪ Open the Find tab.

▪ Replace the Find What text with **lettow**.

▪ Click ▭Find Next▭ .

Because the Match Case option is not selected, Find will look for an exact match regardless of uppercase or lowercase characters.

Your screen should be similar to Figure 2–14.

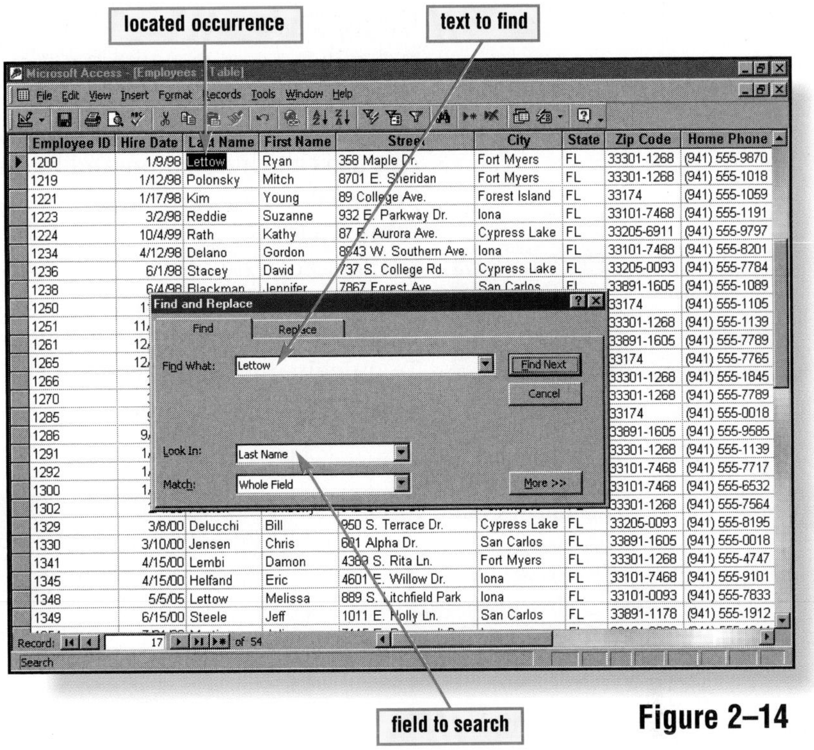

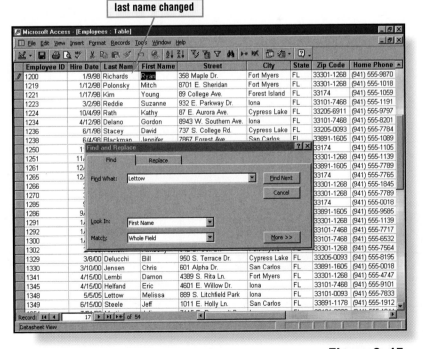

located occurrence

text to find

field to search

Figure 2–14

If the Find command did not locate this record, reissue the command and make sure you enter the name Lettow exactly as shown and you are searching the Last Name field.

Access searches the table and moves to the first occurrence of the entry. The Last Name field is highlighted in record 17. To change the last name to Richards,

8 ▪ Double-click on Lettow in the Last Name field of record 17.

▪ Type **Richards**

▪ Press ⏎Enter .

Your screen should be similar to Figure 2–15.

last name changed

Figure 2–15

Using Undo

Now that the highlight is on the First Name field, you notice this is the record for Ryan Lettow, not Melissa. You changed the wrong record. You can use the Undo command to quickly undo this change. Undo will cancel your last action as long as you have not made any further changes to the table. Even if you save the record or the table, you can undo changes to the last edited record by using the Undo Saved Record command on the Edit menu or by clicking ⤺. Once you have changed another record or moved to another window, however, the earlier change cannot be undone. To quickly undo the change made to this record,

> You can also press **Esc** before leaving the field you are editing to cancel changes you have made.

1 ── ■ Click ⤺ Undo.

> The menu equivalent is **E**dit/**U**ndo, and the keyboard shortcut is **Ctrl** + Z.

Your screen should be similar to Figure 2–16.

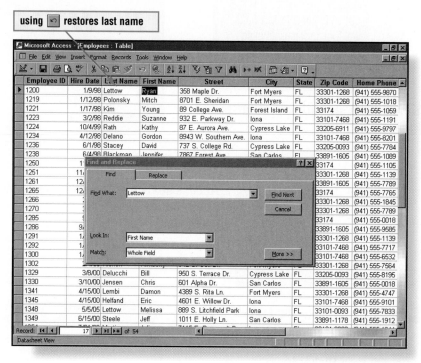

Figure 2–16

The original field value of Lettow is restored. Now you want to continue the search to locate the next record with the last name of Lettow.

2 ── ■ Move back to the Last Name field of record 17.

> Reminder: The insertion point must be on the field you want to search before clicking **Find Next**.

■ Click **Find Next**.

■ Change the last name to **Richards** and the street to **5401 E. Thomas Rd.**

■ Use the Find command to search the table for the following records and correct the entries.

Employee Name	Field	Correction
Peter Torcivia	Street	**4290 E. Alameda Dr.**
Eric Helfand	City, Zip Code	**Cypress Lake 33205-0093**
Jennifer Blackman	Last Name	**Thomas**
Lisa Sutton	Zip Code	**33101-0093**

3 ■ When you are done, close the Find and Replace dialog box and return to the first field of record 1.

Inserting a Field

Additional Information

If you remove a field, Access permanently deletes the field definition and any data in the field. Click 🗐 or use **E**dit/Delete **R**ows to remove a field.

While continuing to use the table, you have realized that you need to include a field of information to hold each employee's gender. Although it is better to include all the necessary fields when creating the table structure, it is possible to add or remove fields from a table at a later time. After looking at the order of the fields, you decide to add the new field, Gender, between the Phone Number and Birth Date fields. To insert the new field in the table and define its properties,

1 ■ Click 🖉 ▾ Design view.

You can also add or delete fields in Datasheet view.

■ Make the Birth Date field current.

■ Click 🖳 Insert Rows.

The menu equivalent is **I**nsert/**R**ows. You can also use the Insert Row command on the shortcut menu.

Your screen should be similar to Figure 2–17.

blank field definition row inserted

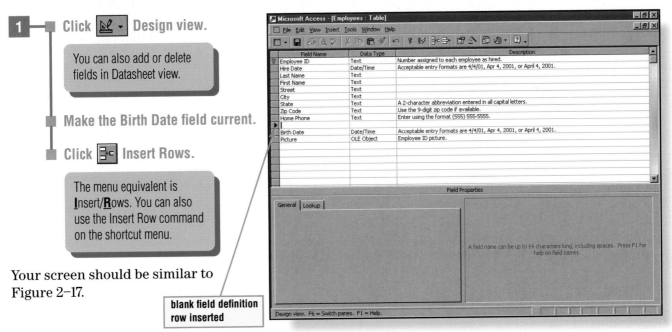

Figure 2–17

2 ━ Enter the new field information as follows:

Field Name: **Gender**

Data Type: **Text**

Description: **Enter M for male or F for female.**

Field Size: **1**

Format: **>**

Your screen should be similar to Figure 2–18.

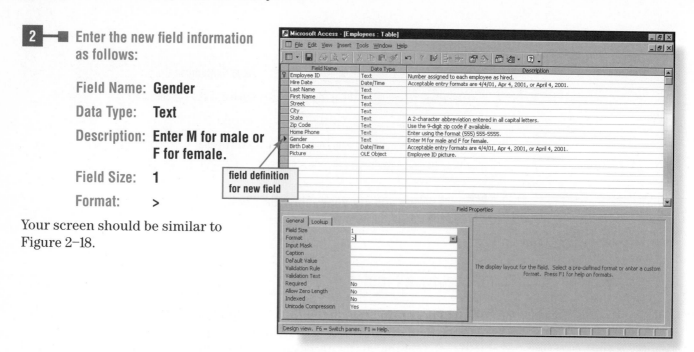

Figure 2–18

Adding Validity Checks

The only two characters you want the Gender field to accept are M for male and F for female. To specify that these two characters are the only entries acceptable in the field, you will include a validity check.

Concept ④ Validity Check

Access automatically performs certain checks, called **validity checks**, on values entered in a field to make sure that the values are valid for the field type. A Text field type has few restrictions, but you can create your own validity checks for a field, which Access will apply during data entry.

A validity check is set by entering an expression to describe acceptable values. An **expression** is a combination of symbols that produces specific results. Expressions are used throughout Access to create validity checks, queries, forms, and reports. These are examples of possible expressions:

Expression	Result
=[Sales Amount] + [Sales Tax]	Sums value in two fields.
="M" OR "F"	Includes M or F entries only.
>--#1/1/95# AND <=#12/31/95#	Includes entries greater than or equal to 1/1/95, and less than or equal to 12/31/95.
="Tennis Rackets"	Includes Tennis Rackets entries only.

You create an expression by combining identifiers, operators, and values to produce the desired result. An **identifier** is an element that refers to the value of a field, a graphical object, or property. In the expression =[Sales Amount] + [Sales Tax], [Sales Amount] and [Sales Tax] are identifiers that refer to the values in the Sales Amount and Sales Tax fields.

An **operator** is a symbol or word that indicates that an operation is to be performed. The Access operators include = (equal to), <> (not equal to), >= (greater than or equal to), <= (less than or equal to), LIKE, OR, and AND. In the expression ="M" OR "F", the = sign and OR are operators. The = operator is assumed if no other operator is specified.

Values are numbers, dates, or character strings. Character strings such as "M," "F," or "Tennis Rackets" are enclosed in quotation marks. Dates are enclosed in pound signs (#), as in >=#1/1/95# AND <=#12/31/95#.

When you add a validity check, you can also add validation text in the Validation Text property box. **Validation text** is an explanatory message that appears if a user attempts to enter invalid information in a text field for which there is a validity check. For example, if you added a validity check to a field to only allow the numbers 1 through 10, you might create validation text that would display the message, "The only valid entries for this field are numbers 1 through 10." If you do not specify a message, Access will display a default error message, which will not clearly describe the reason for the error.

You want to add a validity check to allow only M or F to be entered in the field. You also want to include a validation text message that will be displayed if the wrong character is entered in the Gender field.

1 ━━ ■ Move to the Validation Rule field property text box.

■ Type **M or F**

> You do not need to type the = as it is assumed if no operator is entered.

■ Press ⏎Enter.

■ For the validation text, type **The only valid entries are M or F.**

Your screen should be similar to Figure 2–19.

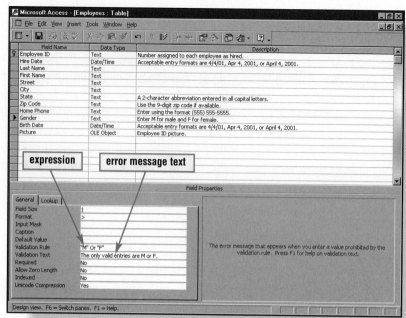

Figure 2–19

The expression states that the acceptable values can only be equal to an M or an F. Notice that Access automatically added quotation marks around the two character strings and changed the "o" in "or" to uppercase. Because the Format property has been set to convert all entries to uppercase, an entry of m or f is also acceptable.

Next you want to add the data for the Gender field to the table.

2 ━━ ■ Click  Datasheet.

■ Click ┌ Yes ┐ to save the table.

Your screen should be similar to Figure 2–20.

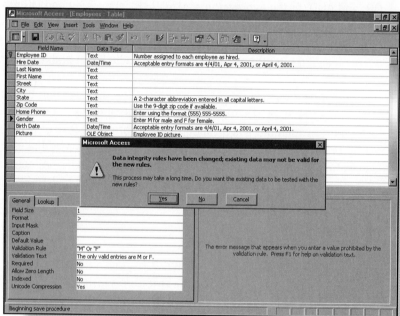

Figure 2–20

A message box advises you that data integrity rules have been changed. When you restructure a table, you often make changes that could result in a loss of data. Changes such as shortening field sizes, creating validity checks, or changing field types can cause existing data to become invalid. Because the field is new, there are no data values to verify, and a validation check is unnecessary. To continue,

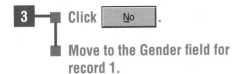

3 ■ Click No .

■ Move to the Gender field for record 1.

Your screen should be similar to Figure 2–21.

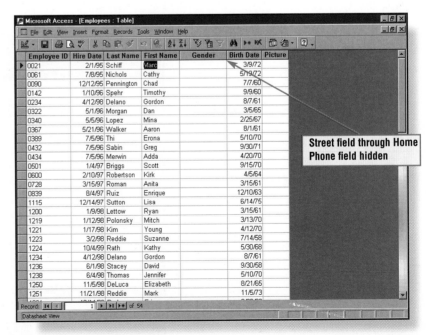

Figure 2–21

The new field was added to the table between the Home Phone and Birth Date fields.

Hiding and Redisplaying Fields

You can most likely tell the gender for each record by looking at the employee's first name. Unfortunately, the First Name field is on the opposite side of the screen from the Gender field. A quick way to view the fields side by side is to hide the fields that are in between.

1 ■ Select the Street field through the Home Phone field.

Drag in the column heads to select the fields.

■ Choose Format/Hide Columns.

Your screen should be similar to Figure 2–22.

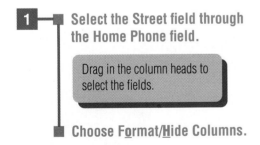

Figure 2–22

Now both the First Name and Gender columns are next to each other, and you can see the first name for record 1 is Marc. Therefore the Gender field for record 1 should be M. To verify that the validity check works, you will enter an invalid field value in the Gender field for this record.

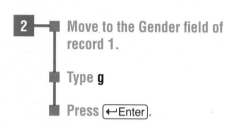

2 — ■ Move to the Gender field of record 1.

■ Type **g**

■ Press ⏎Enter.

Your screen should be similar to Figure 2–23.

invalid entry displays error message text in dialog box

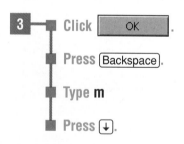

Figure 2–23

Access displays the error message you entered in the Validation Text box of Design view. To clear the error message and correct the entry,

3 — ■ Click [OK].

■ Press Backspace.

■ Type **m**

■ Press ↓.

Your screen should be similar to Figure 2–24.

converted entry to uppercase

Figure 2–24

The entry for the first record is displayed as an uppercase M. Next you will enter the gender for each record and then redisplay the hidden fields.

4 ■ Enter the Gender field values for the remaining records by looking at the First Name field to determine whether the employee is male or female.

■ Reduce the size of the Gender field using the Best Fit command.

Reminder: Double-click on the right column border to best fit the field.

■ Choose Format/Unhide Columns.

Your screen should be similar to Figure 2-25.

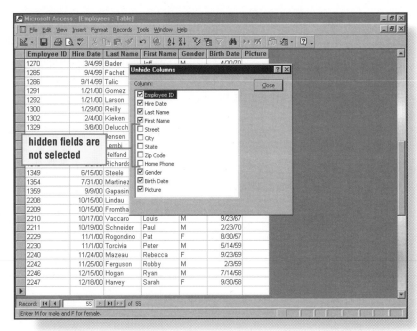

Figure 2-25

5 ■ Select the five fields that do not display checkmarks.

■ Click Close .

Sorting on a Single Field

As you may recall from Tutorial 1, the records are ordered by the primary key field, Employee ID. The Accounting department manager, however, has asked you for an alphabetical list of all employees. To do this you can sort the records in the table.

Concept ⑤ Sort

You can quickly reorder records in a table by **sorting** a table to display in a different record order. Sorting data often helps you find specific information quickly. In Access you can sort data in ascending order (A to Z or 0 to 9) or descending order (Z to A or 9 to 0). You can sort all records in a table by a single field, such as State, or you can select adjacent columns and sort by more than one field, such as State and then City. When you select multiple columns to sort, Access sorts records starting with the column farthest left, then moves to the right across the columns. For example, if you want to quickly sort by State, then by City, the State field must be to the left of the City field. Access saves the new sort order with your table data and reapplies it automatically each time you open the table. To return to the primary key sort order, you must remove the temporary sort.

For the first sort, you want the records arranged in ascending alphabetical order by last name.

1 ■ Move to the Employee ID field of record 1.

■ Move to the Last Name field of any record.

■ Click 🔼 Sort Ascending.

> The menu equivalent is **R**ecords/**S**ort/Sort **A**scending.

Your screen should be similar to Figure 2–26.

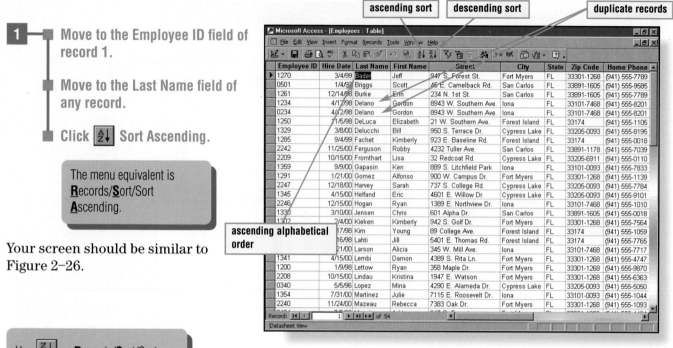

> Use 🔽 or **R**ecords/**S**ort/Sort Des**c**ending to sort in descending alphabetical order.

Figure 2–26

The employee records are displayed in alphabetical order by last name.

Deleting Records

> You cannot use Undo to restore deleted records.

> Records are selected using **E**dit/Se**l**ect Record or by clicking in the row selector when the mouse pointer shape is ➡. In Navigation mode, ⇧Shift + Spacebar selects the current record.

Now that the records are alphabetically arranged, you immediately notice that Gordon Delano's record has been entered into the table twice. The records contain identical information in all the fields except for the Employee ID field. By checking the employee card, you determine that the record with the employee number of 0234 is incorrect. You need to delete the duplicate record.

Records can be removed from a table by selecting the entire record and pressing Del or clicking ✂ Cut. This method is useful when you have multiple records to be deleted that you can select and delete as a group. It is quicker, however, to use the 🗙 Delete Record button when you want to remove records individually. This is because the record is both selected and deleted at the same time.

1 ▪ Move to any field in record 5.

▪ Click 🗙 **Delete Record**.

▪ Click [Yes] to confirm that you want to delete the record.

> The menu equivalent is **E**dit/Cu**t**, and the keyboard shortcut is [Ctrl] + X. The Cut command is also on the shortcut menu when a record is selected.

Your screen should be similar to Figure 2–27.

duplicate record for Delano deleted   delete records

Figure 2–27

Next you want to check the rest of the table to see if you see any other problems.

> As you drag the scroll box, the record location is displayed in the scrolltips box Record: 32 of 53 .

2 ▪ Use the scroll box to scroll down to record 32.

Now you can see that the records for Suzanne and Mark Reddie are sorted by last name but not by first name. You want all records that have the same last name to be further sorted by first name.

Sorting on Multiple Fields

> If the columns are not adjacent, you can hide the columns that are in between. If they are not in the correct order, you can move the columns. You will learn how to do this in Tutorial 3.

To sort first names within same last names, you need to sort using multiple sort fields. When sorting on multiple fields, the fields must be adjacent to each other, and the most important field in the sort must be to the left of the secondary field. The Last Name and First Name fields are already in the correct locations for the sort you want to perform. To specify the fields to sort on, both columns must be selected.

1 ■ Select the Last Name and First Name field columns.

■ Click 🔼 Sort Ascending.

■ Scroll down to record 32 again.

Your screen should be similar to Figure 2–28.

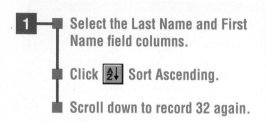

record sorted by last name and by first name

Employee ID	Hire Date	Last Name	First Name	Street	City	State	Zip Code	Home Phone
1251	11/21/98	Reddie	Mark	900 W. Campus Dr.	Fort Myers	FL	33301-1268	(941) 555-1139
1223	3/2/98	Reddie	Suzanne	932 E. Parkway Dr.	Iona	FL	33101-7468	(941) 555-1191
1300	1/29/00	Reilly	Erin	125 N. Marigold St.	Iona	FL	33101-7468	(941) 555-6532
1348	5/5/05	Richards	Melissa	5401 E. Thomas Rd.	Iona	FL	33101-0093	(941) 555-7833
0600	2/10/97	Robertson	Kirk	832 S. William Ave.	Fort Myers	FL	33301-1268	(941) 555-3730
2229	11/1/00	Rogondino	Pat	7583 Turquoise	Cypress Lake	FL	33205-0093	(941) 555-7539
0728	3/15/97	Roman	Anita	2348 S. Bala Dr.	Fort Myers	FL	33301-1268	(941) 555-9870
0839	8/4/97	Ruiz	Enrique	358 Maple Dr.	Cypress Lake	FL	33205-6911	(941) 555-0091
0432	7/5/96	Sabin	Greg	90 E. Rawhide Ave.	Cypress Lake	FL	33205-6911	(941) 555-4455
0021	2/1/95	Schiff	Marc	235 N. Cactus Dr.	Cypress Lake	FL	33205-0093	(941) 555-0010
2211	10/19/00	Schneider	Paul	1731 Jackson Ave.	Fort Myers	FL	33301-1268	(941) 555-7440
0142	1/10/96	Spehr	Timothy	90 Royal Dr.	Forest Island	FL	33174	(941) 555-1038
1236	6/1/98	Stacey	David	737 S. College Rd.	Cypress Lake	FL	33205-0093	(941) 555-7784
1349	6/15/00	Steele	Jeff	1011 E. Holly Ln.	San Carlos	FL	33891-1178	(941) 555-1912
1266	2/4/99	Stueland	Valerie	34 University Dr.	Fort Myers	FL	33301-1268	(941) 555-1845
1115	12/14/97	Sutton	Lisa	4389 S. Hayden Rd.	Iona	FL	33101-0093	(941) 555-1950
1286	9/14/99	Talic	Elvis	45 E. Camelback Rd.	San Carlos	FL	33891-1605	(941) 555-9585
0389	7/5/96	Thi	Erona	7867 Forest Ave.	San Carlos	FL	33891-1605	(941) 555-1089
1238	6/4/98	Thomas	Jennifer	7867 Forest Ave.	San Carlos	FL	33891-1605	(941) 555-1089
2230	11/1/00	Torcivia	Peter	4290 E. Alameda Dr.	Cypress Lake	FL	33205-0093	(941) 555-9870
2210	10/17/00	Vaccaro	Louis	289 E. Heather Ave.	San Carlos	FL	33891-1178	(941) 555-3758
0367	5/21/96	Walker	Aaron	76 Thomas Rd.	San Carlos	FL	33891-1605	(941) 555-2222
*						FL		

Record: 1 of 53

Datasheet View

Figure 2–28

The record for Mark Reddie is now before the record for Suzanne. As you can see, sorting is a fast, useful tool. The sort order remains in effect until you remove the sort or replace it with a new sort order. Although Access remembers your sort order even when you exit the program, it does not actually change the table records. You can remove the sort at any time to restore the records to the primary key sort order. To do this,

2 ■ Choose Records/Remove Filter/Sort.

■ Close the table and save your design changes.

Note: If you are ending your session now, close the database file and exit Access. When you begin again, load Access and open the Employee Records database.

Creating a Form

One of your objectives is to make the database easy to use. You know from experience that long hours of viewing large tables can be tiring. Therefore you want to create an onscreen form to make this table easier to view and use.

Concept ⑥ Forms

A **form** is a database object used primarily to display records onscreen to make it easier to enter new records and to make changes to existing records. Forms are based on an underlying table, and include design control elements such as descriptive text, titles, labels, lines, boxes, and pictures. Forms often use calculations as well, to summarize data that is not listed on the actual table, such as a sales total. Forms make working with long lists of data easier. They enable people to use the data in the tables without having to sift through many lines of data to find the exact record.

You want the onscreen form to be similar to the paper form that is completed by each new employee when hired. The information from that form is used as the source of input for the new record that will be added to the table for the new employee.

As when creating a table, there are several different methods that can be used to create a form. You will use the Form Wizard to guide you through the steps to create a form.

1 ■ **To create a form, click**
   🔲 Forms **to open the Forms object.**

   ■ **Double-click** Create form by using wizard.

Your screen should be similar to Figure 2-29.

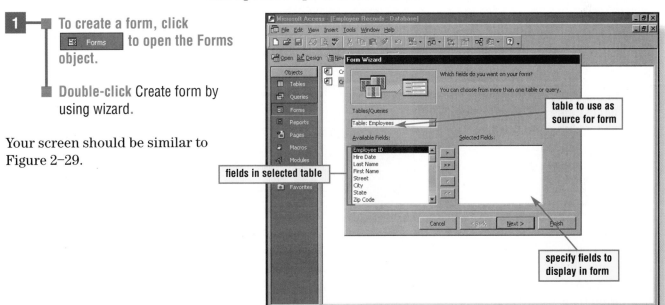

Figure 2-29

The Form Wizard dialog box displays the name of the current table, Employees, in the Tables/Queries list box. This is the underlying table that will be used when creating the form. If your database contained multiple tables, you could open the Tables/Queries drop-down list to select the appropriate underlying table to use for the form.

After selecting the table, you select the fields to include in the form. The fields from the selected table will appear in the Available Fields list box. The order in which you select the fields is the tab order, or the order in which the highlight will move through the fields on the form when you press Tab during data entry. You would like the order to be the same as the order on the paper form. To add the First Name field to the form first, from the Available Fields list box,

2 ■── Select First Name.

■ Click [>].

> You can also double-click on each field name in the Available Fields list box to move the field name to the Selected Fields list box.

> The [>>] button adds all available fields to the Selected Fields list.

Your screen should be similar to Figure 2–30.

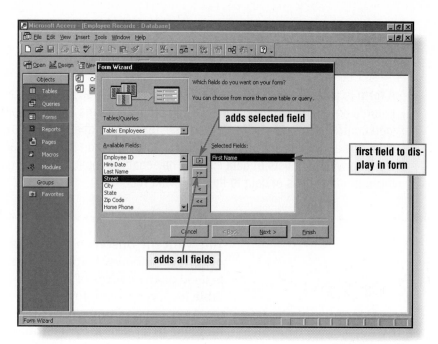

Figure 2–30

The First Name field is removed from the Available Fields list and added to the top of the Selected Fields list box.

3 ■── In the some manner, select the fields in the order shown below and add them to the Selected Fields list.

Last Name
Street
City
State
Zip Code
Home Phone
Gender
Birth Date
Employee ID
Hire Date
Picture

Your screen should be similar to Figure 2–31.

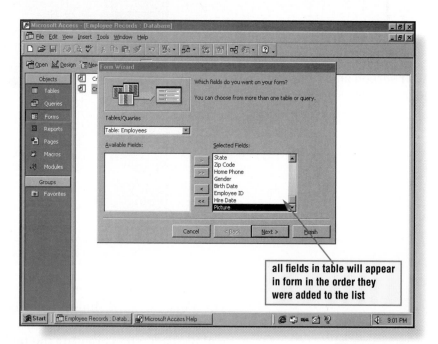

Figure 2–31

When you are done, the Available Fields list box is empty, and the Selected Fields list box lists the fields in the selected order. To move to the next Form Wizard screen,

 **Click** Next > .

Your screen should be similar to Figure 2–32.

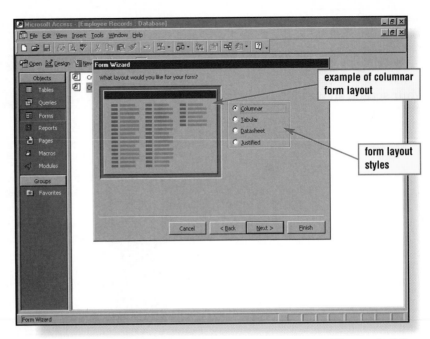

Figure 2–32

In this Wizard dialog box you are asked to select the layout for the form. Four form layouts are available: Columnar, Tabular, Datasheet and Justified. They are described in the table below.

Form	Layout Style	Description
Columnar		Presents data for the selected fields in columns. The field names display down the left side of the page, with the data for each field just to the right of each field name. A single record is displayed in each form window.
Tabular		Presents data in a table layout with field names across the top of the page and the corresponding data in rows and columns under each heading. Multiple records are displayed in Form view, each on a single row.
Datasheet		Displays data in rows and columns similar to the Table Datasheet view, but only selected fields display in the order chosen during form design. Displays multiple records, one per row in the Form window.
Justified		Displays data in rows, with field names across the top of the row and the corresponding field data below it. A single record may appear in multiple rows in the Form window in order to fully display the field name and data.

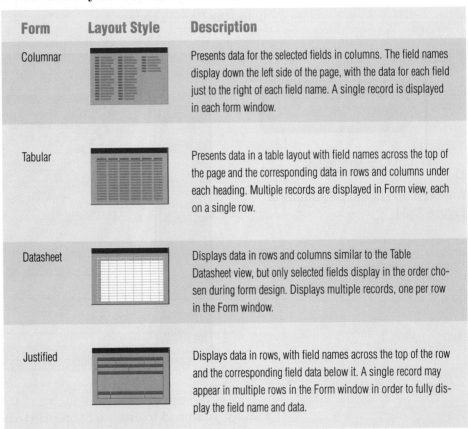

The columnar layout would appear most similar to the paper form currently in use by the personnel department.

5 ■ If necessary, **select** Columnar.

■ **Click** Next > .

Your screen should be similar to
Figure 2–33.

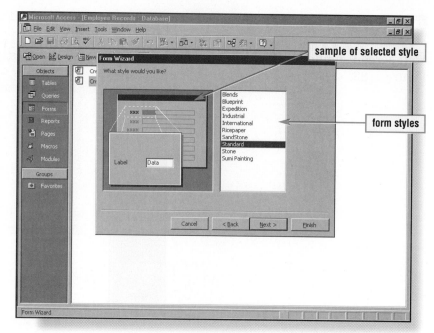

Figure 2–33

From the next dialog box, you select from ten different styles for your
form. A sample of each style as it is selected is displayed on the left side of
the dialog box. Standard is the default selection. You will create the form
using the Blends style.

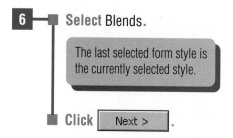

6 ■ **Select** Blends.

> The last selected form style is
> the currently selected style.

■ **Click** Next > .

Your screen should be similar to
Figure 2–34.

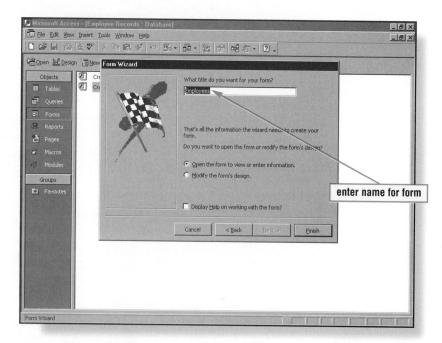

Figure 2–34

Finally, you need to enter a form title to be used as the name of the form,
and you need to specify whether the form should open with data displayed
in it. The Wizard uses the name of the table as the default form title. You
want the form to display data, but you want to change the form's title. To
do this,

7 ■ Type **Employee Data Form**

■ Click [Finish].

■ If necessary, maximize the Form window.

Your screen should be similar to Figure 2–35.

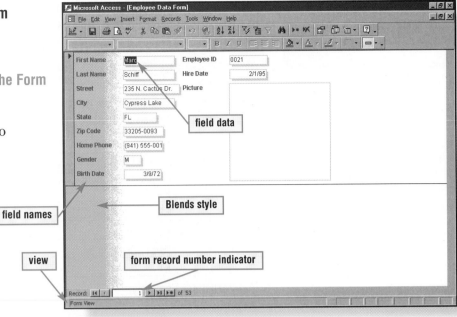

field data

field names

Blends style

view

form record number indicator

Figure 2–35

The completed form is displayed in the Form view window. The form displays the selected fields in columnar layout using the Blends style. The field name labels are in two columns with the field data text boxes in adjacent columns to the right. The employee information for Marc Schiff, the current record in the table, is displayed in the text boxes.

You use the same navigation keys in Form view that you used in Datasheet view. You can move between fields in the form by using the navigation buttons at the bottom of the form, or the [Tab], [←Enter], [⇧Shift] + [Tab], and directional arrow keys on the keyboard. In addition, the [Page Up] and [Page Down] keys allow you to move between records in Form view. You can also use the Find command to locate and display specific records.

8 ■ Display the record for Lisa Sutton.

> If you use the Find command, you can select the name from the Find drop-down list.

Your screen should be similar to Figure 2–36.

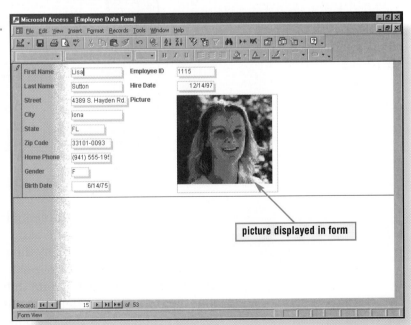

picture displayed in form

Figure 2–36

> Reminder: You would double-click on the picture to see an enlarged view and modify the object.

Lisa Sutton's record is displayed in the form. Because this record contains the inserted picture in the Picture field, the photo is displayed.

Entering Records in Form View

Now you want to add a few new employee records from data on the paper form shown below to the table.

> Use ▶* New Record in the Form toolbar or the ▶* navigation button to display a blank form.

EMPLOYEE DATA

First Name   Kevin   Last Name   Tillman

Street   89 E. Southern Dr.

City   Fort Myers   State __FL__   Zip Code __33301-2316__

Home Phone   (941) 555-3434

Gender   M   Birth Date   April 13, 1971

For Personnel Use Only:

Employee ID   2295

Hire Date   Jan. 12, 2001

---

1 ▪— Move to a new blank entry form and enter the data shown in the paper form for a new record.

> Press [Tab] to move to the next field.

Your screen should be similar to Figure 2–37.

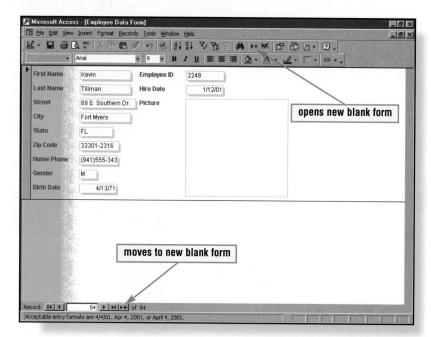

Figure 2–37

> You will learn how to enhance forms in Tutorial 3.

Using the form makes entering the new employee data much faster because the fields are in the same order as the information in the paper Employee Data form used by the personnel department.

When using the Form Wizard most of the field text boxes are appropriately sized to display the data in the field. You probably noticed, however, that the Home Phone field is not quite large enough. You will learn how to fix this problem by sizing the object in the next tutorial.

2 Enter another record using your special Employee ID 9999 and your first and last name. Enter the current date as your Hire Date. The data in all other fields can be fictitious.

To see the records you entered in Form Datasheet view, open the  View button drop-down list and click ▦ ▾ Datasheet view.

> The menu equivalent is **V**iew/Data**s**heet View.

Scroll up a few rows to display both new records.

Your screen should be similar to Figure 2–38.

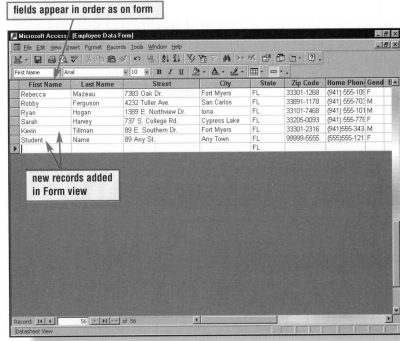

fields appear in order as on form

new records added in Form view

Figure 2–38

Form Datasheet view provides a datasheet view of the form data. Notice that the field columns are in the same order as in the form. Also notice that the new records are not in primary key order by employee number. When you open the table in Datasheet view, the new records will appear in primary key order.

Previewing and Printing a Form

You want to preview, then print just the form displaying your record.

1 Click 🗔 ▾ Form view.

Click 🔍 Print Preview.

Zoom to 100% to see the page better.

Your screen should be similar to Figure 2–39.

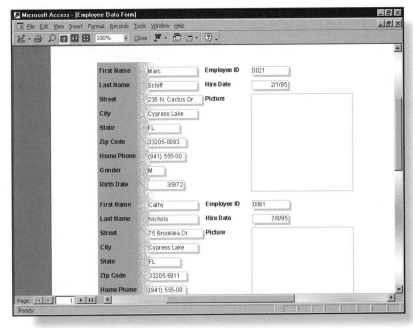

Figure 2–39

Print Preview displays whatever view you were last using. In this case, because you were last in Form view, the form is displayed in the Preview window. Access prints as many records as can be printed on a page in the Form layout. You want to print only the form displaying your record. To do this,

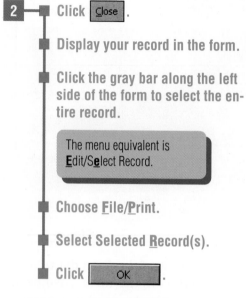

2 ■ Click Close .

■ Display your record in the form.

■ Click the gray bar along the left side of the form to select the entire record.

The menu equivalent is **E**dit/S**e**lect Record.

■ Choose **F**ile/**P**rint.

■ Select Selected **R**ecord(s).

■ Click OK .

Your printed output should be similar to Figure 2–40.

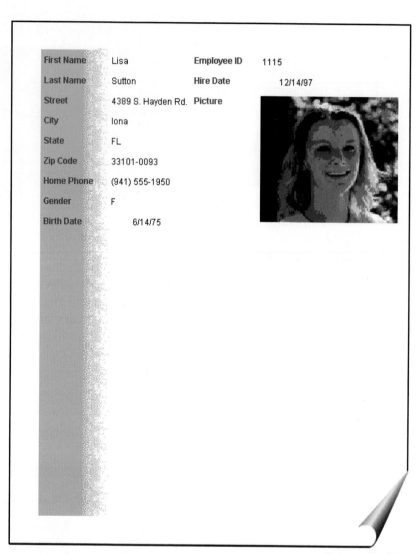

First Name	Lisa	Employee ID	1115
Last Name	Sutton	Hire Date	12/14/97
Street	4389 S. Hayden Rd.	Picture	
City	Iona		
State	FL		
Zip Code	33101-0093		
Home Phone	(941) 555-1950		
Gender	F		
Birth Date	6/14/75		

Figure 2–40

Closing and Saving a Form

Next you will close and save the form.

1 ─■ Close the Form window.

The Database window is displayed, showing the new form object name in the Forms tab object list.

2 ─■ Exit Access.

Warning: Do not remove your data disk from the drive until you exit Access.

Concept Summary

Tutorial 2: Modifying a Table and Creating a Form

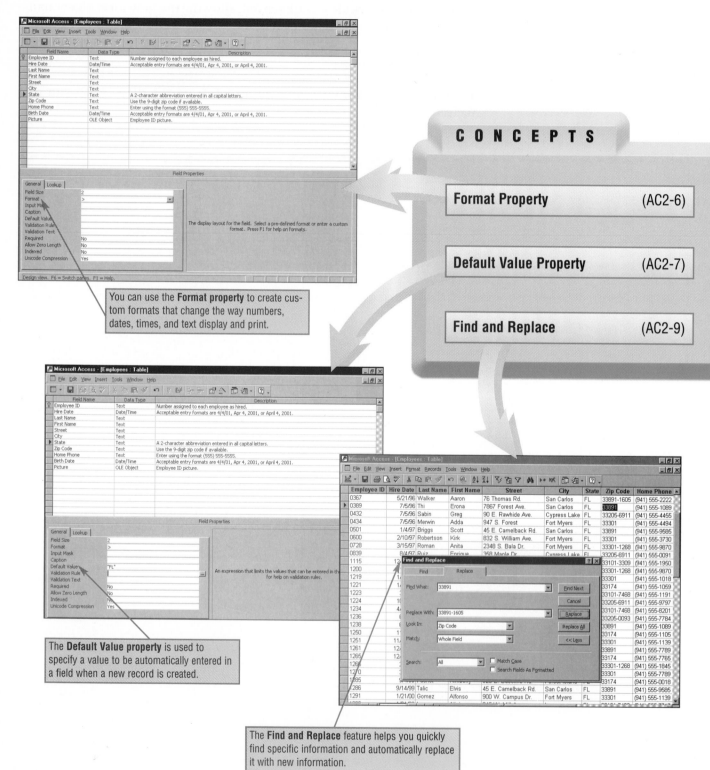

You can use the **Format property** to create custom formats that change the way numbers, dates, times, and text display and print.

C O N C E P T S

Format Property	(AC2-6)
Default Value Property	(AC2-7)
Find and Replace	(AC2-9)

The **Default Value property** is used to specify a value to be automatically entered in a field when a new record is created.

The **Find and Replace** feature helps you quickly find specific information and automatically replace it with new information.

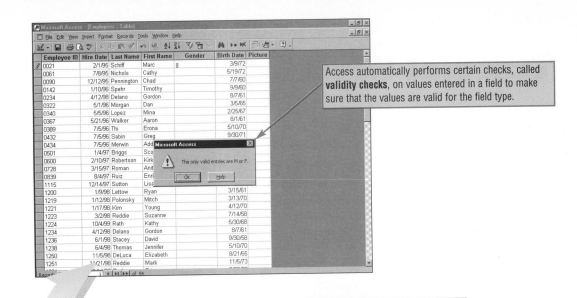

Access automatically performs certain checks, called **validity checks**, on values entered in a field to make sure that the values are valid for the field type.

You can quickly reorder records in a table by **sorting** a table to display in a different record order.

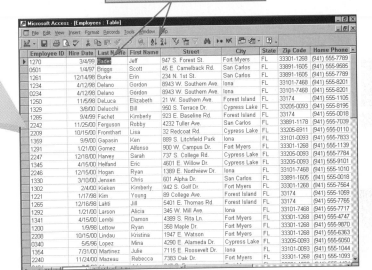

Validity Check	(AC2-17)
Sort	(AC2-21)
Form	(AC2-25)

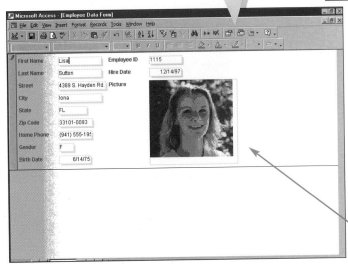

A **form** is a database object used primarily to display records onscreen to make it easier to enter new records and to make changes to existing records.

Tutorial Review

Key Terms

character string   AC2-8
expression   AC2-17
form   AC2-25
identifier   AC2-17

operator   AC2-17
sort   AC2-21
tab order   AC2-27
validation text   AC2-17

validity check   AC2-17
value   AC2-17

Command Summary

Command	Shortcut Keys	Button	Action
Edit/Undo	Ctrl + Z		Cancels last action
Edit/Cut	Ctrl + X or Del	or	Deletes selected record
Edit/Select Record	Shift + Spacebar		Selects current record
Edit/Find	Ctrl + F		Locates specified data
Edit/Replace	Ctrl + H		Locates and replaces specified data
View/Design View			Display Design view
View/Form View			Displays a form in Form view
Insert/Rows			Inserts a new field in table in Design view
Format/Hide Columns			Hides columns in Datasheet view
Format/Unhide Columns			Redisplays hidden columns in Datasheet view
Records/Sort/Sort Ascending			Reorders records in ascending alphabetical order

Screen Identification

In the following screen, several items are identified by letters. Enter the correct term for each item in the spaces that follow.

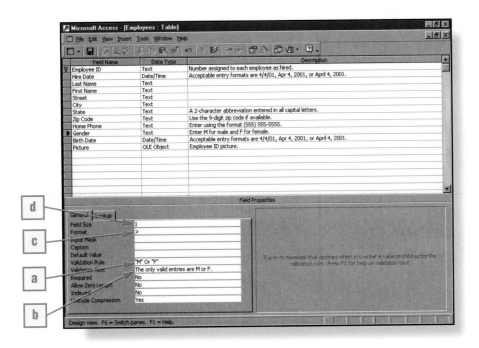

a. _____ b. _____ c. _____ d. _____

Matching

Match the letter to the correct item in the numbered list.

1. match case	_____	**a.**	cancels your last action
2. Ctrl + Home	_____	**b.**	used to check that a value entered in a field is valid for the field type
3.	_____	**c.**	database object used primarily for onscreen display
4. character string	_____	**d.**	moves to the first field of the first record
5. tab order	_____	**e.**	makes the find case sensitive
6. >	_____	**f.**	displays Design view
7. sort	_____	**g.**	order in which pressing [Tab] moves through fields in a form
8. validity check	_____	**h.**	a group of characters
9.	_____	**i.**	changes display order of a table
10. form	_____	**j.**	format character that forces all data in field to uppercase

True/False

Circle the correct answer to the following statements.

1. Format properties do not change the way Access stores data.   True   False

2. The Format property determines the value automatically entered into a field of a new record.   True   False

3. An identifier is a symbol or word that indicates that an operation is to be performed.   True   False

4. The Find command will locate specific values in a field and automatically replace them.   True   False

5. Format properties change the way data is displayed.   True   False

6. The Default Value property is commonly used when most of the entries in a field will be the same for the entire table.   True   False

7. Values are numbers, dates, or pictures.   True   False

8. The Replace command will automatically restore properties to an object.   True   False

9. Sorting reorders records in a table.   True   False

10. Forms are database objects used primarily for report generation.   True   False

Multiple Choice

Circle the letter of the correct answer to the following statements.

1. Format _____ is used to create custom formats that change the way numbers, dates, times, and text display and print.

    a. specification
    b. alignment
    c. range
    d. property

2. Values to be automatically entered into a field are specified in the _____ Value property.

    a. Auto
    b. Initial
    c. Default
    d. Assumed

3. _____ are automatically performed on values entered in a field to make sure that the values are valid for the field type.

    a. Object validations
    b. Security specifications
    c. Form searches
    d. Validity checks

4. You can quickly reorder _____ in a table by sorting.

    a. fields

    b. properties

    c. records

    d. forms

5. Forms are based on the underlying table by using design _____ elements.

    a. control

    b. default

    c. property

    d. object

6. To change the format of a field, different _____ are entered in the Format text box.

    a. symbols

    b. buttons

    c. objects

    d. graphics

7. When users add a record to a table, they can either accept the _____ value or enter another value.

    a. default

    b. initial

    c. last

    d. null

8. Expressions are combinations of _____ that are used to create validity checks, queries, forms, and reports.

    a. symbols

    b. objects

    c. functions

    d. values

9. Data sorted in _____ order is arrange alphabetically A to Z or numerically 0 to 9.

    a. increasing

    b. descending

    c. ascending

    d. decreasing

10. Forms are database objects used primarily to display records _____ to make it easier to enter new records and to make changes to existing records.

    a. numerically

    b. onscreen

    c. in reports

    d. alphabetically

Fill-In

- -

Complete the following statements by filling in the blanks with the correct terms.

1. A(n) _____ is a combination of symbols that produces specific results.

2. The _____ property is used to specify a value that is automatically entered in a field when a new record is created.

3. When _____ are performed, Access makes sure that the entry is acceptable in the field.

4. Records can be temporarily displayed in a different order by using the _____ feature.

5. Forms are primarily used for _____ and making changes to existing records.

6. The _____ property changes the way data appears in a field.

7. The four form layouts are _____ , _____ , _____ , and _____ .

8. Use _____ to cancel your last action.

9. The _____ layout creates a form that displays records with field names across the top of the page and records in rows.

10. To return to _____ order, you must remove the temporary sort.

Discussion Questions

- -

1. Discuss several different format properties and how they are used in a database.

2. Discuss the different types of form layouts and why you would use one layout type over another.

3. Discuss how validity checks work. What are some advantages of adding validity checks to a field? Include several examples.

4. Discuss the different ways records can be sorted. What are some advantages of sorting records?

Hands-On Practice Exercises

Step-by-Step

Rating System   ☆ Easy
                    ☆ ☆ Moderate
                    ☆ ☆ ☆ Difficult

1. Daria O'Dell is very impressed with the work you have done on the spa's database. After an initial review of the database, Ms. O'Dell realizes that the inclusion of additional data in the database can help her with other administrative functions. For example, as part of her future advertising campaigns, she would like to send birthday cards to each of her clients and wonders if it is possible to include birth date information in the database. Also, she would like you to modify some client records, create a form to ease data entry, and print a copy of the form. Your completed form is shown here.

To make the requested changes to the database and create the form, follow these steps:

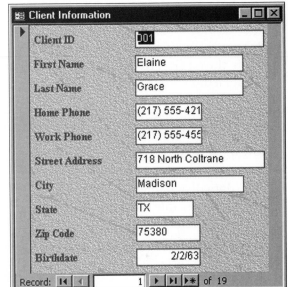

a. Open the database on your data disk named Daria Spa and the table named Clients.

b. In Design view, add the following field to the end of the table:

Field name: **Birthdate**

Data type: **Date/Time**

Description: **Identifies client's birthday**

Field format: **Short date**

c. Make the First Name and Last Name required fields. Hint: Set the Required property to Yes.

d. Save the table design changes and return to Datasheet view. Update the table by filling in the new field for each record.

e. Edit the appropriate records to reflect the client changes that Ms. O'Dell gave you:

■ Sally Grimes has moved to 1499 Parkview. The city, state, and zip code will remain the same.

■ Mr. Lin Chen has a new home telephone number. It is now (217) 555-9076.

■ Debbie Linderson just called and said that she is moving to San Francisco, California. She has asked that her record be deleted from the spa's database.

f. Close the table.

g. Use the Form Wizard to create a form for the Clients table. Include all fields as listed. Use the columnar layout and Expedition style. Title the form **Client Information**.

h. Use the new form to enter the following records:

Record 1	Record 2
023	024
Georgia	[Your first name]
Kendall	[Your last name]
(217) 555-5522	(217) 555-0091
(217) 555-3434	[no work phone]
243 May Avenue	1234 Timber
Bakersville	Alison
TX	TX
75380	76890
3/21/73	8/14/74

i. Preview and print the form for the second new record you added.

2. Your managing editor at the Daily Digest has asked you to expand the advertiser database to include the ad size, rate, and frequency that the client has contracted for. He would also like you to create a data-entry form when you're finished with the basic design. Your completed form is shown here.

To add the new fields to the database and create the form, follow these steps:

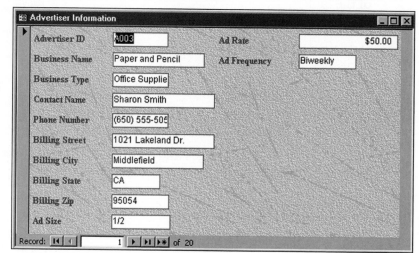

a. Open the database on your data disk named Daily Digest and the table named Advertisers.

b. In Design view, add the following three fields to the table:

Field name:	Ad Size
Data type:	Text
Description:	Enter one of the following: ¼, ½, or Full
Field size:	5

Field name:	Ad Rate
Data type:	Currency
Description:	Contracted rate per ad

Field name:	Ad Frequency
Data type:	Text
Description:	Enter one of the following: Daily, Weekly, Biweekly, or Monthly
Field size:	10

c. Save the table design changes and return to Datasheet View. Update the table by filling in the new fields for each record. Readjust the column widths as necessary.

d. Close the table.

e. Use the Form Wizard to create a form for the Advertisers table. Include all the table fields in their current order. Use the columnar layout and Expedition style. Title the form Advertiser Information.

f. Use the new form to enter the following records:

Record 1	Record 2
E592	A437
Hearth & Home	Fun Stuff
Furniture Store	Toy Store
Doris Francis	[Your Name]
(650) 555-0022	(650) 555-1221
1002 Lincoln Rd.	802 Trenton Way
Temple	Beacon Shores
CA	CA
95056	95055
1/2	Full
50	100
Biweekly	Monthly

g. Preview and print the form for the second new record you added.

3. You and other employees of the Downtown Internet Cafe have been sharing the task of entering product and vendor information into the purchase items database. You are now ready to add fields that show the inventory on hand and to indicate special orders so Evan, the cafe owner, knows when to place an order. However, when you open the database, you noticed that some of the information for the existing fields is missing, incorrect, or inconsistent. You realize that besides adding the new fields, you need to change some of the field properties, specify required fields, correct some errors, and create a form that reflects the cafe's Vendor Information Sheet to make data entry easier. When you are finished, you will end up with an easy-to-use data entry form shown here.

To make the changes and create the form, follow these steps:

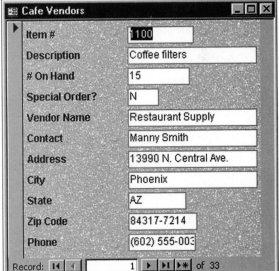

a. Open the database on your data disk named Cafe Purchases and the table named Inventory.

b. Item #6983 was a holiday season special and the cafe is no longer carrying it, so delete that item from the table.

c. Use the Replace command to replace item #2579 with the correct item number, 2575. Use the same command to replace The Beverage Co. with their new name, Better Beverages, Inc. Adjust the Vendor Name column to fit the new name.

d. In Design view, make the Item #, Description, and Vendor Name required fields. Add a Format property to the State field to force the data in that field to display in all capital letters.

e. Add a field before the Vendor Name to specify the inventory on hand for each item:

Field name:	# On Hand
Data type:	Number
Description:	Number of individual units (bags, boxes, etc.) in stock
Field size:	Integer

f. Add another field before the Vendor Name to specify whether the item is a special order (not regularly stocked):

Field name:	Special Order?
Data type:	Text
Description:	Is this a special order item?
Field size:	1
Default value:	N
Validation rule:	Y or N
Validation text:	The only valid entry is Y (yes) or N (no)

g. Return to Datasheet View and update the table by filling in the new fields for each record.

h. Use the Form Wizard to create a columnar form with the SandStone style and include all the table fields in their current order. Title the form Cafe Vendors.

i. Use the new form to add the following purchase items to the table:

Record 1	**Record 2**
1102	2924
Napkins	Coffee mugs
50	12
N	Y
Restaurant Supply	Central Ceramics
Manny Smith	[your name]
13990 N. Central Ave.	772 Hayden Road
Phoenix	Scottsdale
AZ	AZ
84137-7214	85254
(602) 555-0037	(602) 555-1924

j. Preview and print the form for the second new record you added.

4. The EduSoft Company, which develops computer curriculums for grades K–8, has just hired you to update and maintain their software database. Some of the tasks your manager asks you to accomplish involve correcting some known errors and applying some validation rules. She would also like you to create a form, shown here, which will make it easier to enter new software titles. To update the database and create the form, follow these steps:

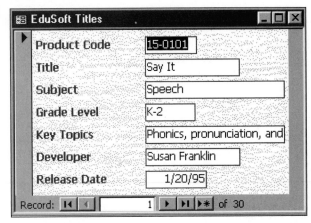

a. Open the database on your data disk named Learning and the table named Software.

b. The corrections you need to make to the table are related to the software titles. Sort the table in ascending order by Title so it will be easier to see the names you need to correct.

c. You have a note that the name of the Figure It series has been changed to Solve It. Use the Replace command (match the Start of Field to retain the numbers) or navigate through the table to find the three records with this title and change them.

d. The program called Reading & Writing was never released and has been replaced by separate reading and writing programs. Find and delete this record.

e. Switch to Design view and add a validity rule and text to the Grade Level field so that it only allows an entry of K–2, 3–5, or 6–8 (all three valid entries must be in quotes).

f. Add a field above Release Date to specify the name of the lead program developer for each title.

Field name:	Developer
Data type:	Text
Description:	Name of lead program developer
Field size:	20

g. Return to Datasheet view and hide the Title through Key Topic columns. Update the table by filling in the new field for each record. Each lead programmer has a unique two-digit prefix on their product numbers. For example, Teri O'Neill worked on products with the 36 prefix. Unhide the columns when you are done.

h. Create a columnar form using the Form Wizard. Use the Sumi Painting style and include all the fields in their current order. Name the form EduSoft Titles.

i. Use the form to enter a new record for a software program called Web Wise, Product Code 90–0103, which is currently in development for grades 6–8 to help them learn to use the Internet and do research. Enter your name as the developer. Preview and print the form for this new record.

5. You have continued to add records to the database for tracking the animals that come into and go out of Animal Angels. Now you need to modify the database structure and customize field properties to control the data entered by the Animal Angels volunteers who are assigned this task. You also want to create a form to make it easier for the volunteers to enter the necessary information, as shown here.

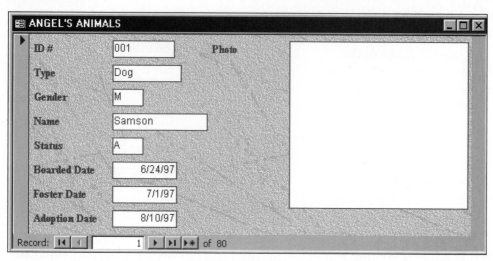

To enhance the Animal Angels database and create the form, follow these steps:

a. Open the database named AA and the table named Animals.

b. In Design view, insert the following field above the Boarded Date field:

Field name:	Status
Data type:	Text
Description:	Enter B (boarded), F (in foster home), or A (adopted)
Field size:	1
Format:	>

c. Make the following additional changes to the database structure:

- Add a validation rule and appropriate validation text to the Gender field to accept only M or F (male or female). Also format the field to display the information uppercase.

- Add a validation rule and appropriate validation text to the Status field to accept only B, F, or A (boarded, foster home, or adopted).

d. Return to Datasheet view and update the table by filling in the new Status field for each record.

e. So you can easily see the current status of the animals to ascertain which still need homes, sort the table in descending order by the Status, Boarded Date, Foster Date, and Adoption Date fields (hold down the ⇧Shift key and click the Status column and then the Adoption Date column). Change the status of Lemon to A and enter today's date as the Adoption Date. Remove the sort filter.

f. Use the Form wizard to create a columnar form. Use the Expedition style and include all the fields in their current order. Title the form ANGEL'S ANIMALS.

g. Add two records using the new form. Enter [your name]'s Pet in the Name field of the second record you add, and then select, preview, and print it.

On Your Own

6. You have heard from the employees of Adventure Travel that the database table you created is a bit unwieldy for them to enter the necessary data, because it now contains so many fields that it requires scrolling across the screen to locate them. You decide to create a form that will make entering data not only easier, but more attractive as well. Open the Adventure database you modified in Practice Exercise 6 of Tutorial 1 and use the Form Wizard to create a form for the Clients table. Use the form to enter one new record with a fictitious client name and another with your name as the client. Select and print the second new record.

7. While creating the basic database table for National Packing, you find out that the sales representatives sell from different product lines: packing cartons, insulation materials, and shipment tracking services. You need to add a field to accommodate this information before creating the final data entry form that you intend to submit to the company as part of your final database package. Open the database and table that you created in Practice Exercise 9 of Tutorial 1. Add a one-character product line field and enter the description Enter 1 (packing cartons), 2 (insulation materials), or 3 (shipment tracking services). Add a corresponding validation rule and message. Update the table to include appropriate values in this new field in the existing records. Close the table, saving the changes. Then use the Form Wizard to create a data entry form for this table. To test the form, enter a new record with your name as the contact and then select and print the record.

8. The single-dentist office for which you created a patient database has now expanded to include a second dentist and receptionist, requiring you to identify required fields and to add more fields that identify which patient is assigned to which dentist. You also decide that creating a form for the database would make it easier for both you and the other receptionist to enter and locate patient information. Open the database and table you created in Practice Exercise 8 of Tutorial 1 and make the patient identification number, name, and phone number required fields. Add a Dentist Name field, with the two dentist's names in the field description and an appropriate validation rule and message. Update the table to "assign" some of the patients to one of the dentists and some patients to the other dentist. Sort the table by dentist name to see the results of your new assignments. "Reassign" one of the displayed patients and then remove the sort filter. Close the table, saving the changes. Create a form for the table using the Form Wizard. Enter two new records, one for each of the dentists. Use the Find command to locate the record form that has your name as the patient, and then select and print the displayed record.

9. The management at Lewis & Lewis, Inc. is quite impressed with the employee database you created. However, they would like you to include home phone numbers and addresses so the database can be used to send mail (such as Christmas cards, 401K information, and tax forms) to employees. Also, you have been asked to create a form that will make it easier for other administrative assistants to enter employee data into the database as well. Open the database and table you created in Practice Exercise 7 of Tutorial 1 and add home address and phone number fields to it. Update the table to include information in the new fields for the existing records. Sort the table by employee last name and use the Replace command or table navigation to locate and change the last name of a female employee who has gotten married since you first created the database. Use the same technique to locate and delete a record for an employee who has left the company. Remove the sort filter and close the table, saving the changes. Create a form for the table using the Form Wizard. Enter two new records. Use the Find command to locate the record form that has your name as the employee, and then select and print the displayed record.

 ☆ ☆ ☆

10. You realize that you have left out some very important fields in the database table you created for the Oldies But Goodies company in Practice Exercise 10 of Tutorial 1—fields that identify the sources where you can obtain the vintage records your customers are looking for. Repeat your Web search for vintage record albums and note the resources (e.g., a company, such as Borders, or an individual collector who is offering these items online) for the titles you have included in your table. Add source name and address fields to the table and update it to include this information in the existing records. Sort the records according to the source name field and adjust the column widths to accommodate the new information. Remove the sort filter and close the table, saving the changes. Now, to make data entry easier for the company's employees, create a data entry form using the Form Wizard. Use the form to enter a new record with your name as the source, and then print it.

Analyzing Tables and Creating Reports

Competencies

After completing this tutorial, you will know how to:

1. Filter table records.
2. Create a query.
3. Move columns.
4. Query two tables.
5. Create a report.
6. Modify a report design.
7. Print a selected page.

Case Study

After modifying the structure of the table of employee records, you have continued to enter many more records. You have also created a second table in the database that contains employee information about location and job titles.

Filtered data displaying only records of employees living in Iona.

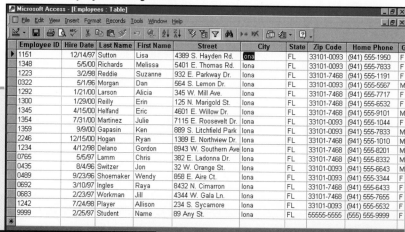

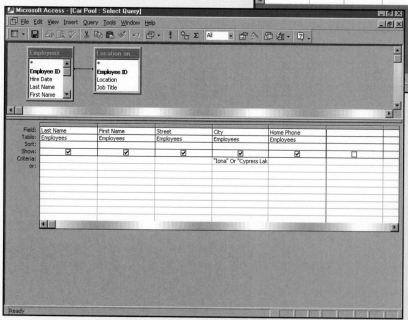

Query design view used to limit information in query results.

Again, the owners are very impressed with the database. They are anxious to see next how the information in the database can be used.

As you have seen, compiling, storing, and updating information in your database is very useful. The real strength of a database program, however, is how it can be used to find the information you need quickly, and manipulate and analyze it to answer specific questions. You will use the information in the tables to provide the answers to several inquiries about the Club employees. As you learn about the analytical features, think what it would be like to do the same task by hand. How long would it take? Would it be as accurate or as well presented? In addition, you will create several reports that present the information from the database attractively.

Employee Address Report

First Name	Last Name	Street	City	State	Zip Code	Home Phone
Jeff	Bader	947 S. Forest St.	Fort Myers	FL	33301-1268	(941) 555-7789
Andrew	Beinbrink	45 Burr Rd.	Fort Myers	FL	33301-1268	(941) 555-5322
Brian	Birch	742 W. Lemon Dr.	Fort Myers	FL	33301-1268	(941) 555-4321
Cindy	Birch	742 W. Lemon Dr.	Fort Myers	FL	33301-1268	(941) 555-4321
William	Bloomquist	43 Kings Rd.	Forest Island	FL	33174	(941) 555-6432
Anna	Brett	23 Suffolk Ln.	Fort Myers	FL	33301-1268	(941) 55
Scott	Briggs	45 E. Camelback Rd.	San Carlos	FL	33891-1605	(941) 55
Erin	Burke	234 N. 1st St.	San Carlos	FL	33891-1605	(941) 55
Gordon	Delano	8943 W. Southern Ave.	Iona	FL	33101-7468	(941) 55
Elizabeth	DeLuca	21 W. Southern Ave.	Forest Island	FL	33174	(941) 55
Bill	Delucchi	950 S. Terrace Dr.	Cypress Lake	FL	33205-0093	(941) 55
Barbara	Ernster	1153 S. Wilson	San Carlos	FL	33891-1605	(941) 55
Kimberly	Fachet	923 E. Baseline Rd.	Forest Island	FL	33174	(941) 55
Daniel	Facqur	5832 Fremont St.	Forest Island	FL	33174	(941) 55
Nancy	Falk	9483 W. Island Dr.	San Carlos	FL	33891-1605	(941) 55
Robby	Ferguson	4232 Tuller Ave.	San Carlos	FL	33891-1178	(941) 55
Lisa	Fromthart	32 Redcoat Rd.	Cypress Lake	FL	33205-6911	(941) 55

Sunday, March 04, 2001   Page

Basic report of all data in table.

Iona to Fort Myers Car Pool Report

First Name	Last Name	City	Street	Home Phone
Bill	Delucchi	Cypress Lake	950 S. Terrace Dr.	(941) 555-8195
Lisa	Fromthart	Cypress Lake	32 Redcoat Rd.	(941) 555-0110
Nichol	Lawrence	Cypress Lake	433 S. Gaucho Dr.	(941) 555-7656
Mina	Lopez	Cypress Lake	4290 E. Alameda Dr.	(941) 555-5050
Cathy	Nichols	Cypress Lake	75 Brooklea Dr.	(941) 555-0001
Marc	Schiff	Cypress Lake	235 N. Cactus Dr.	(941) 555-0010
Eric	Helfand	Iona	4601 E. Willow Dr.	(941) 555-9101
Suzanne	Reddie	Iona	932 E. Parkway Dr.	(941) 555-1191
Name	Student	Iona	89 Any St.	(555) 555-9999
Lisa	Sutton	Iona	4389 S. Hayden Rd.	(941) 555-1950

Report created from query displaying only selected fields.

Concept Overview

The following concepts will be introduced in this lab:

1   **Filter**   A filter is a restriction you place on records in the open datasheet or form to temporarily isolate and display a subset of records.

2   **AND and OR Operators**   The AND and OR operators are used to specify multiple conditions that must be met for the records to display in the datasheet.

3   **Query**   A query is a question you ask of the data contained in a database. You use queries to view data in different ways, to analyze data, and even to change existing data.

4   **Joins and Relationships**   A join is an association that tells Access how data between tables is related. A relationship is established between tables usually through at least one common field.

5   **Report**   Reports are the printed output you generate from tables or queries.

6   **Control**   Reports and forms are linked to the underlying table by using controls. Controls are graphical objects that can be selected and modified.

Using Filter by Selection

You have continued to enter employee records into the Employees table. The updated table has been saved for you as Employees in the Personnel Records database on your data disk.

1 ■ Start Access 2000. Put your data disk in the appropriate drive for your system.

■ Open the Personnel Records database file.

Your screen should be similar to Figure 3–1.

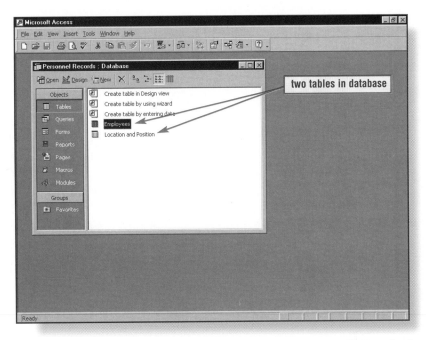

Figure 3–1

The Tables list box of the Database window displays the names of two tables in this database: Employees, and Location and Position. These tables will be used throughout the tutorial.

2 ■ Open the Employees table.

■ If necessary, maximize the Table Datasheet window.

■ Add your information as record number 81 using your special ID number 9999 and the date 2/25/97 as your hire date. Enter your city as Iona.

■ Return to the first field of the first record.

Your screen should be similar to Figure 3–2.

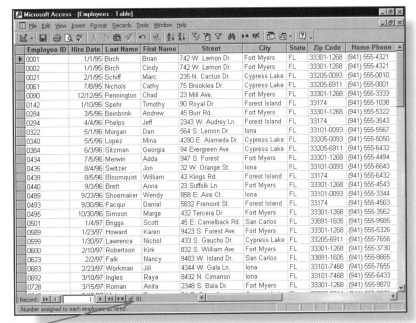

table contains 81 records

Figure 3–2

Julie Martinez, an employee at the Fort Myers location, is interested in forming a car pool. She recently approached you about finding others who may also be interested. You decide this would be a great opportunity to see how you can use the employee table to find this information. To find the employees, you could sort the table and then write down the needed information. This could be time consuming, however, if you had hundreds of employees in the table. A faster way is to apply a filter to the table records to locate this information.

Concept ① Filter

A **filter** is a restriction you place on records in the open datasheet or form to quickly isolate and display a subset of records. A filter is created by specifying a set of limiting conditions, or criteria, you want records to meet in order to be displayed. A filter is ideal when you want to display the subset for only a brief time, then return immediately to the full set of records. You can print the filtered records as you would any form or table. A filter is only temporary and all records are redisplayed when you remove the filter or close and reopen the table or form. The filter results cannot be saved. However, the last filter criteria you specify are saved with the table, and the results can be quickly redisplayed.

Julie lives in Iona, and wants to find others who work at the same location and live in Iona. To do this, you can quickly filter out all the other records using the Filter by Selection method. Filter by Selection is used when you can easily find and select an instance of the value in the table that you want the filter to use as the criterion to meet.

How the value is selected determines what results will be displayed. Placing the insertion point in a field selects the entire field contents. The filtered subset will include all records containing an exact match. Selecting part of a value in a field (by highlighting it) displays all records containing the selection. For example, in a table for a book collection, you could position the mouse pointer anywhere in a field containing the name of the author Stephen King, choose the Filter by Selection command, and only records for books whose author matches the selected name, "Stephen King," would be displayed. Selecting the last name "King" would include all records for authors Stephen King, Martin Luther King, and Barbara Kingsolver.

You want to filter the table to display only those records with a City field entry of Iona. To specify the city to locate, you need to select an example of the data in the table.

> If the selected part of a value starts with the first character in the field, the subset displays all records whose values begin with the same selected characters.

3 ■ Move to the City field of record 9.

■ Click  Filter by Selection

> The menu equivalent is **R**ecords/**F**ilter/Filter by **S**election.

Your screen should be similar to Figure 3–3.

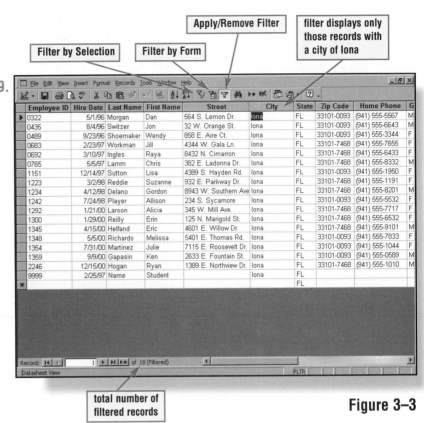

Figure 3–3

> You can print the filtered datasheet like any other datasheet.

> The menu equivalent is **R**ecords/**R**emove Filter/Sort.

The datasheet displays only those records that contain the selected city. All other records are temporarily hidden. The status bar indicates the total number of filtered records (18) and shows that the datasheet is filtered. To remove the filter,

4 ■ Click ▽ Remove Filter.

Using Filter by Form

After seeing how easy it was to locate this information, you want to locate employees who live in the city of Cypress Lake. This information may help in setting up the car pool, because the people traveling from the city of Iona pass through Cypress Lake on the way to the Fort Myers location. To find out this additional information, you need to use the Filter by Form method. This method allows you to perform filters on multiple criteria.

1 ━■ Click 📇 Filter by Form.

> The menu equivalent is **R**ecords/**F**ilter/**F**ilter By Form.

Your screen should be similar to Figure 3–4.

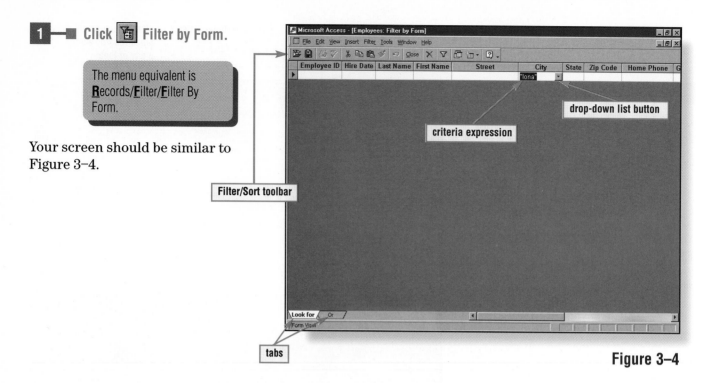

Figure 3–4

The Filter by Form window displays a blank version of the current datasheet with empty fields in which you specify the criteria. This window automatically displays a Filter/Sort toolbar that contains the standard buttons as well as buttons (identified below) that are specific to the Filter by Form window.

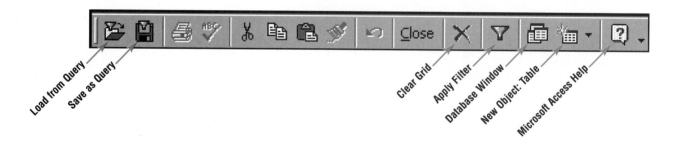

The window also includes two tabs, Look For and Or, where you enter the filter criteria. The criteria are entered in the blank field space of the record row as an expression. A **criteria expression** specifies the criteria for the filter to use. You can either type values or choose values from a drop-down list in the desired field to create the criteria expression.

Currently the City field displays the criterion you last specified using Filter by Selection as the criteria expression. Notice that the field displays a drop-down list button. Each field will display a drop-down button when the field is selected. Clicking the button displays a list of values that are available in that field from which you can select to help you enter the criteria expression. Since the City field already contains the correct criterion, you do not need to enter a different one.

Next you need to add the second criterion to the filter to include all records with a City field value of Cypress Lake. To instruct the filter to locate records meeting multiple criteria, you use the AND or OR operators.

Concept ② AND and OR Operators

The AND and OR operators are used to specify multiple conditions that must be met for the records to display in the filter datasheet. The AND operator narrows the search, because a record must meet both conditions to be included. The OR operator broadens the search, because any record meeting either condition is included in the output.

The AND operator is assumed when you enter criteria in multiple fields. Within a field, typing the word "AND" between criteria in the same field establishes the AND condition. For example, in the book table you could enter "Stephen King" in the author name field, then you could enter "Horror" in the category field to display records where the author's name is Stephen King and the category is Horror.

The OR operator is established by entering the criterion in the Or tab, or by typing "OR" between criteria in the same field. For example, you could enter "Stephen King" in the author name field, select the Or tab, then enter "Horror" in the category field. This filter would display those records where the author's name is Stephen King or where the category is Horror.

In this filter you will use an OR operator so that records meeting either city criterion will be included in the output. To include the city as an OR criterion, you enter the criterion in the Or tab.

2 ■ Open the Or tab.

> A value must be entered in the Look For tab before the Or tab is available.

Your screen should be similar to Figure 3–5.

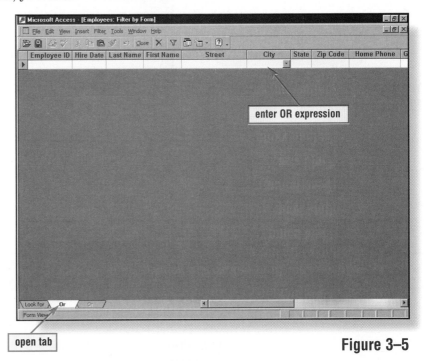

enter OR expression

open tab

Figure 3–5

The Or tab is opened, and a new blank row is displayed. You will enter the expression specifying the criterion by selecting the criterion from the City drop-down list.

3 ■ Click ▼ (in the City field).

■ Choose Cypress Lake.

> You could also have typed the expression "Iona" or "Cypress Lake" directly in the City field.

Your screen should be similar to Figure 3–6.

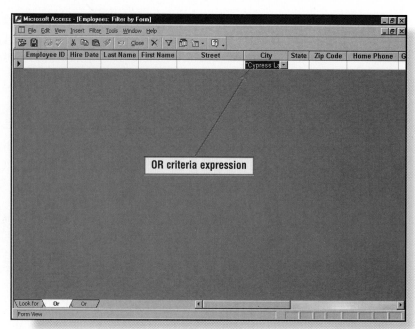

Figure 3–6

The selected criterion is displayed in the City field. It is surrounded by quotes as required of all text entries used in an expression. The Look For tab still contains the criterion for the city of Iona. To apply the filter,

4 ■ Click ▼ Apply Filter.

> The menu equivalent is Filter/Apply Filter/Sort.

Your screen should be similar to Figure 3–7.

filter results in 33 records with a city of Iona OR Cypress Lake

Figure 3–7

The filtered datasheet displays the records for all 33 employees who live in the city of Iona or Cypress Lake. To redisplay all records in the table,

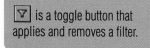

> ▼ is a toggle button that applies and removes a filter.

5 ■ Click ▼ Remove Filter.

The filter criteria you last specified are stored with the table, and the results can be redisplayed simply by applying the filter. To see the results again,

6 ■ Click 🔽 Apply Filter.

■ Redisplay all records.

■ Close the Employees table and save your changes.

Creating a Query

Using the filters does not help you determine which employees travel to the Fort Myers location from Iona or Cypress Lake. You also do not need all the employee information for the car pool. To obtain exactly what information you need, you will use a query.

Concept ③ Query

A **query** is a question you ask of the data contained in a database. You use queries to view data in different ways, to analyze data, and even to change existing data. Since queries are based on tables, you can also use a query as the source for forms and reports. The five types of queries are described in the table below.

Query Type	Description
Select query	Retrieves the specific data you request from one or more tables, then displays the data in a query datasheet in the order you specify. This is the most common type of query.
Crosstab query	Summarizes large amounts of data in an easy-to-read, row-and-column format.
Parameter query	Displays a dialog box prompting you for information, such as criteria for locating data. For example, a parameter query might request the beginning and ending dates, then display all records matching dates between the two specified values.
Action query	Makes changes to many records in one operation. There are four types of action queries: a make-table query creates a new table from selected data in one or more tables; an update query makes update changes to records, such as when you need to raise salaries of all sales staff by 7 percent; an append query adds records from one or more tables to the end of other tables; and a delete query deletes records from a table or tables.
SQL query	Created using SQL (Structured Query Language), an advanced programming language used in Access.

To create a new query,

1 Click  to open the Queries object window.

Click New .

Your screen should be similar to Figure 3–8.

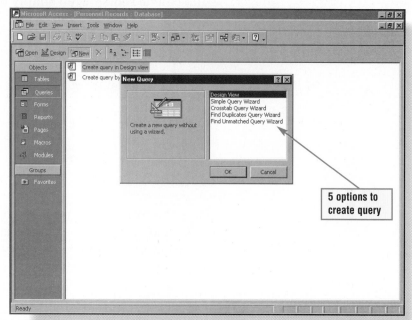

Figure 3–8

The New Query dialog box contains five options for creating queries. You can create a query from scratch in Query Design view or by using one of the four Query Wizards. The table below explains the type of query each of the four Wizards creates.

Query Wizard	Type of Query Created
Simple	Select query
Crosstab	Crosstab query
Find Duplicates	Locates all records that contain duplicate values in one or more fields in the specified tables.
Find Unmatched	Locates records in one table that do not have records in another. For example, you could locate all employees in one table who have no hours worked in another table.

To create a select query using the Simple Query Wizard,

2 ▪ Select Simple Query Wizard.

▪ Click ☐ OK ☐.

The dialog box on your screen should be similar to Figure 3–9.

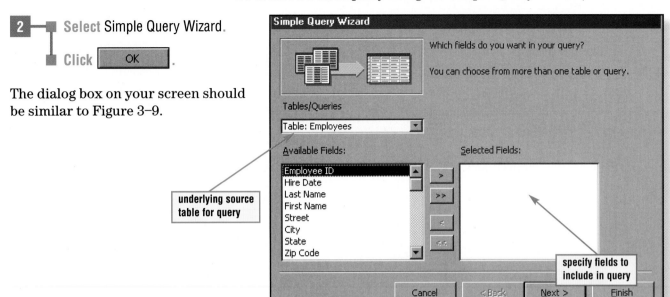

underlying source table for query

specify fields to include in query

Figure 3–9

In the first Simple Query Wizard window, you specify the underlying table and the fields from the table that will give you the desired query result, just as you did when creating a form. You will use data from the Employees table, which is already selected. You need to select the fields you want displayed in the query output.

3 ▪ Add the Last Name, First Name, Street, City, and Home Phone fields to the Selected Fields list.

Double-click the field name in the Available Fields list to add it to the Selected Fields list.

The dialog box on your screen should be similar to Figure 3–10.

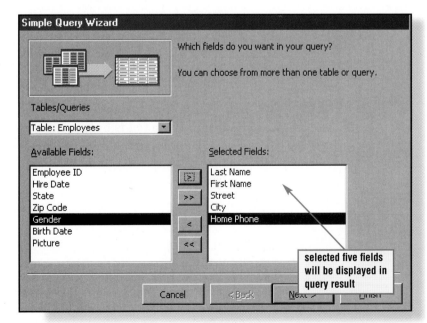

selected five fields will be displayed in query result

Figure 3–10

4 Click [Next >].

Replace the suggested title in the text box with **Car Pool**.

Click [Finish].

After a few moments, your screen should be similar to Figure 3–11.

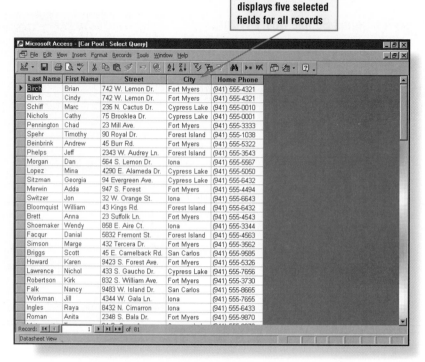

Query Datasheet view displays five selected fields for all records

Figure 3–11

The result or answer to the query is displayed in a **query datasheet.** The query datasheet displays only the five specified fields for all records in the table. Query Datasheet view includes the same menus and toolbar buttons as in Table Datasheet view.

Moving Columns

The order of the fields in the **query datasheet** reflects the order they were placed in the Selected Fields list. You want the list of names to be organized with the first name before the last name. You can change the display order of the fields by moving the columns. To reorder columns, first select the column you want to move and then drag the selection to its new location. You want to move the Last Name column to the right of the First Name column.

1 ━━■ Select the Last Name column.

> Reminder: Click on the Last Name column heading when the mouse pointer is a ↓ to select it.

■ **Click and hold the mouse button on the Last Name column heading.**

> When the mouse pointer is a ⬚, it indicates you can drag to move the selection.

■ **Drag the Last Name column to the right until a thick black line is displayed between the First Name and Street columns. Release the mouse button.**

■ **Clear the selection.**

> You can also press Ctrl + F8 to turn on Move mode. Then press ← or → to move the column in the desired direction, then press Esc.

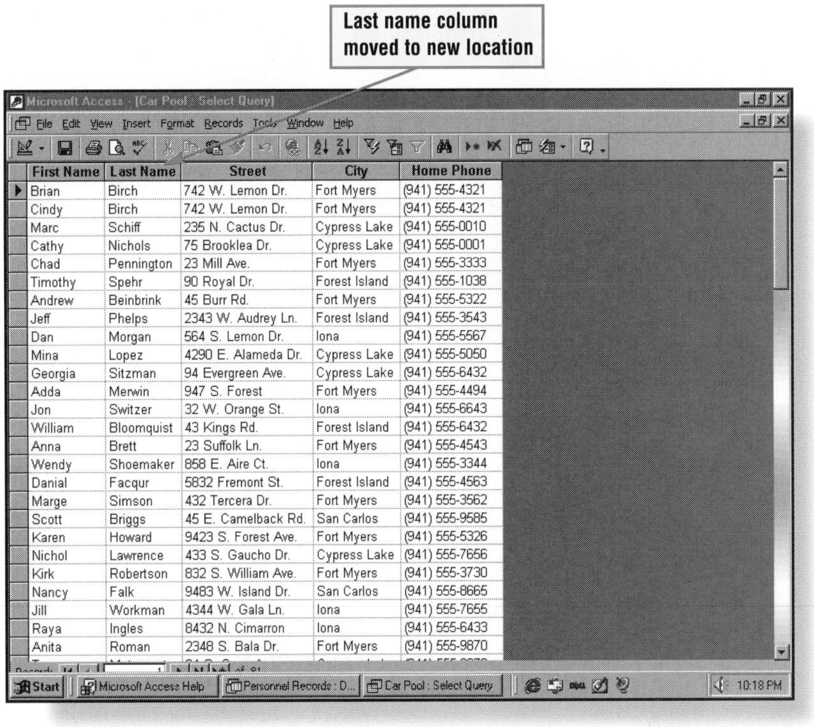

Your screen should be similar to Figure 3–12.

> Last name column moved to new location

Figure 3–12

Additional Information
- - - - - - - - - -
You can move fields in Table Data-sheet view in the same manner.

Changing the column order in the query datasheet does not affect the field order in the table, which is controlled by the table design.

Specifying Multiple Criteria in a Query
- -

Although the query result displays only the fields you want to see, it displays all the records in the database. To refine the query to display only selected records, you need to specify the criteria in the Query Design view window.

1 ▬■ Click 🖉 ▾ View to switch to the Query Design view.

Your screen should be similar to Figure 3–13.

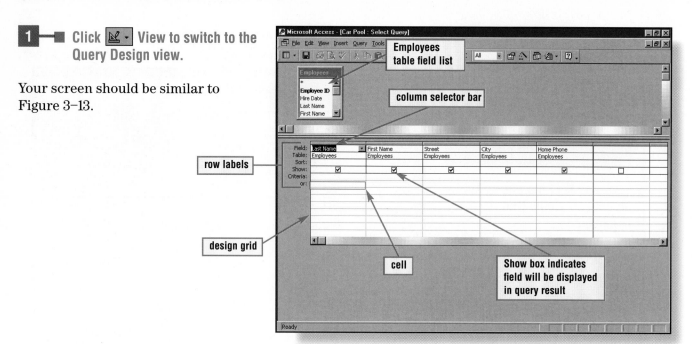

Figure 3–13

The Query Design view is used to create and modify the structure of the query. This view automatically displays a Query Design toolbar that contains the standard buttons as well as buttons (identified below) that are specific to the Query Design view window.

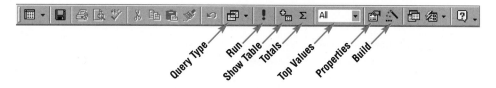

The Query Design window is divided into two areas. The upper area displays a list box of all the fields in the selected table. This is called the **field list.** The lower portion of the window displays the design grid, where you enter the settings to define the query are displayed. Each column in the grid holds the information about each field to be included in the query datasheet. The design grid currently displays the fields you specified in the Query Wizard. Above the field names is a narrow bar called the **column selector bar.** It is used to select an entire column. Each row label identifies the type of information that can be entered. The intersection of a column and row creates a **cell.** This is where you enter expressions to obtain the query results you need. Notice the boxes, called Show boxes, in the Show row. The Show box is checked for each field. This indicates that the query result will display the field column.

In the Criteria row of the City column, you first need to enter a criteria expression to locate only those records where the city is Iona. To specify the criterion, you will enter an expression that contains a comparison operator. A **comparison operator** is used to compare two values. The comparison operators are = (equal to) <> (not equal to), < (less than), >

(greater than), <= (less than or equal to), and >= (greater than or equal to). You will use the equal to comparison operator to find all records with a city of Iona. You do not need to enter the = sign for the equal to comparison, as this is the assumed comparison if none is entered.

2 ■ Move to the City Criteria cell.

■ Type **Iona**.

■ Press ⏎Enter.

> The criteria expression is not case sensitive.

Your screen should be similar to Figure 3–14.

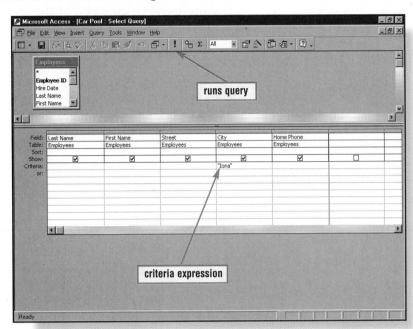

Figure 3–14

The expression is enclosed in quotes because it is a string. To display the query results, you run the query.

3 ■ Click  Run.

Your screen should be similar to Figure 3–15.

> The menu equivalent is **Q**uery/**R**un. You can also click 🖽▾ Datasheet View to run the query and display the query datasheet.

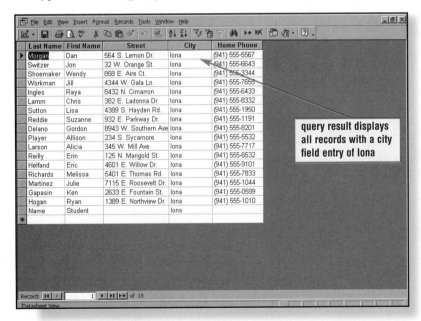

Figure 3–15

The query datasheet displays only those records meeting the city criterion. This is the same result as the first filter except that it displays only the specified fields.

Next you will add a second criteria to include the city of Cypress Lake in the result. In the Query Datasheet, the AND condition is established by typing the AND operator in the Criteria cell as part of the expression. An OR condition in a single field is established by entering the second criterion in the Or row cell of the same field. To see how this works, you will add Cypress Lake as the Or criteria.

4 ■ **Switch to Query Design view.**

■ **Type Cypress Lake in the Or cell of the City column.**

■ **Press** ⎆Enter.

Your screen should be similar to Figure 3–16.

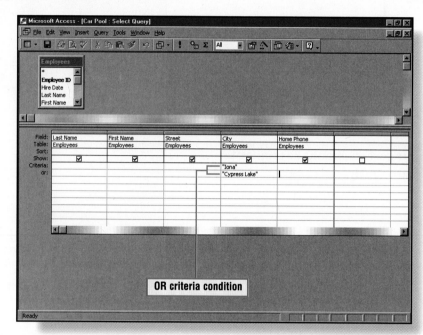

Figure 3–16

5 ■ **Run the query.**

> If an expression is entered incorrectly, an informational box will be displayed indicating the source of the error.

Your screen should be similar to Figure 3–17.

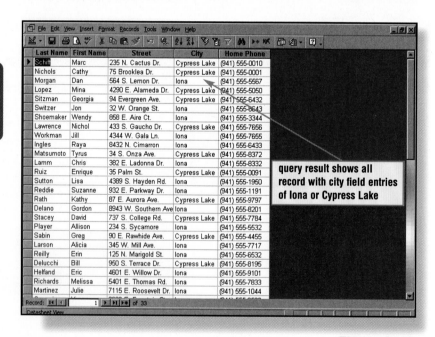

Figure 3–17

Thirty-three records were located in which the employee met the specified criteria. Notice that the fields are again in the order in which they appear in the Design grid.

6 ── ■ Move the Last Name column after the First Name column.

While you are working on the carpool query, Brian, the owner, stops in and asks if you can find some information quickly for him. Because you plan to continue working on the carpool query, you will save the query so you do not have to recreate it. This is another advantage of queries over filters. Filters are temporary, whereas queries can be permanently saved with the database.

7 ── ■ Click ▣ Save.

■ Close the Query Datasheet window.

Your screen should be similar to Figure 3-18.

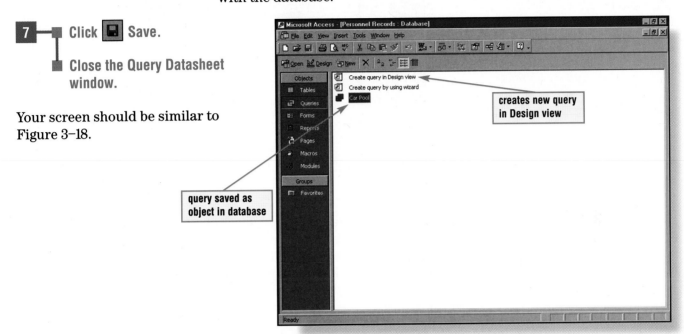

Figure 3-18

The query name, Car Pool, is displayed in the Queries object list.

Creating a Query in Design View

Brian is planning a ten-year anniversary celebration party and plans to recognize those employees who have worked with Lifestyle Fitness Club for 3, 5 or more years. He needs to know how many people are in each category so that he can order the correct number of awards. To help Brian locate these employees, you will create a new query using the Query Design view.

1 ■ **Double-click** Create query in Design view.

Your screen should be similar to Figure 3–19.

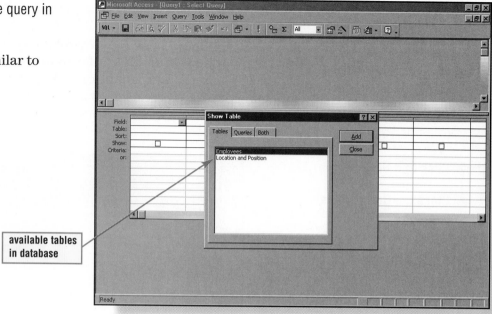

available tables in database

Figure 3–19

The Query Design window is open with the Show Table dialog box open on top of it. The dialog box is used to specify the underlying table or query to use to create the new query. The three tabs—Tables, Queries, and Both—contain the names of the existing tables and queries that can be used as the information source for the query. You need to add the Employees table to the query design.

2 ■ **If necessary, open the Tables tab and select the Employees table.**

■ **Click** Add .

You can also double-click the table name to add it to the query design.

■ **Click** Close .

■ **If necessary, maximize the Query Design window.**

Your screen should be similar to Figure 3–20.

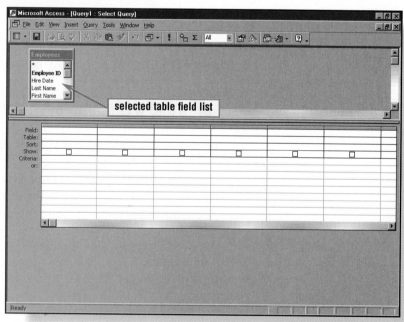

selected table field list

Figure 3–20

A field list for the selected table appears above the design grid. From the field list, you need to add the fields to the grid that you want to use in the query. The methods you can use to add fields to the design grid are described below.

■ Drag the field name from the field list to the grid. You can add several fields at once by pressing ⇧Shift and clicking to select adjacent fields, or by pressing Ctrl and clicking to select nonadjacent fields. When you drag multiple fields at a time, Access places each field in a separate column.

■ Double-click on the field name. The field is added to the next available column in the grid.

■ Select the Field cell drop-down arrow in the grid, then choose the field name.

> To select all fields, double-click the field list title bar.

In addition, if you select the asterisk in the field list and add it to the grid, Access displays the table or query name in the field row followed by a period and asterisk; all fields in the table will be included in the query results. Using this feature also will automatically include any new fields that may later be added to the table, and will exclude deleted fields. You cannot sort records or specify criteria for fields, however, unless you also add those fields individually to the design grid.

3 ■ **Double-click** Hire Date **in the field list to add it to the grid.**

■ **Add the** First Name **and** Last Name **fields to the grid next.**

Your screen should be similar to Figure 3–21.

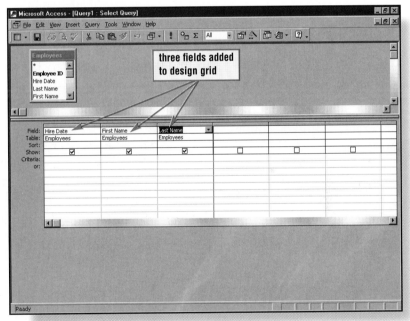

Figure 3–21

First you want to locate all employees who have at least 3 years with the club. To do this you will use the < operator to locate all records with a hire date less than 1/1/98. To specify the criterion,

4 ■ **In the Hire Date Criteria cell,
type <1/1/98**

■ **Press** ⏎Enter.

Your screen should be similar to
Figure 3–22.

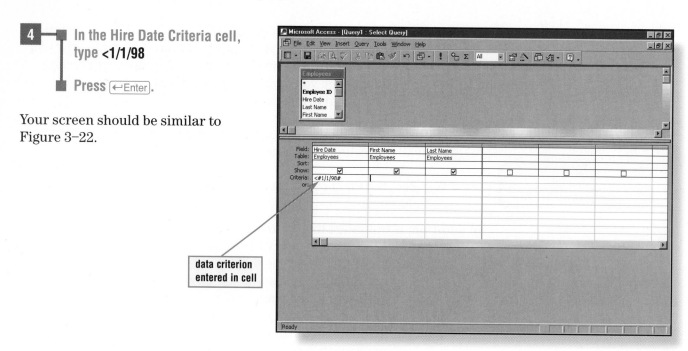

data criterion
entered in cell

Figure 3–22

The expression appears in the cell as <#1/1/98#. Access adds # signs
around the date to identify the values in the expression as a date.

5 ■ **Click** 🛈 **Run.**

Your screen should be similar to
Figure 3–23.

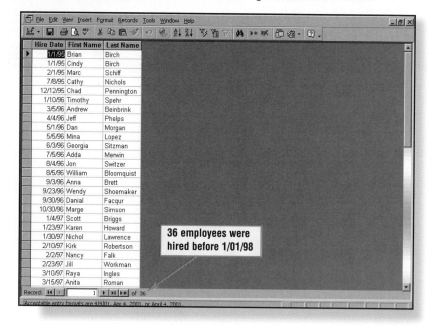

36 employees were
hired before 1/01/98

Figure 3–23

The query datasheet displays only those records meeting the date criterion. The record number indicator of the query datasheet shows that 36
employees were hired before January 1998. Next you will refine the search
to locate employees with more than 3 years service, but less than 5 years.

6 — Return to Query Design view.

  Enter **>1/1/96 and <1/1/98** in the Hire Date Criteria cell.

  Click **!** Run.

Your screen should be similar to Figure 3–24.

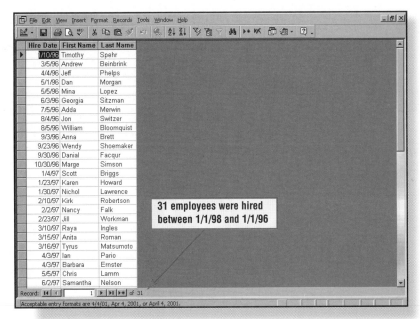

31 employees were hired between 1/1/98 and 1/1/96

Figure 3–24

The number of employees with between 3 and 5 years with the Club is 31. Brian also wants a printed list of these employees. And just in case Brian wants this information again, you will save the query.

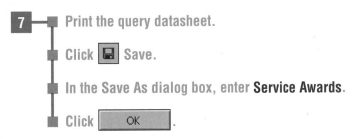

Click ☐ Print or use **F**ile/**P**rint if you need to specify printer settings.

7 — Print the query datasheet.

  Click 🖫 Save.

  In the Save As dialog box, enter **Service Awards**.

  Click **OK**.

You can quickly clear all criteria from the grid using **E**dit/Cle**a**r Grid.

Knowing the total with over 3 years was 36, this means there are 5 employees with more than 5 years. To verify this,

8 — Return to Query Design view and enter **<1/1/96** in the Hire Date Criteria cell.

  Run the query.

  Print the query datasheet.

  Close the Query Datasheet without saving the changes.

The query result confirms your calculation.

Querying Two Tables

Now that you have provided Brian with the answers he needed, you can get back to work on the car pool query. The car pool list would be more helpful if it had only the people that work at the Fort Myers location.

Unfortunately, the Employees table does not contain this information. This information, however, is available in the Location and Position table.

1 ── Click ▦ Tables and open the Location and Position table.

Your screen should be similar to Figure 3–25.

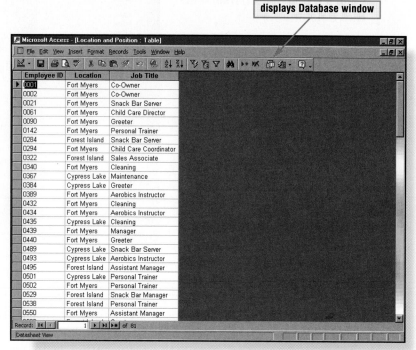

Figure 3–25

The Location and Position table contains three fields of data for each employee: Employee ID, Club Location, and Job Title. The Employee ID field is the key field and is the common field between the two tables. To display the information on the Fort Myers employees, you need to create a query using information from this table and from the Employees table. A query that uses more than one table is called a **multitable query.**

To open the Car Pool query you saved,

2 ▪ Click 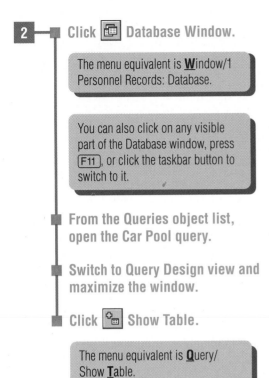 Database Window.

> The menu equivalent is **W**indow/1 Personnel Records: Database.

> You can also click on any visible part of the Database window, press F11, or click the taskbar button to switch to it. ✓

▪ From the Queries object list, open the Car Pool query.

▪ Switch to Query Design view and maximize the window.

▪ Click 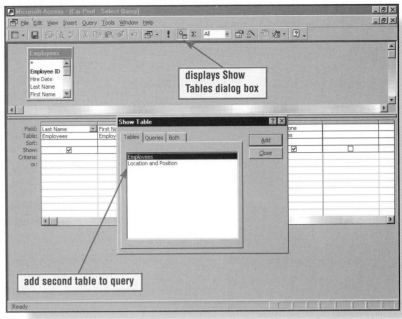 Show Table.

> The menu equivalent is **Q**uery/ Show **T**able.

Figure 3–26

Your screen should be similar to Figure 3–26.

From the Query Design window, you need to select the name of the table you want to add to the query.

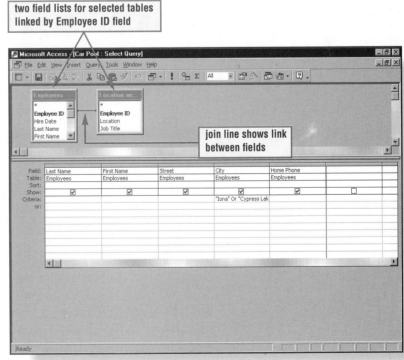

3 ▪ If necessary, open the Tables tab and select **Location and Position**.

▪ Click  Add.

▪ Close the Show Table dialog box.

Your screen should be similar to Figure 3–27.

Figure 3–27

The field list for the second table is added to the Query Design window. The line between the two field lists indicates that the two tables have been temporarily joined.

Concept ④ Joins and Relationships

More information and examples of relationships are available through the Office Assistant.

Use **T**ools/**R**elationships to define permanent relationships between tables.

A **join** is an association that tells Access how data between tables is related. Joining tables allows you to bring information from different tables in your database together. A **relationship** is established between tables usually through at least one common field. The common fields must be of the same data type and contain the same kind of information, but can have different field names. When you add multiple tables to a query, Access automatically joins tables based on the common fields if one of the common fields is a primary key. This is called the default join or **inner join.** If the common fields have different names, Access does not automatically insert the line and create the join. You can create the join manually by dragging from one common field to the other. The join instructs the query to check for matching values in the joined fields. When matches are found, the matching data is added to the query datasheet as a single record.

The three types of relationships, one-to-many, many-to-many, and one-to-one, are described in the table below. The most common type is a one-to-many relationship.

Relationship Type	Description
One-to-many	A record in table A can have many matching records in table B, but a record in table B has only one matching record in table A.
Many-to-many	A record in table A can have many matching records in table B, and a record in table B can have many matching records in table A. This requires a third table in the relationship, known as a junction table, that serves as a bridge between the two tables.
One-to-one	A record in table A has only one matching record in table B, and a record in table B has only one matching record in table A.

In a one-to-many relationship, there is a primary table and a related or foreign table. The primary table is usually the "one" side of two related tables in a one-to-many relationship, and the related table is usually on the "many" side of a one-to-many relationship.

Using Tools/Relationships, you can also define permanent relationships between tables that will enforce the rules of referential integrity. These rules help ensure that the database always contains accurate and complete data. When these rules are enforced, you cannot add records to a related table when there is no associated record in the primary table. You also cannot change values in the primary table that would result in records that do not have a match in a related table, or delete records from the primary table when there are matching related records in a related table.

The diagram below shows that when the Employee ID fields of the two tables are joined, a query can be created using data from both tables to provide the requested information.

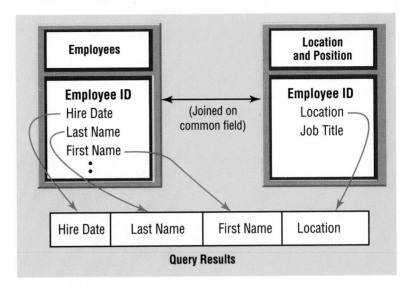

The type of relationship created using these two tables is a one-to-one relationship. This is because each record in the first table has one matching record in the second table.

Next you need to add the fields to the grid that you want to use in the query.

4 ■ Add the Location field to the design grid.

■ To specify the location criterion, enter the expression **Fort Myers** in the Location Criteria cell.

Your screen should be similar to Figure 3–28.

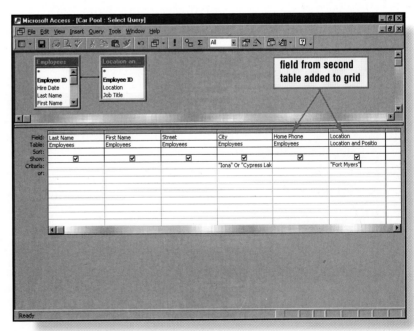

Figure 3–28

ACCESS 2000

5 — ■ Run the query.

Your screen should be similar to
Figure 3–29.

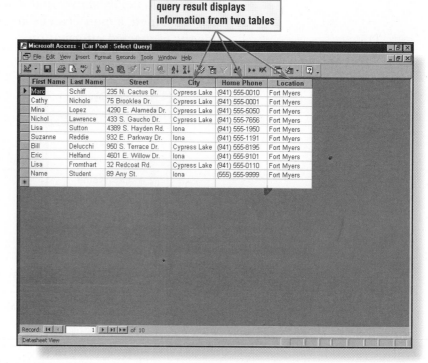

Figure 3–29

The query result shows there are ten employees who live in either Iona or
Cypress Lake and work at the Fort Myers location. Each record consists
of information from both tables. Both tables must contain matching
records in order for a record to appear in the query's result.

Next you want to sort the query datasheet by City and Last Name.

6 — ■ Move the City column to the left
of the Last Name column.

■ Select both columns.

■ Click 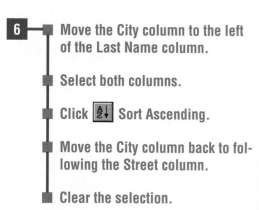 Sort Ascending.

■ Move the City column back to following the Street column.

■ Clear the selection.

Your screen should be similar to
Figure 3–30.

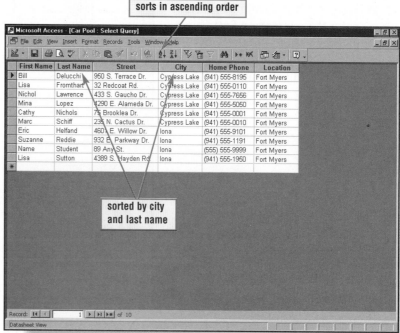

Figure 3–30

7 ━■ Close the query, saving your changes.

Note: If you are running short on time, this is an appropriate point to end this session. When you begin again, open the Personnel Records database.

Using the AutoReport Wizard

Brian showed Cindy the printout you gave him of the employees that will get service awards. She sees many uses for the information generated by Access, including the ability to quickly analyze information in the database. As a starter, she has asked you to create an address report for all employees sorted by name. You have already created and printed several simple reports using the Print command on the File menu. This time, however, you want to create a custom report of this information.

Concept ⑤ Report

Reports are the printed output you generate from tables or queries. It might be a simple listing of all the fields in a table, or it might be a list of selected fields based on a query.

Access also includes a custom report feature that allows you to create professional-appearing reports. The custom report is a document that includes text formats, styles, and layouts that enhance the display of information. In addition, you can group data in reports to achieve specific results. You can then display summary information, such as totals, by group to allow the reader to further analyze the data. Creating a custom report displays the information from your database in a more attractive and meaningful format.

You will create the address list report using the data in the Employees table.

1 ■ Open the Reports Object window.

■ Click .

> The menu equivalent is
> Insert/Report.

Your screen should be similar to
Figure 3–31.

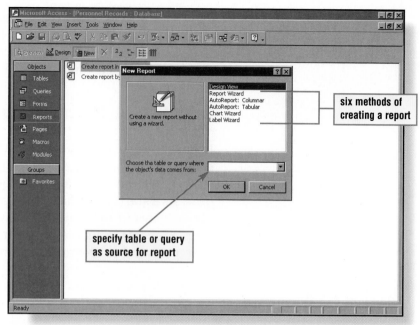

Figure 3–31

The New Report dialog box presents six ways to create a report. You can
create a report from scratch in Design view, or by using the Report Wizard
or one of the AutoReport Wizards. The Report Wizard lets you choose the
fields to include in the report and helps you quickly format and lay out the
new report. The AutoReport Wizard creates a report that displays all
fields and records from the underlying table or query in a predesigned report layout and style.

You decide to use the AutoReport Wizard to create a columnar report
using data in the Employees table.

2 ■ Select AutoReport: Columnar.

■ Select Employees from the
Choose the Table or Query drop-
down list.

■ Click 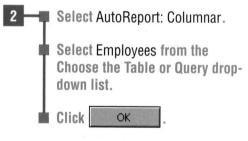 OK .

Your screen should be similar to
Figure 3–32.

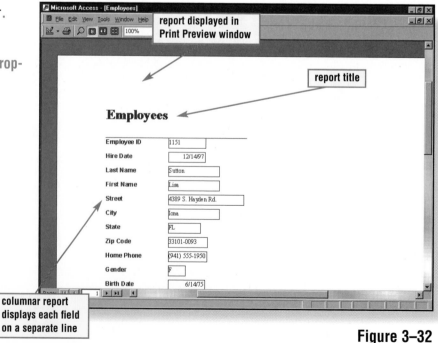

Figure 3–32

After a few moments, the report is created and displayed in the Print Preview window. The AutoReport Wizard creates a columnar report that displays each field on a separate line in a single column for each record. The fields are in the order they appear in the table. The report appears in a predefined report style and layout. The report style shown in Figure 3–32 uses the table name as the report title and includes the use of text colors, typefaces and sizes, and horizontal lines and boxes.

> You will learn about many of these features shortly.

Your report may be displayed with a different style. This is because when creating an AutoReport, Access remembers the last autoformat report style used to create a report on your machine, then applies that same style to the new report. If the Autoformat command has not been used, the report will use the basic style.

> You will learn how to change styles later in this tutorial.

Zooming the Window

Only the upper part of the first page of the report is visible in the window. To see more of the report in the window at one time, you can toggle between 100% and Fit by clicking on the window, or you can decrease the on-screen character size by specifying a smaller magnification percentage using the Zoom command. You can increase the character size up to two times normal display (200%) or reduce it to 10%.

1 ■ **Open the** `100% ▼` **Zoom Control drop-down list.**

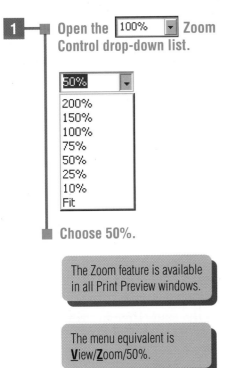

■ **Choose 50%.**

> The Zoom feature is available in all Print Preview windows.

> The menu equivalent is **V**iew/**Z**oom/50%.

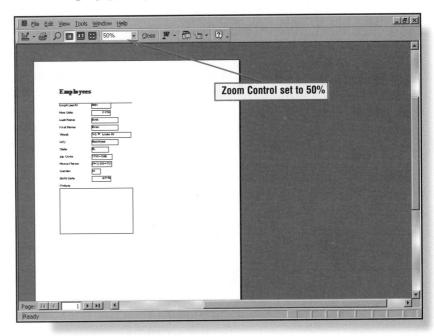

Figure 3–33

Your screen should be similar to Figure 3–33.

The text is reduced in size by half, allowing you to view more of the page in the window. You can now see three sides of the page. This is very close to the magnification level you get using the Fit option.

2 ━■ Click on the page to change the magnification to Fit.

> The menu equivalent is **V**iew/**Z**oom/**F**it to Window.

Your screen should be similar to Figure 3–34.

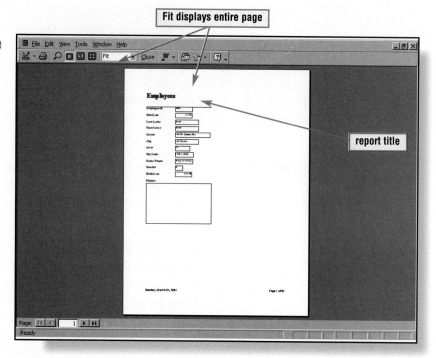

Figure 3–34

Now the entire page is visible, and although most of the text is too small to read, you can now see the entire page layout. The report title appears at the top of the page, and each field of information is displayed on a separate line in a single column for each record. The current date and page number appear at the bottom of the page in the footer. The first record from the Employees table is displayed on the first page of the report.

Now, because the last magnification level you used was 50%, clicking on the page again will switch between the last-used magnification level and the Fit magnification. The location of the pointer on the report when you click indicates the area of the report that will appear in the window.

3 ━■ With the mouse pointer as ⊕ , click on the report title.

The page is displayed at 50% magnification again.

4 ━■ Return the magnification level to 100%.

You can also view multiple report pages at the same time in Print Preview. To view six pages,

5 ■ Click 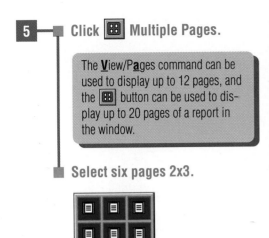 Multiple Pages.

The **V**iew/**Pa**ges command can be used to display up to 12 pages, and the 🔲 button can be used to display up to 20 pages of a report in the window.

■ Select six pages 2x3.

Your screen should be similar to Figure 3–35.

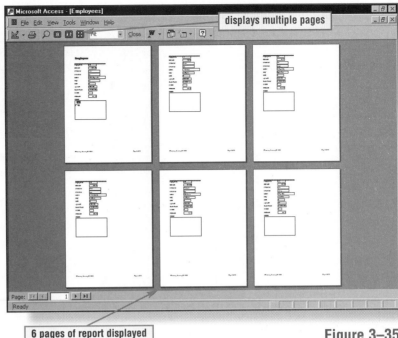

displays multiple pages

6 pages of report displayed

Figure 3–35

After looking over the columnar report, you decide the layout is inappropriate for your report because only one record is printed per page. In addition, you do not want the report to include all the fields from the table. To close the report file without saving it,

Do not click `Close` on the toolbar. This closes the Print Preview window, but does not close the report file.

6 ■ Click ☒.

■ Click No

Using the Report Wizard

You want the report to display the field contents for each record on a line rather than in a column. The Report Wizard will create this type of report. From the Reports tab,

1 ■ **Double-click** Create report by using wizard.

Fields are added just as in Form Wizard.

The Report Wizard consists of a series of dialog boxes, much like the Form Wizard. In the first dialog box (see Figure 3–36) you specify the table or query to be used in the report and select the fields.

2 ■ Select Table: Employees from the Tables/Queries drop-down list.

■ Add the First Name field to the Selected Fields list.

■ Then add the Last Name, Street, City, State, Zip Code, and Home Phone fields in that order.

> You do not have to include all the fields in the table or query on a report.

Your screen should be similar to Figure 3–36.

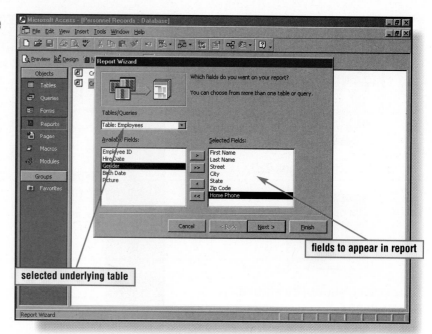

Figure 3–36

3 ■ Click  Next > .

In the second Report Wizard dialog box, you specify how to group the data in the report. Cindy does not want the report grouped by any category. To move to the next dialog box,

4 ■ Click Next > .

The next dialog box (see Figure 3–37) is used to specify a sort order for the records. A report can be sorted on up to four fields. Again, you want the report sorted in ascending order by last name and first name within same last names.

5 Select the Last Name field from
the number 1 drop-down list and
the First Name field from the
number 2 drop-down list.

> Clicking [↕] toggles between
> ascending and descending
> sort order.

Your screen should be similar to
Figure 3–37.

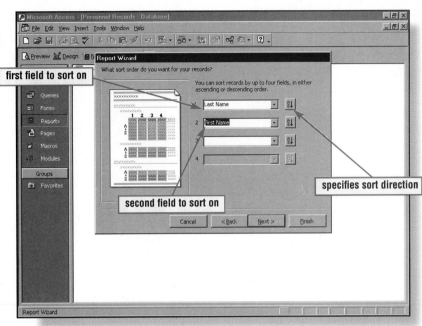

Figure 3–37

6 Click **Next >** .

Your screen should be similar to
Figure 3–38.

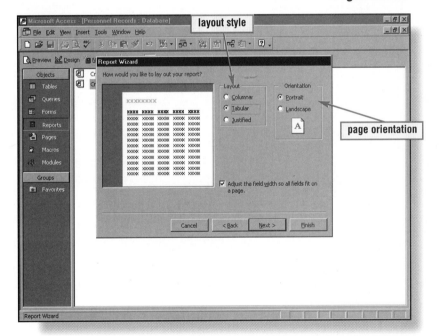

Figure 3–38

The next dialog box is used to change the report layout and orientation.
Orientation refers to the direction text prints on a page. Normal orientation is to print across the width of an 8½-inch page. This is called **portrait**
orientation. You can change the orientation to print across the length of
the paper. This is called **landscape** orientation. The default report settings
create a tabular layout using portrait orientation. In addition, the option
to adjust the field width so all fields fit on one page is selected. Because
this report is only five columns, the default settings are acceptable.

7 ■ Click  .

Your screen should be similar to
Figure 3–39.

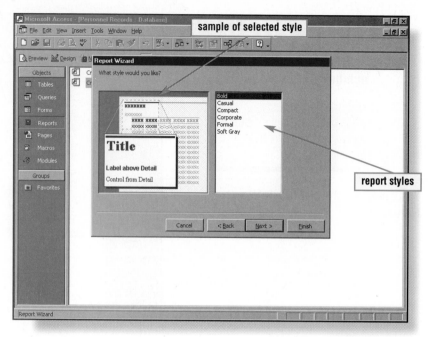

Figure 3–39

From this dialog box you select a style for the report. The preview area displays a sample of each style as it is selected.

8 ■ Select each style to preview the style options.

■ You believe the Bold style is most appropriate for this report.

■ Select Bold.

■ Click 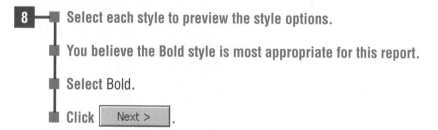 .

The last Report Wizard dialog box is used to add a title to the report and to specify how the report should be displayed after it is created. The only change you want to make is to replace the table name with a more descriptive report title.

9 Type **Employee Address Report.**

Click **Finish**.

Your screen should be similar to Figure 3–40.

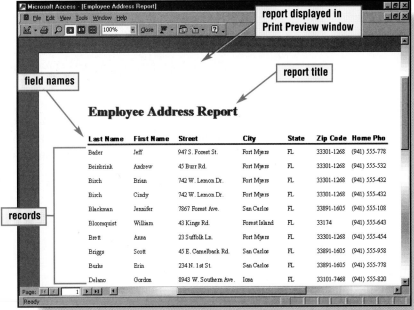

Figure 3–40

The program takes a minute to generate the report, during which time Report Design view is briefly displayed. In a few moments, the completed report with the data from the underlying table is displayed in the Print Preview window.

The Print Preview window displays the report using the selected Bold report style. The report title reflects the title you specified using the Wizard. The names of the selected fields are displayed on the first line of the report, and each record appears on a separate row below the field names. Notice that the Last Name field is the first field, even though you selected it as the second field. This is because the sort order overrides the selected field order.

10 Change the magnification to Fit.

Your screen should be similar to Figure 3–41.

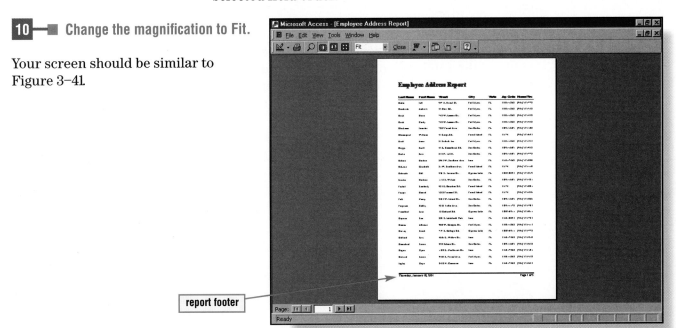

Figure 3–41

You can now see the layout of the report on the entire page. The report information easily fits across the page with the orientation set to portrait.

Modifying the Report Design

You like the layout of this report, but you still want the Last Name field to follow the First Name field. You also notice that you need to fix the Home Phone field label so that it displays the label fully. To make these changes, you need to modify the report design.

1 ━━ Click 📝 ▾ **Design View.**

Your screen should be similar to Figure 3–42.

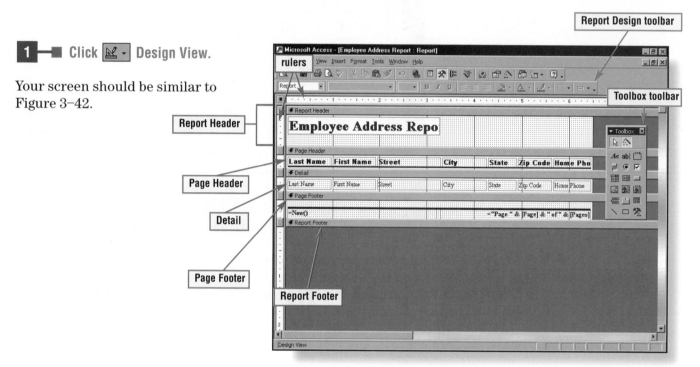

Figure 3–42

Report Design view displays the report in a window that is bordered along the top by a horizontal ruler and along the left by a vertical ruler. The rulers help you correctly place items in the Report Design window.

The Report Design view automatically displays three toolbars: Report Design, Formatting, and Toolbox. The Report Design toolbar contains the standard buttons as well as buttons that are specific to the Report Design view window. The Formatting toolbar displayed below the menu bar contains buttons that allow you to make text enhancements. The Toolbox toolbar contains buttons that are used to add and modify report design objects.

If the Toolbox is not displayed use **V**iew/T**o**olbox or click 🛠 to display it.

2 ■ **If necessary, move the Toolbox toolbar to the right side of the window.**

The Report Design window is divided into five areas: Report Header, Page Header, Detail, Page Footer, and Report Footer. The contents of each section appear below the horizontal bar containing the name. The sections are described in the table below.

Section	Description
Report Header	Contains information to be printed once at the beginning of the report. The report title is displayed in this area.
Page Header	Contains information to be printed at the top of each page. The column headings are displayed in this section.
Detail	Contains the records of the table. The field column widths are the same as the column widths set in the table design.
Page Footer	Contains information to be printed at the bottom of each page, such as the date and page number.
Report Footer	Contains information to be printed at the end of the report. The Report Footer section currently contains no data.

Selecting, Moving, and Sizing Controls

Every object in a report is contained in a control.

Concept ⑥ Control

Reports and forms are linked to the underlying table by using controls. **Controls** are graphical objects that can be selected and modified. Once a control is selected, it can be sized, moved, or enhanced in other ways.

The most common type of control is a text box. A **text box control** creates a link to the underlying source, usually a field from a table, and displays the field entry in the report or form. This type of control is called a **bound control** because it is tied to a field in an underlying table.

The report or form usually also includes a label with each text box control. A **label control** initially displays the field name from the underlying table associated with the text box control. Label controls can also display custom names you specify instead of the field name, or other descriptive text entries such as a title or instructions for the user. These controls are **unbound controls** because they are not connected to a field. Other unbound controls contain elements that enhance the appearance of the form, such as lines, boxes, and pictures.

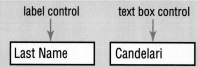

A third type of control is a **calculated control,** which displays the results of a calculation in the form or report. It contains an expression that uses data from the underlying table or another control as its source of data.

Finally, some text box and label controls are connected and act as one when manipulated. These controls are called **compound controls**.

You select, size and move controls in Form Design view just like in Report Design view.

In this report design, the label controls are displayed in the Page Header section, and the text box controls are in the Detail section. You need to select controls to modify them. To select the Last Name control,

3 ■ **Click on the Last Name label control in the Page Header section.**

> The mouse pointer must be ⌖ when selecting controls.

Your screen should be similar to Figure 3–43.

> When you first click on a control, the 🖑 shape appears and will display as long as you hold down the mouse button.

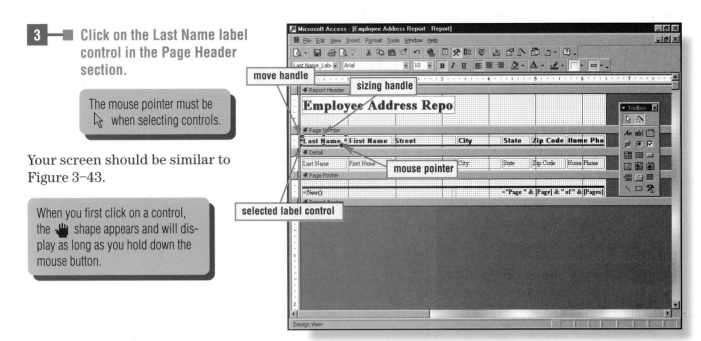

Figure 3–4

The Last Name label control is surrounded by eight small boxes called **sizing handles** that indicate the label control is selected. The sizing handles are used to size the control. In addition, a large box in the upper left corner is displayed. This is a **move handle** that is used to move the selected control.

You also want to select the Last Name text box control.

4 ■ **Hold down ⇧Shift and click on the Last Name text box control in the Detail section.**

> You can also delete controls by selecting them and pressing Delete.

Your screen should be similar to Figure 3–44.

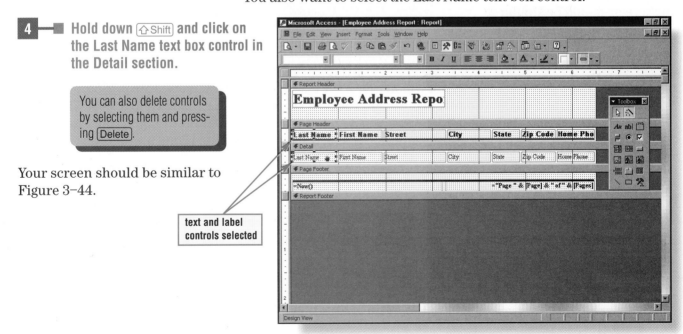

Figure 3–44

Now both controls are selected. Once controls are selected, they can be modified. In this case, you want to move the Last Name controls to the right of the First Name controls. Controls are moved by dragging them to the new location. When you can move a selected control, the mouse

You can also move controls using (Ctrl) + the directional arrow keys.

pointer shape appears as 🖑. You can then drag the control to any location in the report design. The grid of dots helps you position the controls on the form. It not only provides a visual guide to positioning and sizing controls, but controls are "snapped" to the grid, or automatically positioned on the nearest grid line.

Because you need to swap positions of the two fields, you will first move the Last Name controls to the right, then you will move the First Name controls to the left.

5 ■ Drag the Last Name controls to the right until they overlap part of the Street controls.

Do not point to a sizing or move handle.

■ Select the First Name controls and drag them to the left edge of the grid.

■ Select the Last Name controls again and drag them to between the First Name and Street controls.

Your screen should be similar to Figure 3–45.

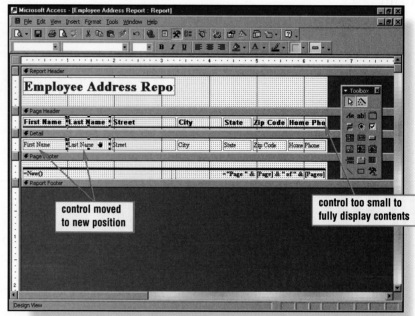

control moved to new position

control too small to fully display contents

Figure 3–45

Next you will increase the size of the Home Phone control. When you position the mouse pointer on a sizing handle, it changes to a ↔. The direction of the arrow indicates in which direction dragging the mouse will alter the shape of the object. This is similar to sizing a window.

6 Select the Home Phone text box and label controls.

Point to the middle handle on the right end of either selected control.

When the mouse pointer appears as ↔, drag the control to the right until the entire field label is displayed.

> The right edge of the form will automatically increase as you increase the size of the control.

Your screen should be similar to Figure 3–46.

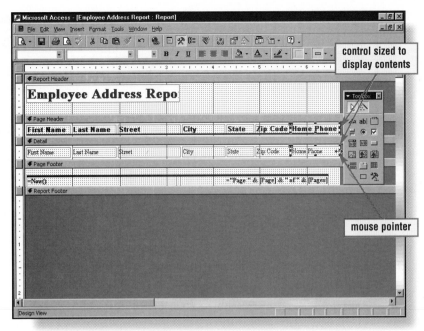

Figure 3–46

Then to see the change in the report,

7 Click  Print Preview.

Zoom the window to 100%.

Your screen should be similar to Figure 3–47.

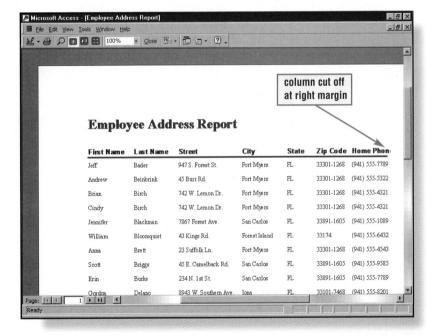

Figure 3–47

The Home Phone label is still cut off because it extends beyond the right margin. To change the page orientation to landscape so the entire width of the report will print on the page,

8 ■ Choose File/Page Setup.

■ Open the Page tab.

■ Select Landscape.

■ Choose [OK].

■ Zoom the preview window to Fit.

Your screen should be similar to Figure 3–48.

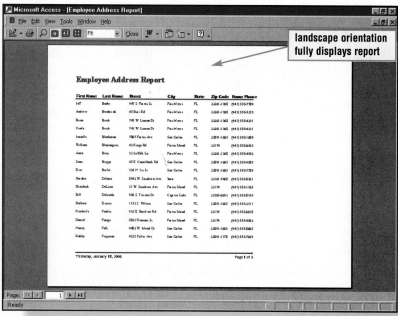

Figure 3–48

Printing a Selected Page

The report is now in the order you want it to appear. Now you will print the page containing your record.

1 ■ Move to the page of the report that contains your name.

> Increase the magnification to locate your record more easily.

■ Choose File/Print.

> The 🖨 Print button prints the entire report.

■ If necessary, select the appropriate printer for your system.

■ Select Pages.

> The page number is displayed in the page indicator box.

■ Type the page number containing your record in the From and To text boxes.

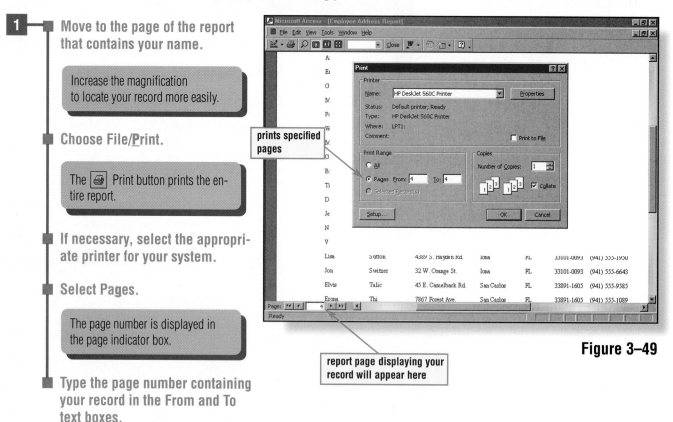

Figure 3–49

Your screen should be similar to Figure 3–49.

2 ■ Click | OK | .

■ Close the Report window, saving the changes you have made.

The Database window is displayed again, and the report object name is listed in the Reports object list. The Report Wizard automatically saves the report using the report title as the object name.

Creating a Report from a Query

You have seen how easy it is to create a report from a table, so you would like to create a report from the car pool query.

1 ■ Use the Report Wizard to create a tabular report based on the car pool query using the following specifications:

■ Include all fields except Club Location.

■ Sort on City first, then Last Name and First Name. Use the casual style.

■ Title the report **Iona to Fort Myers Car Pool Report**.

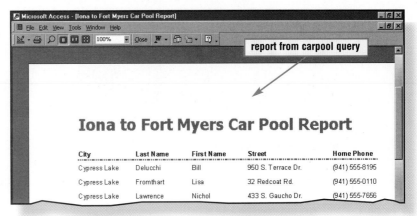

report from carpool query

Iona to Fort Myers Car Pool Report

City	Last Name	First Name	Street	Home Phone
Cypress Lake	Delucchi	Bill	950 S. Terrace Dr.	(941) 555-8195
Cypress Lake	Fromthart	Lisa	32 Redcoat Rd.	(941) 555-0110
Cypress Lake	Lawrence	Nichol	433 S. Gaucho Dr.	(941) 555-7656

Figure 3–50

When the Wizard finishes, your screen should be similar to Figure 3–50.

2 ■ Use Report Design view to move the fields into First Name, Last Name, City, Street, and Home Phone order.

■ Print the report.

Your completed report should look like the report shown in the Case Study at the beginning of the tutorial.

Compacting the Database

Additional Information

A file is fragmented when it becomes too large for your computer to store in a single location on your disk. When this happens, the file is split up and stored in pieces in different locations on the disk, making it slower to access.

As you modify a database the changes are saved to your disk. When you delete data or objects the database file can become fragmented and use disk space inefficiently. To make the database perform optimally, you should compact the database on a regular basis. Compacting makes a copy of the file and rearranges how the file is stored on your disk. To compact the database,

1 ■ Choose **T**ools/**D**atabase Utilities/**C**ompact and Repair Database.

■ Close the Database file and exit Access.

Concept Summary

Tutorial 3: Analyzing Tables and Creating Reports

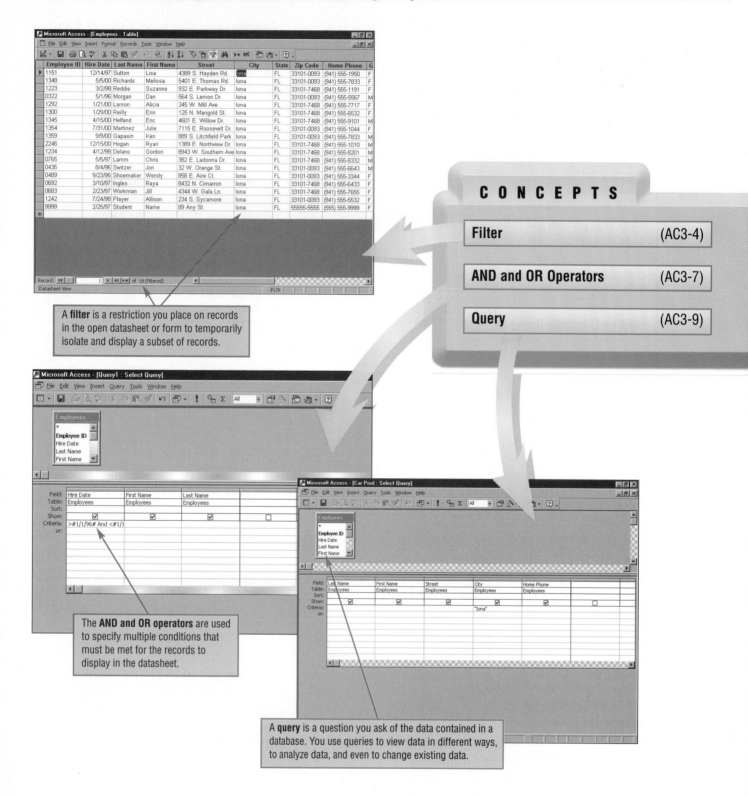

CONCEPTS

Filter	(AC3-4)
AND and OR Operators	(AC3-7)
Query	(AC3-9)

A **filter** is a restriction you place on records in the open datasheet or form to temporarily isolate and display a subset of records.

The **AND and OR operators** are used to specify multiple conditions that must be met for the records to display in the datasheet.

A **query** is a question you ask of the data contained in a database. You use queries to view data in different ways, to analyze data, and even to change existing data.

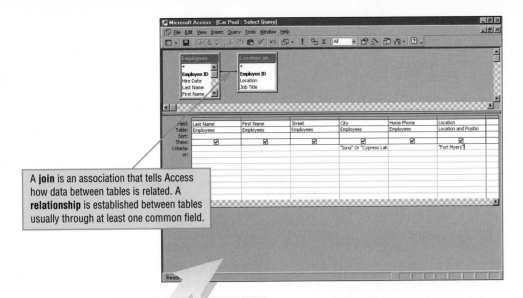

A **join** is an association that tells Access how data between tables is related. A **relationship** is established between tables usually through at least one common field.

Joins and Relationships (AC3-24)

Report (AC3-27)

Control (AC3-38)

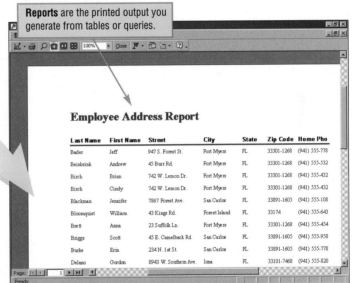

Reports are the printed output you generate from tables or queries.

Employee Address Report

Last Name	First Name	Street	City	State	Zip Code	Home Pho
Bader	Jeff	947 S. Forest St.	Fort Myers	FL	33301-1268	(941) 555-778
Beinbrink	Andrew	45 Burr Rd.	Fort Myers	FL	33301-1268	(941) 555-532
Birch	Brian	742 W. Lemon Dr.	Fort Myers	FL	33301-1268	(941) 555-432
Birch	Cindy	742 W. Lemon Dr.	Fort Myers	FL	33301-1268	(941) 555-432
Blackman	Jennifer	7867 Forest Ave.	San Carlos	FL	33891-1605	(941) 555-108
Bloomquist	William	43 Kings Rd.	Forest Island	FL	33174	(941) 555-643
Brett	Anna	23 Suffolk Ln.	Fort Myers	FL	33301-1268	(941) 555-454
Briggs	Scott	45 E. Camelback Rd.	San Carlos	FL	33891-1605	(941) 555-958
Burke	Erin	234 N. 1st St.	San Carlos	FL	33891-1605	(941) 555-778
Delano	Gordon	8943 W. Southern Ave.	Iona	FL	33101-7468	(941) 555-820

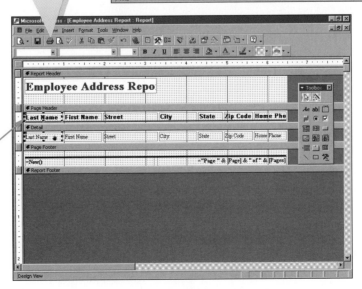

Reports and forms are linked to the underlying table by using **controls**. Controls are graphical objects that can be selected and modified.

Tutorial Review

Key Terms

bound control   AC3-38
calculated control   AC3-38
cell   AC3-14
column selector bar   AC3-14
comparison operator   AC3-14
compound control   AC3-38
control   AC3-38
criteria expression   AC3-6
field list   AC3-14

filter   AC3-4
inner join   AC3-24
join   AC3-24
label control   AC3-38
landscape   AC3-33
move handle   AC3-39
multitable query   AC3-22
orientation   AC3-33

portrait   AC3-33
query   AC3-9
query datasheet   AC3-12
relationship   AC3-24
report   AC3-27
sizing handles   AC3-39
text box control   AC3-38
unbound control   AC3-38

Command Summary

Command	Shortcut Keys	Button	Action
File/Page Set**u**p/Page/**L**andscape			Changes page orientation to landscape
File/**P**rint/Pa**g**es/**F**rom			Prints selected pages
Edit/Cle**a**r Grid			Clears query grid
Insert/**R**eport			Creates a new report object
View/**Z**oom/%.			Displays previewed document at specified percentage
View/**Z**oom/**F**it to Window			Displays entire previewed document page
View/P**a**ges			Displays specified number of pages of previewed document
Records/**F**ilter/**F**ilter by Form			Displays blank datasheet for entering criteria to display specific information
Records/**F**ilter/Filter by **S**election			Displays only records that contain a specific value
Records/Appl**y** Filter/Sort			Applies filter to table
Records/**R**emove Filter/Sort			Removes filter from table
Tools/**R**elationships			Defines permanent relationship between tables
Tools/**D**atabase Utilities/**C**ompact and Repair Database			Compacts and repairs database file
Filte**r**/Appl**y** Filter/Sort			Applies filter to table
Query/**R**un			Displays query results in Query Datasheet view
Query/Show **T**able			Displays Show Table dialog box
Window/**1** <name>			Displays Database window

Screen Identification

In the following screen, several items are identified by letters. Enter the correct term for each item in the spaces that follow.

a. _____   f. _____

b. _____   g. _____

c. _____   h. _____

d. _____   i. _____

e. _____

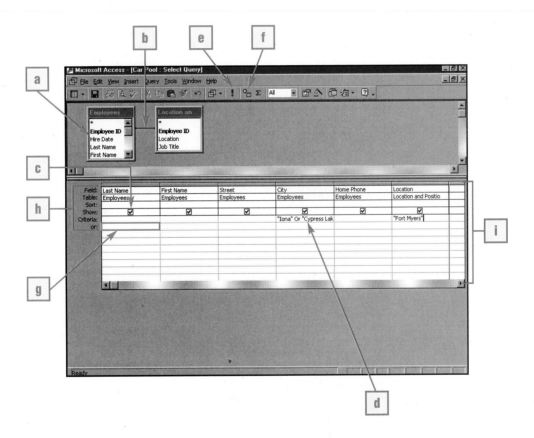

Matching

Match the letter to the correct item in the numbered list.

1. ☒   _____ **a.** intersection of a column and row

2. query   _____ **b.** a control that is tied to a field in an underlying table

3. multitable query   _____ **c.** temporary restriction placed on displayed data to isolate specific records

4. criteria   _____ **d.** includes any records containing either condition

5. ☒   _____ **e.** object that links a form or report to the underlying table

6. filter   _____ **f.** runs a query and displays query datasheet

7. OR   _____ **g.** used to ask questions about database tables

8. bound   _____ **h.** query that uses data from more than one table

9. control   _____ **i.** set of limiting conditions

10. cell   _____ **j.** accesses Filter By Form feature

True/False

Circle correct answer to the following statements.

1. Multiple filter results can be saved.	True	False
2. The OR operator narrows a search.	True	False
3. Queries are used to view data in different ways, to analyze data, and to change existing data.	True	False
4. Outer join is the default join in Access.	True	False
5. Access includes a custom report feature to assist in creating professional-appearing reports.	True	False
6. Filters use reports to set limiting conditions.	True	False
7. The AND operator is assumed when you enter criteria in multiple fields.	True	False
8. The most common type of relationship is many-to-many.	True	False
9. Reports are printed output generated from tables and queries.	True	False
10. Controls are text objects.	True	False

Multiple-Choice

- -

Circle the letter of the correct answer to the following statements.

1. A(n) _____ is a restriction placed on records in the open datasheet or form to quickly isolate and display a subset of records.

    a. filter

    b. query

    c. join

    d. property

2. AND and OR are _____.

    a. criteria

    b. operators

    c. elements

    d. properties

3. Select, crosstab, parameter, action, and SQL are different types of _____.

    a. action elements

    b. formats

    c. queries

    d. property elements

4. One-to-many, many-to-many, and one-to-one are different types of _____.

    a. relationships

    b. queries

    c. filters

    d. reports

5. Reports and forms are linked to the underlying table by using _____.

   a. filters

   b. criteria

   c. controls

   d. keys

6. A filter is created by specifying a set of limiting conditions or _____.

   a. forms

   b. controls

   c. criteria

   d. objects

7. The operator that broadens a search, because any record meeting either condition is included in the output, is _____.

   a. AND

   b. OR

   c. MOST

   d. ALL

8. A(n) _____ is a question asked of the data contained in a database.

   a. form

   b. inquiry

   c. request

   d. query

9. A(n) _____ is an association that tells Access how data between tables is related.

   a. join

   b. criteria

   c. query

   d. object

10. Text box, bound, unbound, label, and calculated are _____.

    a. buttons

    b. forms

    c. properties

    d. controls

Fill-In

Complete the following statements by filling in the blanks with the correct terms.

1. A(n) _____ is used to isolate and display a specific group of records.

2. The _____ operator narrows the search for records that meet both conditions.

3. The _____ operator narrows the search for records that meet either condition.

4. A(n) _____ is an association that shows how data between tables is related.

5. A(n) _____ retrieves specific data from one or more tables and displays the results in a query datasheet.

6. The _____ of the Query window is where the fields to be displayed in the query datasheet are placed.

7. Tables are joined by defining a(n) _____ between the tables.

8. _____ are used to link the underlying table or query to the report.

9. Custom names in a report are _____ because they are not connected to a field.

10. The _____ comparison operator is used to find values that are less than or equal to another value.

Discussion Questions

1. Discuss what filters are and how they can be used in a database. When would it be appropriate to use a filter?

2. Discuss the differences between the AND and OR filter conditions.

3. Discuss what a query can do and some advantages of using queries.

4. Discuss the three types of relationships. Give an example of how an inner join could be created in a database.

Hands-On Practice Exercises

Step by Step

☆

Rating System   ☆ Easy
       ☆☆ Moderate
       ☆☆☆ Difficult

1. Daria O'Dell, the owner of Daria's Day Spa, is thinking of offering a "Young Again" spa package that would include various skin treatments and massages. To get an idea of how much interest there would be in this package among her current clientele, Ms. O'Dell has asked you for a list of clients who are over the age of 35. (She does not need anything as formal as a report.) You decide that the simplest way to do this is to filter the table and print the filtered datasheet (which you completed in Practice Exercise 1 of Tutorial 2). The printed datasheet is shown here.

								Clients			1/22/01

Client ID	First Name	Last Name	Home Phone	Work Phone	Street Address	City	State	Zip Code	Birthdate
001	Elaine	Grace	(217) 555-4215	(217) 555-4557	718 North Coltrane	Madison	TX	75380	2/2/63
017	Pauline	Kelly	(217) 555-3822	(217) 555-8989	1723 Edwards Drive	Madison	TX	75380	5/11/54
002	Polly	Trawe	(217) 555-0091	(217) 555-2831	619 Portland Drive	Alison	TX	76890	11/27/54
003	Nadine	Richmond	(217) 555-1748	(217) 555-4279	1248 Trammell Avenue	Alison	TX	76890	9/10/50
009	Bobbi	Miller	(217) 555-3844		7435 Red Robin Lane	Madison	TX	75380	2/21/57
010	Charlene	Riley	(217) 555-0975	(217) 555-2499	2424 Eastern	Murray	TX	75377	3/16/58
011	Fen	Woo	(217) 555-5380	(217) 555-1441	8547 Lindsey Avenue	Murray	TX	75377	1/25/54

To filter the report, follow these steps:

a. Open the Daria Spa database and the Clients table. Best Fit the columns.

b. Select Filter by Form and enter <1/1/64 in the Birthdate field. Apply the filter.

c. Enter your name in the last of the displayed fields and print the filtered data sheet in landscape orientation.

d. Remove the filter. Close the table, saving the changes.

2. The managing editor of the Daily Digest periodically contacts businesses that are currently advertising in the publication only once a month to see if they would like to increase the frequency of their ads. To do this, he needs a datasheet from you that contains the contact information for these businesses, as shown here.

Monthly Advertisers									1/22/01		
Advertiser ID	Business Name	Business Type	Contact Name	Phone Number	Billing Street	Billing City	Billing State	Billing Zip	Ad Size	Ad Rate	Ad Frequency
E233	Prints	Print Shop	Richard Jones	(650) 555-4217	58 Lantana Ln.	Beacon Shores	CA	95055	1/4	$50.00	Monthly
A437	Fun Stuff	Toy Store	[Your Name]	(650) 555-1221	802 Trenton Way	Beacon Shores	CA	95055	Full	$100.00	Monthly
D504	Little Feet	Daycare	Joanne Kramer	(650) 555-3008	29B Roake Ct.	Beacon Shores	CA	95055	Full	$100.00	Monthly
B121	Fancy Pants	Clothing Store	Lucy Stevens	(650) 555-1938	222 Redwood Ln.	Beacon Shores	CA	95055	Full	$100.00	Monthly

To produce this datasheet, you will perform a query on the Advertisers table (which you completed in Practice Exercise 2 in Tutorial 2).

a. Open the Daily Digest database and select the Queries tab.

b. Use the Query Wizard to run a detail query on the Advertisers table. Include all the fields in the order listed. Title the query **Monthly Advertisers**.

c. In Query Design view, enter **Monthly** in the Ad Frequency criteria field. Run the query. Sort the Ad Size field in ascending sort order. Print the query using landscape orientation.

d. Close the query, saving the changes.

3. Now that you have your Cafe Purchases database set up for the Downtown Internet Cafe (which you completed in Practice Exercise 3 of Tutorial 2), you are ready to actually use it to track inventory. In addition to performing your daily query of the database for low-quantity items, Evan, the owner, has asked you for a datasheet that shows all special-order items. He would also like a report (shown here) by the end of the day that shows the results of your low-quantity query so he can place the necessary orders.

To create the datasheet, query, and report, follow these steps:

a. Open the Cafe Purchases database and the Inventory table. Filter the table to display only those records where the Special Order? field is Y. Hide the address columns. Print the filtered data sheet to give to Evan. Unhide the hidden columns and remove the filter.

Cafe Items To Be Ordered

Vendor Name	Better Beverages, Inc.
Contact	Mae Yung
Phone	(415) 555-1122
Description	Darjeeling tea
# On Hand	39
Special Order?	N
Vendor Name	Better Beverages, Inc.
Contact	Mae Yung
Phone	(415) 555-1122
Description	Orange Pekoe tea
# On Hand	21
Special Order?	N
Vendor Name	Better Beverages, Inc.
Contact	Mae Yung
Phone	(415) 555-1122
Description	Earl Grey tea
# On Hand	17
Special Order?	N

Monday, January 22, 2001

b. Use the Query Wizard to create a query based on the Inventory table. Include all fields except Item # in their current order. Name the query To Be Ordered. In Design view, enter the criteria to display only those records with an On-Hand # that is less than 25, and run the query. Review the resulting datasheet.

c. Upon reviewing the datasheet, you realize that it is not in a very useful order. Also, since Evan typically places orders by phone, the address information is not really necessary. Return to Design view and do the following:

- Apply an ascending sort to the Vendor Name column.

- Delete the four address columns.

- Move the Vendor Name, Contact, and Phone columns to the left of the Description column.

d. Run the query and review the resulting data sheet. Since the query now looks satisfactory enough to create a report from it, close the query window, saving the changes.

e. Use the Report Wizard to create a report based on the To Be Ordered query you just saved. Include the listed fields in the following order:

- Vendor Name

- Contact

- Phone

- Description

- # On Hand

- Special Order?

f. Select Vendor Name as the only sort field. Select the Columnar layout and Bold style. Name the report Cafe Items To Be Ordered.

g. Preview and print the page of the report that contains your name in the Contact field, and then close the Report window, saving the changes.

4. As the database manager for the EduSoft curriculum software company, you need to periodically submit reports to the head of marketing so she can use them to canvass school systems for potential customers. You just received a memo from her requesting a report, shown here, on titles for grades 3–8.

To create the requested report, follow these steps:

a. Open the database named Learning, which you completed in Practice Exercise 4 of Tutorial 2.

b. Use the Query Wizard to create a query based on the Software table. Include the following fields in this order: Grade Level, Title, Subject, Key Topics. Name the query **Marketing**.

c. In Query Design view, enter **3-5** in the first Grade Level criteria cell, and **6-8** in the second (Or) cell. Run the query and review the resulting datasheet. Close the query window, saving the changes.

EduSoft Programs for Grades 3-8

Grade Level	Subject	Title	Key Topics
3-5	Art	Create It II	Art styles

Grade Level	Subject	Title	Key Topics
3-5	Astronomy	Seeing Stars	Solar system exploration and discoveries

Grade Level	Subject	Title	Key Topics
3-5	Composition	Write It II	Idea organization and theme writing

Grade Level	Subject	Title	Key Topics
3-5	Geography	Find It II	U.S. geography

Grade Level	Subject	Title	Key Topics
3-5	History	Remember It II	U.S. history

Grade Level	Subject	Title	Key Topics
3-5	Math	Solve It II	Logic and problem-solving

Grade Level	Subject	Title	Key Topics
3-5	Meteorology	Rain or Shine	Weather systems and how to predict them

Grade Level	Subject	Title	Key Topics
3-5	Reading	Read It II	Literature and thinking strategies

Grade Level	Subject	Title	Key Topics
3-5	Science	Try It II	Scientific reasoning, systems and patterns

Grade Level	Subject	Title	Key Topics
3-5	Spelling	Spell It II	Spelling mastery and assessment

Monday, January 22, 2001   *Page 1 of 2*

d. Use the Report Wizard to create a report based on the Marketing query you just saved. Include all the fields in the order listed. Select Grade Level as the first sort field and Subject as the second sort field. Select the Justified layout, landscape orientation, and Corporate style. Name the report **EduSoft Programs for Grades 3–8**.

e. Center the Report Header control at the top of the page.

f. Preview and then print the report. Close the Report window, saving the changes you made.

5. The Animal Angels volunteers are successfully using the database you created to enter information for all the animals picked up by the organization and boarded, placed in foster care, and/or adopted. Meanwhile, you created another table containing information about the adoptive homes (including names, addresses, and phone numbers). The Animal Angels owners have now asked you for a report, shown below, of all animals adopted in the past six months and by whom so the appropriate thank you notes can be sent.

To create the requested report, follow these steps:

a. Open the database named Angels.

b. Open the Queries tab and create a query in Design view. Join the Animals and Adopters tables, and add the following fields to the design grid in the order listed below:

■ Animal Type

■ Status

■ Adoption Date

■ Adopter First Name

■ Adopter Last Name

■ Adopter Street

■ Adopter City

■ Adopter State

■ Adopter Zip

Animal Angels Adoption Report

Adopter First Name	Adopter Last Name	Adopter Street	Adopter City	Adopter State	Adopter Zip	Type
Blair	Castillo	382 E. Meadow Ave.	Chandler	AZ	83174-2311	Cat

Adopter First Name	Adopter Last Name	Adopter Street	Adopter City	Adopter State	Adopter Zip	Type
Craig	Nelson	77 E. Lincoln Dr.	Mesa	AZ	84101-8475	Iguana

Adopter First Name	Adopter Last Name	Adopter Street	Adopter City	Adopter State	Adopter Zip	Type
Daniel	Klinger	289 E. Heather Ave.	Phoenix	AZ	82891-1605	Cat

Adopter First Name	Adopter Last Name	Adopter Street	Adopter City	Adopter State	Adopter Zip	Type
Dianne	Trenton	899 High St.	Mesa	AZ	84101-8475	Horse

Adopter First Name	Adopter Last Name	Adopter Street	Adopter City	Adopter State	Adopter Zip	Type
Erica	Snider	234 N. 1st St.	Tempe	AZ	86301-1268	Cat

Adopter First Name	Adopter Last Name	Adopter Street	Adopter City	Adopter State	Adopter Zip	Type
Helen	Cady	34 University Dr.	Tempe	AZ	86301-1268	Dog

Adopter First Name	Adopter Last Name	Adopter Street	Adopter City	Adopter State	Adopter Zip	Type
Kate	Broeker	23 Price Rd.	Tempe	AZ	86301-1268	Dog

Adopter First Name	Adopter Last Name	Adopter Street	Adopter City	Adopter State	Adopter Zip	Type
Kevin	Hanson	235 W. Camelback Rd.	Tempe	AZ	86301-1268	Dog

Adopter First Name	Adopter Last Name	Adopter Street	Adopter City	Adopter State	Adopter Zip	Type
Kurt	Ehmann	7867 Forest Ave.	Phoenix	AZ	82891-1605	Cat

Adopter First Name	Adopter Last Name	Adopter Street	Adopter City	Adopter State	Adopter Zip	Type
Scott	Briggs	45 E. Camelback Rd.	Phoenix	AZ	82891-1605	Dog

Monday, January 22, 2001   Page 1 of 2

c. Specify A as the Status criteria and >9/1/98 as the Adoption Date criteria. Run the query and review the resulting datasheet. Select an ascending sort in the Adopter Last Name column. Save the query as Adoptees and close the Query window.

d. Use the Report Wizard to create a report based on the Adoptees query you just saved. Include the following fields in the order listed below:

■ Adopter First Name

■ Adopter Last Name

■ Adopter Street

■ Adopter City

■ Adopter State

■ Adopter Zip

■ Type

e. Select Adopter First Name as the first sort field and Adopter Last Name as the second sort field. Select the Justified layout, landscape orientation, and the Casual style. Name the report Animal Angels Adoption Report.

f. Center the Report Header control at the top of the page.

g. Preview and then print the report. Close the report window, saving the changes you made.

On Your Own

6. The program manager for the EduSoft Company is requesting a list of software titles that were worked on by Teri O'Neill so he can use it for Teri's review. Open the database named Learning and the Software table you updated in Practice Exercise 4 of Tutorial 2. Filter the table to include only those records that have Teri O'Neill in the Developer field. Add your name to one of the software titles (e.g., "[Your Name]'s Solve It") and print the filtered datasheet.

7. As an administrative assistant at Lewis & Lewis, Inc., you are responsible for sending out W2 forms to all of the employees. Use the employee database that you updated in Practice Exercise 9 of Tutorial 2 and create a query that includes only the employee name and home address fields. Run and print the resulting query datasheet.

8. Based on the overwhelming positive response from the Hawaiian Islands tour, Adventure Travel is planning a reunion trip and would like to contact the clients who took the first trip. Open the Adventure database that you updated in Practice Exercise 6 of Tutorial 2 and create a query that includes the client name, address, and phone fields as well as the tour name fields. Enter query sort criteria to find only those records that have Hawaiian Islands in one of the tour name fields, and apply an ascending sort to the Last Name field. Save the query and then use the Report Wizard to create a report based on the query. Include all the fields except the Client # field, and reverse the order of the Last Name and First Name fields. Sort the report by the Last Name and then First Name fields. Preview and print the report.

9. The Animal Angels owners have finished sending thank you cards to those who adopted animals in the last six months, and would now like to send cards to those who have provided foster care in the same time period. Using the same techniques you used in Practice Exercise 5 of this tutorial, create a query in the Angels database that joins the Animals and Fosters tables; includes the animal type, status, and foster home information; and specifies F and >9/1/98 as the Status and Foster Date criteria. Save and close the query, and then use the Report Wizard to create a report based on this query. Include all fields except the status field, with the foster home name and address information fields first and the type field last. Preview and print the report.

 ☆☆☆

10. Oldies But Goodies has expanded to include out-of-print books as well as vintage record albums. Revisit the Web to obtain some book titles and resources and add the appropriate fields to the table you updated in Practice Exercise 10 of Tutorial 2. To create a list of only the new products, filter the table to include the client and book fields (not the record album fields), and print the filtered datasheet. Then create a query that includes the records for both product types (record and book), sorted by category. Use the Report Wizard to create a report that is based on the query; include the customer name, product type, category, and source fields; and sort it by customer last name. Preview and print the report.

Working Together: Linking Access and Word

Case Study Brian, the Club owner, recently asked you to provide him with a list of all employees who have 3 years service with the Club. He also wanted the same information for all employees with over 5 years service. You queried the Employee table in the Personnel Records database and were quickly able to obtain this information. Now you want to include the query results with a brief memo to Brian.

All Microsoft Office applications have a common user interface such as similar commands and menu structures. In addition to these obvious features, they have been designed to work together, making it easy to share and exchange information between applications. You will learn how to share information between applications while you create the memo. Your memo containing the query results generated by Access will look like that shown here.

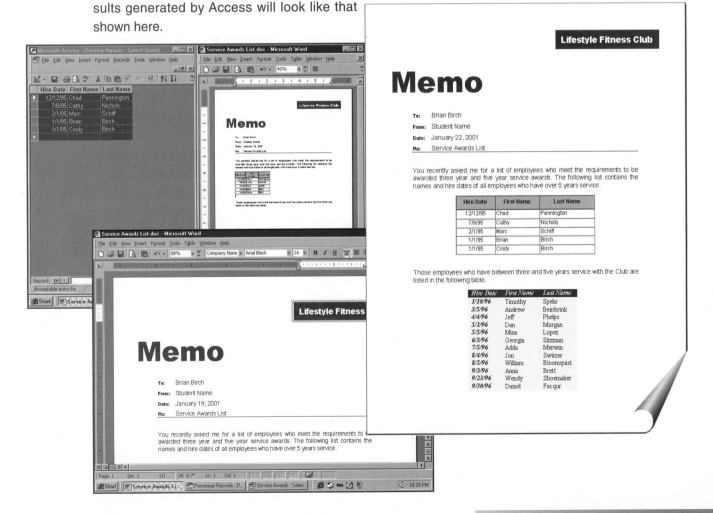

Note: This tutorial assumes that you already know how to use Word 2000 and that you have completed Tutorial 3 of Access. You will need the data file Personnel Records you saved at the end of Tutorial 3.

Copying Between Applications

You have already created the memo to the owner of the Club, and just need to add the information from Access to the memo. To see the memo,

1 ■ **Start Word 2000 and open the document Service Awards List from your data disk.**

■ **If necessary, maximize the application and document windows.**

Your screen should be similar to Figure 1.

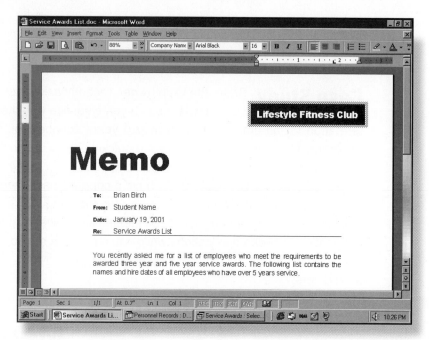

Figure 1

This document contains the text of the memo to the owner.

2 ■ **Replace "Student Name" in the memo header with your name.**

■ **Scroll the memo so you can see the two paragraphs in the body of the memo.**

Your screen should be similar to Figure 2.

insert Access query results

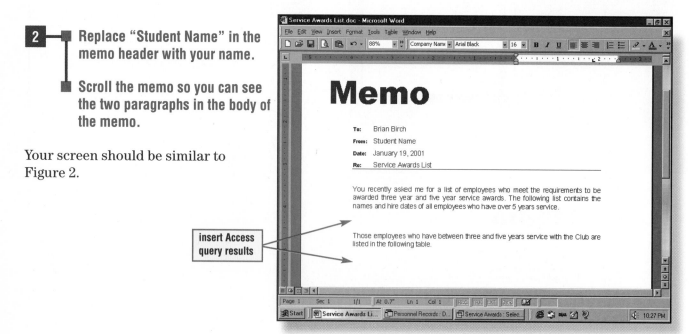

Figure 2

Below each of the paragraphs, you want to display the appropriate list of employees. This information is available in the Personnel Records database file and can be obtained using the Service Awards query you created and saved.

3
- Start Access 2000.
- Open the Personnel Records database from your data disk.
- Open the Service Awards query.
- If necessary, maximize the query datasheet window.

Your screen should be similar to Figure 3.

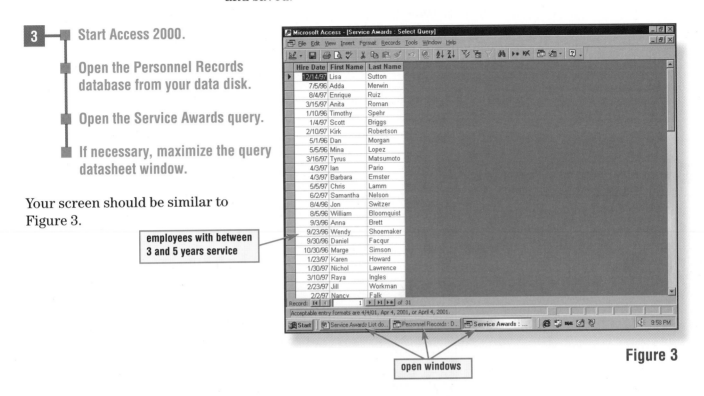

employees with between 3 and 5 years service

open windows

Figure 3

There are now two open applications, Word and Access. Word is open in a window behind the Access application window. Application buttons for all open windows are displayed in the taskbar. Access is the active application, and Service Awards: Select Query is the active file.

The 31 employees who have between 3 and 5 years service with the Club are listed in the query datasheet. Below the first paragraph of the memo, you want to display those employees with 5 years or more of service. To obtain this information, you need to modify the query.

4
- Display Design view.
- Change the criteria in the Hire Date cell to **<1/1/96**
- Run the query.

Your screen should be similar to Figure 4.

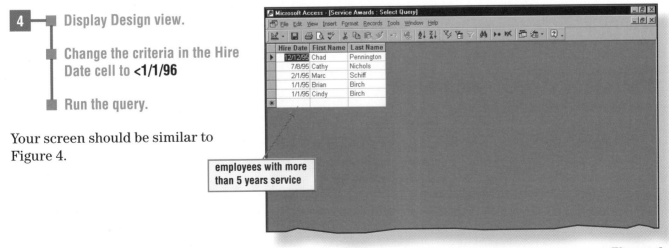

employees with more than 5 years service

Figure 4

You want to copy the output from the query below the first paragraph of the memo. As with all Office applications, you can cut, copy, and paste selections within and between tables and objects in an Access database. You can also perform these operations between Access databases and other applications. For example, you can copy a database object or selection into a Word document. The information is inserted in a format the application can edit, if possible.

To do this, you can use Copy and Paste or drag and drop between applications to copy the database object. To use drag and drop, both applications must be open and visible in the window. To display both applications at the same time on the desktop, you will tile the two open applications vertically in the window.

5 ■ **Right-click on a blank area of the taskbar to open the Shortcut menu.**

■ **Select Tile Windows Vertically.**

Your screen should be similar to Figure 5.

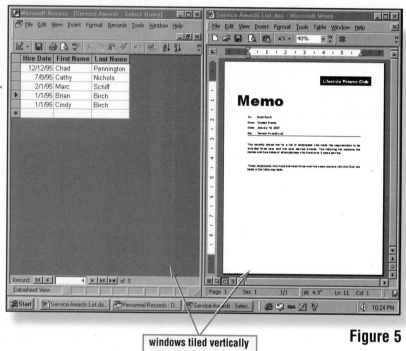

windows tiled vertically

Figure 5

6 ■ Click in the Access application window to make it active.

■ Use **E**dit/Select **A**ll Records to select the query datasheet table.

■ Copy and Paste the selected table to the space below the first paragraph of the memo in the document.

Your screen should be similar to Figure 6.

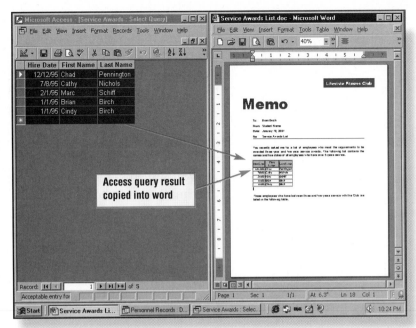

Access query result copied into word

Figure 6

The query results have been copied into the Word document as a table that can be edited and manipulated within Word. Much of the formatting associated with the copied information is also pasted into the document. You think the memo would look better if it was larger and centered between the margins.

7 ■ Choose **U**ndo Tile from the taskbar Shortcut menu.

■ Select the table and increase the size of the table by dragging the lower right sizing handle.

■ Select the entire table.

■ Click 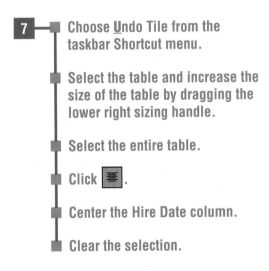.

■ Center the Hire Date column.

■ Clear the selection.

Your screen should be similar to Figure 7.

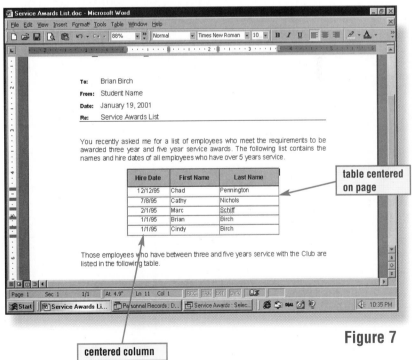

table centered on page

centered column

Figure 7

Linking an Access Object to Another Application

Next you need to insert the query results showing all employees who have more than 3 years and less than 5 years with the Club. As you consider the memo, you are concerned that Brian, when he sees the large number of employees meeting the criteria, may ask you to modify the query to provide a different analysis. If this request is made, you want the memo to be automatically updated when you modify the query. To do this you will link the query object to the memo.

You will insert the query result into the memo as a **linked object**. Information created in one application can also be inserted as a linked object into a document created by another application. When an object is linked, the data is stored in the **source file** (the document it was created in). A graphic representation or picture of the data is displayed in the **destination file** (the document in which the object is inserted). A connection between the information in the destination file to the source file is established by the creation of a link. The link contains references to the location of the source file and the selection within the document that is linked to the destination file.

When changes are made in the source file that affect the linked object, the changes are automatically reflected in the destination file when it is opened. This is called a **live link**. When you create linked objects, the date and time on your machine should be accurate, because the program refers to the date of the source file to determine whether updates are needed when you open the destination file.

To create a link to the query, you use the ▣ Insert Database button on the Database toolbar of Word.

1 ■ Display the Database toolbar.

■ Move to below the second paragraph of the memo.

■ Click ▣ Insert Database.

Your screen should be similar to Figure 8.

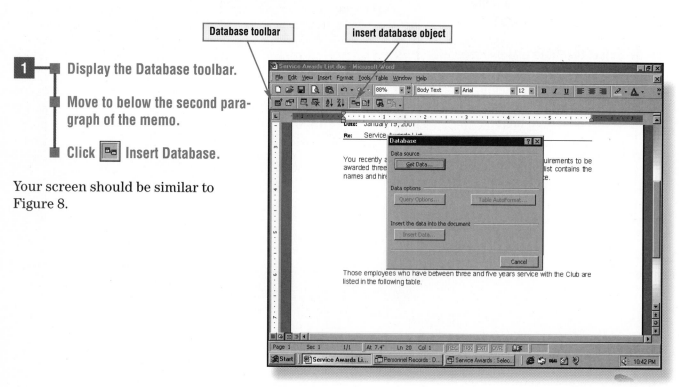

Database toolbar

insert database object

Figure 8

From the Database dialog box, you need to first select the database file to be inserted into the memo.

2 ■ Click [Get Data...].

■ If necessary, select the drive containing your data disk from the Look In drop-down list.

■ To display Microsoft Access file types, select **MS Access Databases** from the Files of Type drop-down list.

■ Select the file **Personnel Records**.

■ Click [Open].

Your screen should be similar to Figure 9.

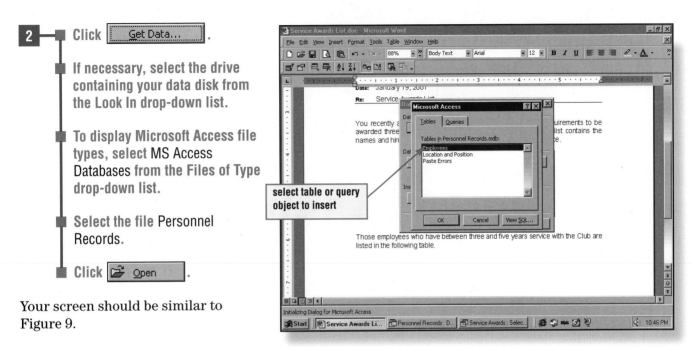

Figure 9

In the Microsoft Access dialog box, you select the table or query you want to insert in the Word document.

3 ■ Open the Queries tab and select **Service Awards**.

Your screen should be similar to Figure 10.

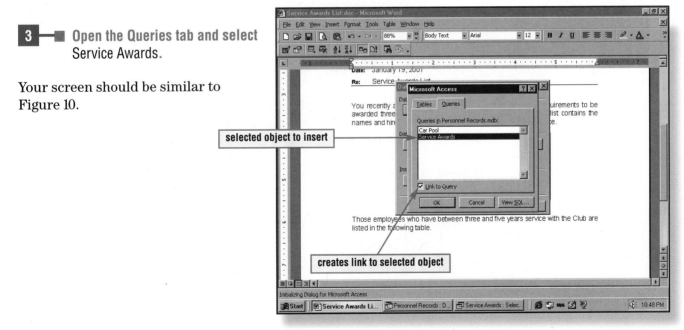

Figure 10

Notice that the Link to Query option is preselected. This option establishes the link between the query object and the Word document.

4 ━■ Click  .

The Database dialog box is displayed again. The Query Options button allows you to modify the query settings. Since you want it to appear as it is, you do not need to use this option. The AutoFormat button lets you select a format to apply to the table. If you do not select a format style, the datasheet is copied into the document as an unformatted table.

5 ━■ Click  .

Your screen should be similar to Figure 11.

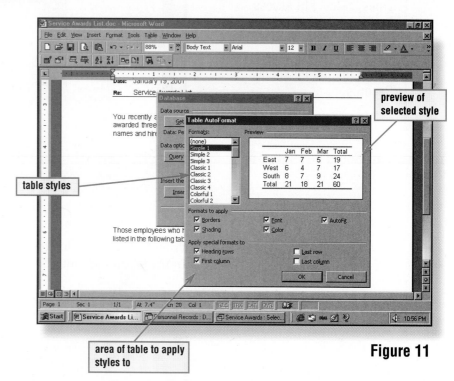

Figure 11

From the Table Autoformat dialog box, you select the style you want to use and the parts of the table you want to apply it to. You want the formats applied to the heading rows and first column.

6 ━■ If necessary, select the Heading rows and First column options as the only two areas to apply special formats.

■ Select a style of your choice.

■ Click OK .

The Database dialog box is displayed again. Finally, to insert the data into the document.

7 ■ Click [Insert Data...].

Your screen should be similar to Figure 12.

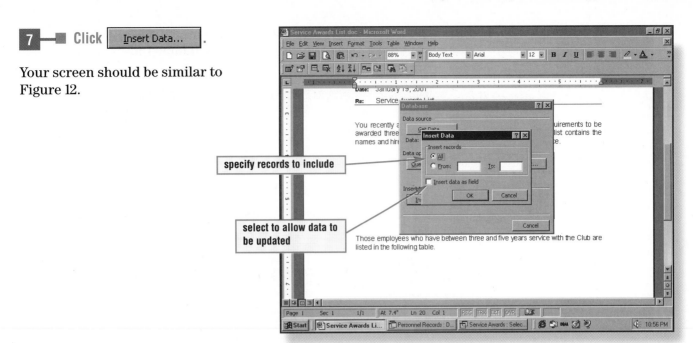

Figure 12

From the Insert Data dialog box, you specify what records to include in the inserted table and whether to insert the data as a field. Inserting it as a field allows the data to be updated whenever the source changes.

8 ■ If necessary, select **A**ll.

■ Select **I**nsert data as field.

■ Click [OK].

■ Scroll the memo to see more of the inserted table.

> The table continues on the second page of the memo.

Your screen should be similar to Figure 13.

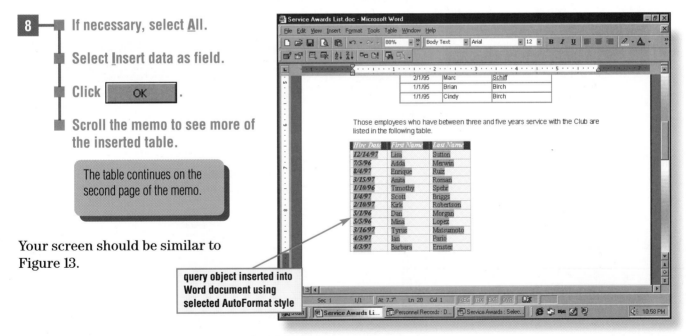

Figure 13

The link to the database file and to the query object is established, and the database table is inserted into the document in the selected format style. The table lists the 31 employees who have between 3 and 5 years with the Club. Even though you modified the query earlier, the original query results are displayed. This is because you did not save the changes you made to the query. Consequently, the inserted table reflects the results of the original query.

9 Center the table on the page.

Click above the table to clear the selection.

If necessary, insert a blank line between the paragraph and the table.

Your screen should be similar to Figure 14.

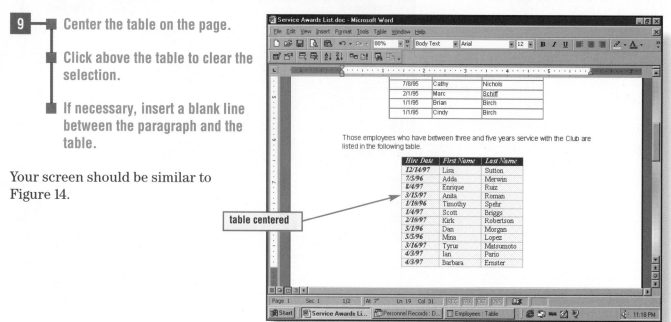

Figure 14

You think the information in the table should be sorted by hire date. To make this change to the table,

10 Select the Hire Date column.

Click ![Sort Ascending icon] Sort Ascending.

Click above the table to clear the selection.

Your screen should be similar to Figure 15.

You may need to scroll to the second page to see the record with the misspelled name.

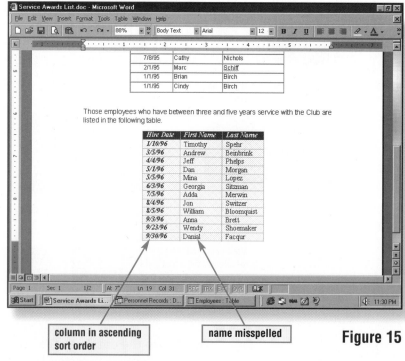

Figure 15

Updating a Linked Object

Now you notice that Daniel Facquer's first name is misspelled. You want to correct this in both the table in Access and in the memo. By making the change in Access, you can then update the memo to reflect the change because it is a linked object.

1 ■ **Switch to the Access Query datasheet window.**

■ **If necessary, maximize the Access window.**

■ **Close the query without saving the changes.**

■ **Open the Employees table.**

■ **Change the spelling of Danial Facqur's first name to Daniel (record 17).**

Your screen should be similar to Figure 16.

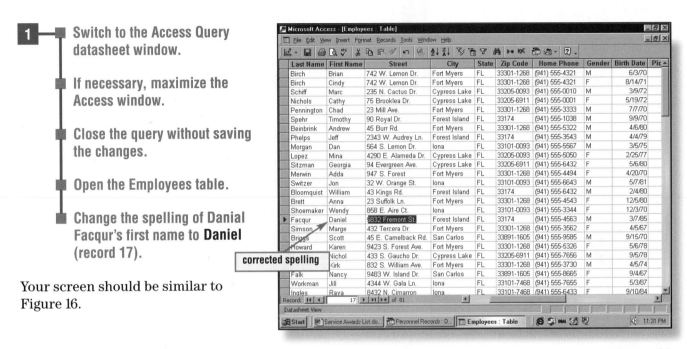

Figure 16

2 ■ **Switch to the Word memo.**

■ **Click** 🔲 **Update Field to update the table contents.**

Your screen should be similar to Figure 17.

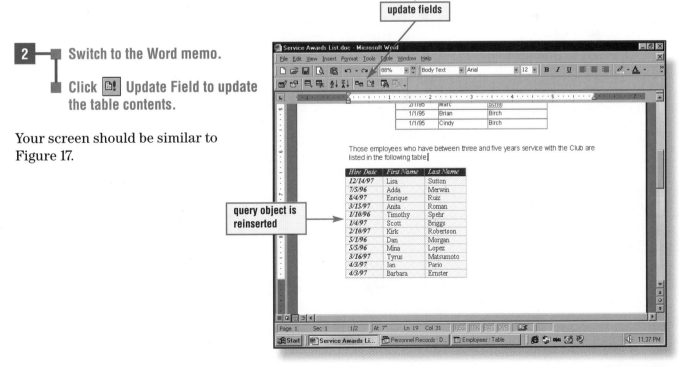

Figure 17

The query results are regenerated and inserted into the document again.

3 ■ Scroll the memo to confirm that Daniel's name is now corrected in the table.

■ If necessary, sort by the Hire Date field again. Center the table on the page.

Your screen should be similar to Figure 18.

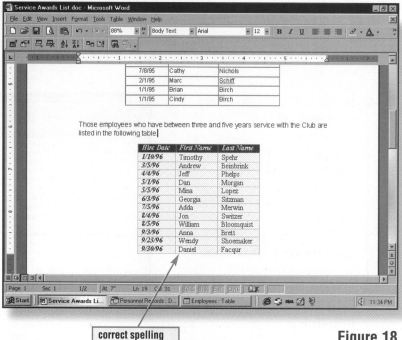

Hire Date	First Name	Last Name
7/8/95	Cathy	Nichols
2/1/95	Marc	Schiff
1/1/95	Brian	Birch
1/1/95	Cindy	Birch

Those employees who have between three and five years service with the Club are listed in the following table.

Hire Date	First Name	Last Name
1/10/96	Timothy	Spehr
3/5/96	Andrew	Beinbrink
4/4/96	Jeff	Phelps
5/1/96	Dan	Morgan
5/5/96	Mina	Lopez
6/3/96	Georgia	Sitzman
7/5/96	Adda	Merwin
8/4/96	Jon	Switzer
8/5/96	William	Bloomquist
9/3/96	Anna	Brett
9/23/96	Wendy	Shoemaker
9/30/96	Daniel	Facqur

correct spelling

Figure 18

4 ■ Save the memo as **Service Awards Linked**.

■ Close the Database toolbar.

■ Print the memo and exit Word.

■ Close the Personnel Records database.

Key Terms

Destination file   ACW-6
Linked object   ACW-6
Live link   ACW-6
Source file   ACW-6

Hands-On Practice Exercises

Step by Step

1. This problem is a continuation of Practice Exercise 1 in Tutorial 3. Daria O'Dell, the owner of Daria's Day Spa, has asked you for a list of clients who are over the age of 35 to get an idea of how much interest there would be in a "Young Again" spa package she is considering offering. You already filtered the Clients table to locate this information and now want to include the results in a memo to Daria.

    a. Open the Daria Spa database and the Clients table. Apply the filter. (If you did not save the table with the filter, create the filter again by following the instructions in Hands-on Practice Exercise 1 of Tutorial 3).

    b. Hide the Client ID, Home Phone, and Work Phone fields.

    c. Open Word and enter the following text.

        TO: Daria O'Dell
        FROM: [your name]
        DATE: [current date]

        Below is the information you requested on clients over the age of 35.

    d. Copy the query results into the Word document.

    e. Save the memo as Daria Clients. Print the document.

    f. Unhide the three fields. Remove the filter. Close the table and database.

2. This problem is a continuation of Practice Exercise 2 in Tutorial 3. You have queried the Daily Digest database to locate all businesses that are currently advertising in the publication only once a month. Now you want to send this information in a memo to the managing editor. You want to link the database query results to the memo, as this information is periodically requested. Then each time this request is made, all you would need to do is rerun the query to get the updated results and update the memo.

    a. Open the Daily Digest database and the Monthly Advertisers query.

    b. Modify the query to display the following fields only: Business Name, Business Type, Contact Name, Phone Number, Ad Size, and Ad Frequency. *Hint:* Clear the Show box of the fields you do not want displayed.

    c. Open Word, and enter the following text.

        TO: Dan Lenz, Managing Editor
        From: [your name]
        DATE: [current date]

        Below is the information you requested on monthly advertisers.

   d. Copy the query results into the Word document as a linked object.

   e. Change the Ad Frequency of one of the Biweekly ads to Monthly. Run the query again.

   f. Update the memo.

   g. Save the memo as Daily Digest Memo. Print the document.

   f. Save the query changes. Close the table and database.

3. This problem is a continuation of Practice Exercise 4 in Tutorial 3. EduSoft's marketing director has asked you to locate the same information for grade levels K–2. You will quickly modify the marketing query to get this information and include it in a memo to the director.

   a. Open the Learning database and the Marketing query.

   b. Modify the query to display the grade levels K–2 only. Save the modified query as **Marketing K2**. Best fit the fields.

   c. Open Word and enter the following text.

      TO: Marketing Director, Valerie McLaughlin
      From: [your name]
      DATE: [current date]

      Below is the information you requested on grade levels K–2.

   d. Copy the query results into the Word document as a linked object.

   e. Add a new title to the table using the following information: **90-0102; Tell It; Speech; K–2; Story Telling; your name; current date**.

   f. Run the query again.

   g. Update the memo.

   h. Save the memo as EduSoft. Print the document.

   i. Save the query changes. Close the table and database.

Glossary of Key Terms

Best Fit: A feature that automatically adjusts column width to fit the longest entry.

Bound control: A control that is tied to a field in an underlying table.

Calculated control: Displays the results of a calculation in the form or report.

Cell: The space created by the intersection of a vertical column and a horizontal row.

Clip art: A collection of graphics that is usually bundled with a software application.

Column selector bar: In Query Design view, the thin gray bar just above the field name in the grid. It is used to select an entire column.

Column width: The number of characters that are displayed in a column in Datasheet view.

Comparison operator: A symbol used in expressions to compare two values. The > (greater than) and < (less than) symbols are examples of comparison operators.

Compound control: Text box and label controls that are connected and act as one when manipulated.

Control: In Form and Report Design views, graphical objects that can be selected and modified.

Criteria expression: An expression that will select only the records that meet certain limiting criteria.

Character string: A sequence of characters (letters, numbers, or symbols) that must be handled as text, not as numeric data.

Current record: The record, containing the insertion point, that will be affected by the next action.

Database: An organized collection of related information.

Data type: Attribute for a field that determines what type of data it can contain.

Design grid: The part of the Design window which displays settings that are used to define a table design or define a query.

Design view: Used to create new database objects and modify the design of existing objects.

Destination file: The document in which a linked object is inserted.

Drawing object: A graphic consisting of shapes, such as lines and boxes, that can be created using a drawing program such as Paint.

Edit mode: Used to enter and edit data in a field.

Expression: A combination of symbols that produces specific results.

Field: The smallest unit of information about a record, the values of which appear in a column of the database.

Field list: A small window that lists all fields in an underlying table.

Field name: Label used to identify the data stored in a field.

Field property: A character associated with a field that affects its appearance or behavior.

Field selector: A small gray box or bar in datasheets and queries that can be clicked to select an entire column. The field selector usually contains the field names.

Field size: Field property that limits a text data type to a certain size or limits numeric data to values within a specific range.

Filter: A restriction placed on records in an open datasheet or form to temporarily isolate a subset of records.

Form: A database object used primarily for onscreen display of records, to make it easier to enter data and to make changes to existing records.

Graphic: A non-text element or object, such as a drawing or picture, that can be added to a database.

Identifier: A part of an expression that refers to the value of a field, a graphical object, or property.

Inner join: The default Access join that joins tables based on the common fields if one of the common fields is a primary key.

Input mask: Used in fields and text boxes to format data and provide control over what values can be entered into a field.

Join: An association that tells Access how data between tables is related.

Label control: Displays descriptive text associated with the text box control.

Landscape: Printing orientation that prints a report across the length of the page.

Linked object: An object that is pasted into another application. The data is stored in the source document, and a graphic representation of the data is displayed in the destination document.

Live link: When a source document is edited, the changes are automatically reflected in the linked object in the destination document.

Many-to-many relationship: Records in both tables can have many matching records in the other table.

Move handle: A large box that is used to move a selected control.

Multitable query: A query that uses more than one table.

Navigation buttons: Used to move through records with a mouse.

Navigation mode: Used to move from field to field and to delete a field entry.

Object: An item such as a table, form, or report that can be selected and manipulated as a unit.

Object bar: Used to quickly access the different database objects.

Object list box: Displays a list of objects associated with the selected object type.

One-to-many relationship: Records in one table can have many matching records in a second table, but the second table can only have one match in the first table.

One-to-one relationship: Records in both tables only have one matching record.

Operator: A symbol or word that indicates that an operation is to be performed.

Orientation: The direction text prints on a page, either landscape or portrait.

Picture: An illustration such as a scanned photograph.

Portrait: Printing orientation that prints the report across the width of a page.

Primary key: One or more fields in a table that uniquely identify a record.

Query: A question you ask of the data contained in a database. Used to view data in different ways, to analyze data, and to change data.

Query datasheet: Where the result or answer to a query is displayed.

Record: A row of a table, consisting of all the information about one person, thing, or place.

Record number indicator: Displays the current record number and total number of records in the lower left corner of most views.

Record selector: Displayed to the left of the first column; it indicates which record is the current record.

Relational database: A database containing multiple tables linked by a common field.

Relationship: A link made between tables, usually through at least one common field.

Report: Printed output generated from queries or tables.

Sizing handles: Small boxes surrounding a selected control that are used to size the control.

Sort: A temporary record order in the datasheet that reorders records in a table.

Source file: The document in which a linked object is created.

Tab order: The order in which Access moves through a form or table when the [Tab ⇆] key is pressed.

Table: Consists of vertical columns and horizontal rows of information about a particular category of things.

Text box control: Creates a link to the underlying source, usually a field from a table, and displays the field entry in the report or form.

Unbound control: A control that is not connected to a field in an underlying table.

Validation text: Text that is displayed when a validation rule is violated.

Validity check: Process of checking to see whether data meets certain criteria.

Value: A part of an expression that is a number, date, or character.

View: An Access window format for viewing objects in a database.

Command Summary

Command	Shortcut Key	Button	Action
File/**N**ew	Ctrl + N	🗋	Creates a new database
File/**O**pen	Ctrl + O	📂	Opens an existing database
File/**C**lose			Closes open window
File/**S**ave	Ctrl + S	💾	Saves table
File/Page Set**u**p/Page/**L**andscape			Changes page orientation to landscape
File/**P**rint/Pa**g**es/**F**rom			Prints selected pages
File/Print Pre**v**iew		🔍	Displays file as it will appear when printed
File/**P**rint	Ctrl + P	🖨	Prints contents of file
File/**E**xit		✖	Closes Access and returns to Windows 98 desktop
Edit/**U**ndo	Ctrl + Z	↺	Cancels last action
Edit/Cu**t**	Ctrl + X or Delete	✂ or ✂	Deletes selected record
Edit/Se**l**ect Record	⇧Shift + Spacebar		Selects current record
Edit/Select **A**ll Records	Ctrl + A		Selects all controls on a form in
Edit/**F**ind	Ctrl + F	🔍	Locates specified data
Edit/R**e**place	Ctrl + H		Locates and replaces specified data
Edit/Delete **R**ows			Deletes selected field in Design view
Edit/Primary **K**ey		🔑	Defines a field as a primary key field
Edit/Cle**a**r Grid			Clears query grid
View/**D**esign View		▣ ▾	Displays form in Design view
View/**F**orm View			Displays form in Form view
View/**D**atasheet View		▦ ▾	Display a form in Datasheet view
Insert/**R**ows			Inserts a new field in table in Design view
Insert/**O**bject			Inserts object into database

Command	Shortcut Key	Button	Action
Insert/Report			Creates a new report object
Filter/Apply Filter/Sort		▽	Applies filter to table
Query/Run		!	Displays query results in Query Datasheet view
Query/Show Table			Displays Show Table dialog box
Format/Column Width			Changes width of table columns in Datasheet view
Format/Column Width/Best Fit			Sizes selected columns to accommodate longest entry or column header
Format/Hide Columns			Hides columns in Datasheet view
Format/Unhide Columns			Redisplays hidden columns in Datasheet view
Records/Data Entry			Hides existing records and displays Data Entry window
Records/Sort/Sort Ascending		ᴀ↓	Reorders records in ascending alphabetical order
View/Zoom/%.			Displays previewed document at set percentage
View/Zoom/Fit to Window			Displays entire previewed document page
View/Pages			Displays specified number of pages of previewed document
Records/Filter/Filter by Form			Displays blank datasheet for entering criteria to display specific information
Records/Filter/Filter by Selection			Displays only records that contain a specific value
Records/Apply Filter/Sort		▽	Applies filter to table
Records/Remove Filter/Sort		▽	Removes filter from table
Tools/Relationships			Defines permanent relationship between tables
Tools/Database Utilities/Compact and Repair Database			Compacts and repairs database file
Window/1 <name>			Displays Database window

Index

Notes